HISTORY JUST AHEAD

A Guide to
Wisconsin's Historical Markers

D1286980

HISTORY JUST AHEAD

A Guide to Wisconsin's Historical Markers

Edited by Sarah Davis McBride

Historical Markers Coordinator,
Division of Historic Preservation

State Historical Society of Wisconsin
Madison, 1999

ACKNOWLEDGEMENTS

I am indebted to the following people who have helped me bring this book to fruition. I thank Larry Reed and George Meyer for their commitment to revitalize the Wisconsin Historical Markers Program and their vision for a new historical markers guidebook; Paul Hass and Michael Stevens for their sound editorial advice and keen eye; Debbie Cerra for her design expertise and indefatigable patience; Roger Bjorge, Steve Meyer, Darell Smith and Monty Raskin for their on-site inventories of our official state markers; and Leif Hubbard at the Department of Transportation for administering the ISTEA Enhancement Funds that helped produce this book. For assisting me with photographs at the State Historical Society of Wisconsin I thank Nicolette Bromberg, Andrew Kraushaar, Tracy Will, Lisa Hinzman, Jim Draeger, Marsha Weisiger, Susie Wirka and, at the City of Milwaukee, Brian Pionke. I also wish to thank Bill Philpott and John Broihahn in the Division of Historic Preservation for their counsel.

Library of Congress cataloging-in-publication
History Just Ahead: a guide to Wisconsin's historical markers
edited by Sarah Davis McBride
p.   cm.
Includes index
ISBN 0-87020-317-7
1. Historical markers--Wisconsin Guidebooks.
2. Wisconsin-History, Local
3. Wisconsin Guidebooks
I. McBride, Sarah Davis, 1952- .
II. State Historical Society of Wisconsin.
917.7504'43--dc21

TABLE OF CONTENTS

INTRODUCTION

Wisconsin has a healthy respect for its past and for those who make sense of it. The state's compelling history is the subject of countless books. Its material remnants are carefully stored and exhibited on museum shelves and in historic houses. It is enlivened by costumed interpreters who dramatize the daily living patterns of Wisconsin's rural past and every year it is re-enacted by history devotees donning buckskin or Civil War regalia.

Frederick Jackson Turner, one of the nation's most influential historians, was born and developed his groundbreaking "frontier thesis" in Wisconsin. The State Historical Society of Wisconsin was founded in 1846, two years before Wisconsin became a state. From early statehood through the Progressive Era and up to the present, the Society has carefully preserved the historical record, making it available to the public. Wisconsin's reverence for its past is surpassed only by its encouragement of historians who interpret it for us.

For almost fifty years, Wisconsin's Historical Markers Program has been making sense of both important small incidents and monumental events that together contribute to the state's multi-layered past. Whether a marker commemorates Wisconsin's involvement in World War II or the invention of the ice cream sundae, the markers program commits to memory Wisconsin's significant history, helping to identify, describe, record, and commemorate the state's collective cultural and natural heritage.

The Historical Markers Program took root in 1944, when Governor Walter Goodland appointed an advisory committee to study "how best to mark historic sites in Wisconsin." In a spirit of surprising optimism, Goodland predicted that "thousands of tourists will come to Wisconsin in increasing numbers after the war is over." In keeping with the state's progressive tradition, Goodland thought Wisconsin should educate and inspire its tourists.

After World War II, the tourists did, indeed, come to Wisconsin, and the state began a historic sites and markers program, erecting a series of bronze plaques and wooden signs to commemorate great events like Jean

Nicolet's landing on Green Bay's shores, to inspire an appreciation for the natural environment like the wild St. Croix River in the northwest and to designate state architectural landmarks such as the Old Wade House Stagecoach Inn on the plank road from the Port of Sheboygan to Fond du Lac.

Although these early markers were attractive, they lacked physical uniformity. So in 1950, the Wisconsin Historical Sites and Markers Committee adopted a standardized marker design. Thenceforth, state markers were made of cast aluminum and painted in brown and cream enamel. The markers were crowned by an official seal enclosing a rather ferocious-looking badger, Wisconsin's state animal. "The Badger State" actually owes its nickname not to the burrowing mammal but to lead miners who arrived in southwestern Wisconsin early in the 19th century. Too preoccupied with digging for "gray gold," the miners lived in abandoned mine shafts and temporary burrows instead of houses.

In 1951, Wisconsin erected its first official standardized marker at the "Pestigo Fire Cemetery" and in 1953 enacted legislation for an official Historical Markers Council to establish a uniform system of marking. Since that time, Wisconsin has placed markers along highways, in state and county parks, and in dozens of communities, enriching every region of the state. To date, Wisconsin has erected 412 markers in small, medium, and large sizes and continues to add new ones to the list every year.

Perhaps the most important aspect of Wisconsin's marking program is that it is truly a program of the people. Every new marker subject is initiated by the public. The State Historical Society of Wisconsin processes and approves new marker applications, but individuals and organizations pay for their own markers and choose subjects of their own interest--so long as these are significant on a local, state, or national level. Marker subjects must also address at least one aspect of Wisconsin history in the following categories: archaeology, architecture, culture, events, ethnic associations, geology, legends, natural history, and people.

Thanks to the Wisconsin public, then, you can find markers in almost all of the state's 72 counties, covering subjects of seemingly infinite variety. Along with markers for famous and infamous characters, great events, industrial and agricultural inventions, engineering feats, military forts, roads and trails, ethnic settlements, communities, and places of natural wonder and beauty, you can also find markers for lost villages, mythical creatures, disasters, and even for dogs. This diversity helps us to understand the breadth of Wisconsin history and, although far from a chronology of state history, it offers insight into the ways Wisconsinites' interests have changed and continue to change over time.

In 1994, Wisconsin enacted new legislation to expand the Historical Markers Program, including hiring a markers coordinator, compiling a markers guidebook, and extending the program's eligible criteria to include local history. In addition, the program received four limited grants to reimburse sponsors for the cost of their new markers. All of these factors have helped to renew interest in Wisconsin's official markers, offering a fresh perspective on history as experienced in Wisconsin communities. As a result, from 1995 through 1998 alone, the program has placed more than 100 new historical markers.

Under the newly expanded program, the state has initiated and erected a series of thematic markers. These series are named: Wisconsin Veterans markers, Green Bay Ethnic Trail markers and Black Hawk War Trail markers. The veterans markers are found throughout the state. The ethnic trail markers are found in the northeast and southeast regions of the state along a corridor of immigrant settlement. The Black Hawk War Trail markers follow the path Sac leader Black Hawk and his band took during the spring and summer of 1832. These markers are found in the south central and southwest regions of the state. An identifying bronze seal of Black Hawk appears on each of the markers in this series.

Historical markers, like any recorded histories, are rooted in the time and place in which they were written. Wisconsin markers have appeared on the landscape for over fifty years, and during that time the language and perspectives of both academic and popular history have evolved and changed significantly. Historians are now much more attuned to the accomplishments and historical significance of women, of ethnic and racial minorities, and of ordinary people in general. Historical markers no longer deal exclusively with "great men" and "great events." Today, the markers program is encouraging sponsors to nominate historical subjects woefully neglected in the past and is working towards updating the language of some of the older markers.

Official markers are an important element in telling Wisconsin's story. Placed on the very landscapes where significant events occurred, markers evoke an immediacy of the past that no history book can ever provide. Whether or not any tangible evidence actually remains nearby, the markers allow the visitor a sense of discovery, awakening the imagination to a specific time and place. Most importantly, markers commemorate the lives and the sacrifices of those who went before us, inspiring and connecting us to our past.

HOW TO USE THIS GUIDEBOOK

History Just Ahead is organized for the convenience of both the traveler and the casual reader. The book is divided into five regional sections: the Southeast, the South Central, the Southwest, the Northwest, and the Northeast. Within each regional section, counties are arranged alphabetically. These sections are used solely as a method of organizing this guidebook; these divisions do not necessarily reflect geographical or cultural boundaries. Within each county, marker texts are generally organized by their proximity to the nearest city or town.

This guidebook also contains six maps. A large map of Wisconsin at the beginning of the book introduces the state, illustrating its principal cities and highways. Each marker location is flagged with a marker number so that the reader can see how the markers are spread across the state. The five other maps are regional maps for the Southeast, South Central, Southwest, Northwest, and Northeast. These maps occur at the beginning of each regional section. Each regional map illustrates the major highways, cities, and county divisions within that region and marker locations are flagged with the marker number within each county. (All six maps should be used in conjunction with a good Wisconsin highway map.)

State of Wisconsin icon maps are found on every right-hand page. These little maps highlight regional divisions, visually orienting the reader to the area where the markers on that page will be found. Further, the regional divisions are written vertically along the edge of the page so that the reader will always know which regional map to reference when trying to locate a specific marker. When driving to a site, the reader should turn to the regional map at the beginning of each regional section to find the desired marker.

The oval shields containing numbers represent the official marker numbers assigned to each marker soon after it is placed. The reader should reference this official marker number when locating a particular marker on the map. At the end of the book is a numerical list of Wisconsin's official markers and a useful cross-referencing index arranged by name, place and subject.

WISCONSIN HISTORICAL MARKERS

0 10 20 30 40

Miles

June 1999   *University of Wisconsin Cartographic Laboratory*

PLACING A STATE HISTORICAL MARKER

Photo Courtesy of Jim Widmer, Theresa, WI.

In 1997, state and village employees erect a large historical marker in Theresa. Wisconsin's official markers are made of cast aluminum, painted in brown and cream enamel. They are identified by a badger emblem at the top of each marker.

Markers
Southeast Region

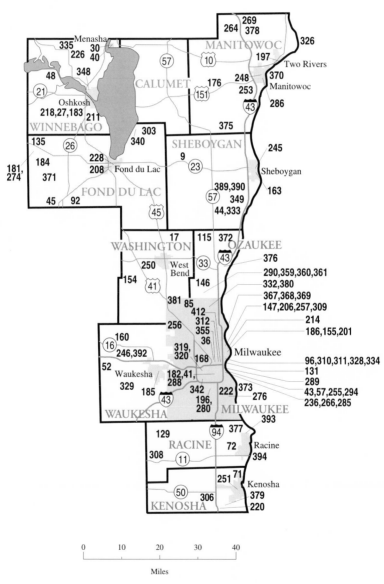

```
0        10        20        30        40
└────────┴─────────┴─────────┴─────────┘
                  Miles
```

June 1999

University of Wisconsin Cartographic Laboratory

1

Fond du Lac County

274 **CARRIE CHAPMAN CATT** Erected 1984
In Pedrick Wayside, Hwy. 23, Ripon

A national leader of the woman suffrage movement, Carrie Chapman Catt was born in Ripon, Wisconsin, in 1859 and spent most of her life as a tireless crusader for women's rights. A gifted organizer, political strategist, and public speaker, Catt succeeded Susan B. Anthony as president of the nation's most important suffrage group, the National American Woman Suffrage Association, from 1900-4 and 1915-20. She transformed the movement into a purposeful organization and led the successful campaign for ratification of the 19th Amendment to the United States Constitution, guaranteeing women the right to vote. After passage of the amendment in 1920, Catt helped found and served as first president of the League of Women Voters. Her concern with women's rights was worldwide, and in 1904 she was elected first president of the International Woman Suffrage Alliance and served in the post until 1923. In later years, she was active in the international peace and disarmament movement. She died in New Rochelle, New York, in 1947.

> "How I pity those who have not felt the grip of the oneness of women struggling, serving, suffering, sacrificing for the righteousness of women's emancipation!"

Carrie Chapman Catt, ca. 1911.
SHSW Visual Materials Archive (X3) 31951.

Fond du Lac County

135 **BIRTHPLACE OF REPUBLICAN PARTY** Erected 1964
Hwy. 23, Ripon

In 1852 Alvan Early Bovay of Ripon met with Horace Greeley in New York and advocated dissolution of the Whig Party and formation of a new party to fuse together antislavery elements. At the same time he suggested the name "Republican" because he felt "it was a good name...with charm and prestige." The opportunity to act came in January 1854 when Senator Stephen Douglas of Illinois introduced the Kansas-Nebraska Bill, which permitted the extension of slavery beyond the limits of the earlier Missouri Compromise. Three months of debate on the bill created upheavals in all the existing political parties. When the bill passed the Senate on March 3, 1854, Bovay recalled: "We went into the little meeting, Whigs, Free Soilers, and Democrats. We came out Republicans, and we were the first Republicans in the Union." On February 22, 1856, a convention was held at Pittsburgh to establish a national organization, and the name "Republican" was adopted for the new party. Among those present were Horace Greeley and Abraham Lincoln.

Fond du Lac County

184 **RIPON COLLEGE** Erected 1972
Ripon College campus, Ripon

Incorporated January 29, 1851. The first college building, East Hall, was staked out that spring by Ripon city founders David Mapes and Alvan Bovay. Chartered as Brockway College, it was renamed Ripon College in 1864 and graduated its first class, four women, in 1867. Although private and nonsectarian, it was given support by the Winnebago convention of Presbyterian and Congregational churches until 1868. A regiment of the 1st Wisconsin Cavalry was mobilized here during the Civil War. The three original buildings are still in use.

181 CERESCO   Erected 1972
In Park on Union St., 1 block S of Hwy. 23, Ripon

The Long House is one of the few visible remains of the pioneer settlement of Ceresco. Founded in 1844 and named for Ceres, the Roman goddess of agriculture, Ceresco was the home of the Wisconsin Phalanx, an experiment in communal living according to the rule of the French social philosopher Charles Fourier. Under the leadership of Warren Chase, the Phalanx attracted a membership of about two hundred persons. The company enjoyed a few years of vigorous life, then declined and disbanded in 1851. The village became a part of Ripon in 1853.

Long House Dormitory at Ceresco, a Wisconsin Fourierite community.
University of Wisconsin-Madison (X313) 3148-E.

Fond du Lac County

 THE MILITARY ROAD   Erected 1975
S. Military Rd. and W. 2nd St., Fond du Lac

The Military Road, built in 1835, became the first highway to cross the state. Congress appropriated $5,000 to connect the St. Lawrence and Mississippi River basins. The troops at Fort Crawford constructed the road from Prairie du Chien to Portage; those at Fort Winnebago extended it to Fond du Lac, and those at Fort Howard completed it to Green Bay. Blazed trees and plowed furrows marked the route. Brush laid in riverbeds made wagon crossings possible. The early thoroughfare followed many Indian trails. The army officials who supervised the work became interested in the future of the territory and invested their own finances in its development. The Military Road, the first influence of the federal government in Wisconsin, encouraged settlers to come to this territory.

Fond du Lac County

 EDWARD S. BRAGG   Erected 1996
Hwy. 151, 6 mi. N of Fond du Lac

Born in New York in 1827, Edward S. Bragg was admitted to the bar in 1848 and moved to Fond du Lac in 1850, where he practiced law and played an active role in politics. When the Civil War broke out in 1861, Bragg joined other "War Democrats" in supporting the military suppression of the Confederacy. Bragg recruited and later commanded a volunteer militia company after it was amalgamated with the 6th Wisconsin Infantry Regiment. Serving with valor and distinction, Bragg won a colonelcy in 1863 and command of the famed Iron Brigade in 1864. By the war's end he was brigadier general. Resuming his political career after the war, Bragg became a state senator, won two terms in Congress, and chaired several Wisconsin delegations to national Democratic conventions. A fiscal conservative, Bragg refused to support the Democratic ticket in 1896 and became a Republican. He served as minister to Mexico and consul general at Havana, culminating his long career as consul general at Hong Kong. Bragg died in 1912.

Fond du Lac County

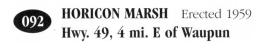

228 **WISCONSIN PROGRESSIVE PARTY** Erected 1979
30 E. 2nd St., Fond du Lac

Near this site on May 19, 1934, the Wisconsin Progressive Party was formally
organized. The Party was the result of a movement begun forty years before on the
principle that the will of the people should be the law of the land. The legislation
it initiated in Wisconsin was later adopted throughout the nation. Laws fostered by
the party protected the workers of Wisconsin against the calamities of injury and
unemployment. To commemorate the Progressive Party's contribution to workers'
welfare, the Fond du Lac County Wisconsin Labor Council, AFL-CIO,
dedicated this plaque on its 75th, and our nation's 200th, birthday.

Fond du Lac County

092 **HORICON MARSH** Erected 1959
Hwy. 49, 4 mi. E of Waupun

Horicon Marsh, an area of 31,653 acres, was scoured out by the Wisconsin glacier
at least 10,000 years ago. Gradually the upper Rock River made deposits which
slowed its current and spread its waters over the marshland. The Marsh became a
haunt of the earliest Indians, whose mounds remain. To promote lumbering, transportation, and agriculture, white pioneers built a dam in 1846. Horicon Lake, covering 51 square miles, became famous for hunting and fishing. The dam was
removed in 1869, restoring the marsh, which was subjected to various development
schemes that changed its character. Climaxing a twenty-year struggle by conserva-
tionists, Horicon National Wildlife Refuge was established July 16, 1941. The state
controls the south 10,857 acres; the federal government the north 20,796. A wide
range of wildfowl, many varieties of small birds, and numerous fur-bearing animals
constitute the population of Horicon Marsh.

Fond du Lac County

371 **THE RAUBE ROAD SITE**   Erected 1998
W11413 Hwy. TC, Brandon

The Raube Road Site is one of Wisconsin's few remaining intact Old Military Road segments from the state's territorial period. Located on farmland purchased by Albert and Martha Raube in 1911, this 123-foot-long Military Road segment was part of the first constructed roadway to cross Wisconsin. Originally planned as an army supply and communication route between Fort Crawford at Prairie du Chien, Fort Winnebago at Portage, and Fort Howard at Green Bay, the 234-mile-long road was surveyed and built between 1832 and 1837. Fort Winnebago troops constructed the Poynette to Fond du Lac River section using oxen and hand tools during the summer of 1835. The road's marshy areas were filled with bundles of brush, tree limbs, and stone, while smaller streams were bridged with large logs. Preserved by the Raube family, the "Old Road" was listed in the National Register of Historic Places in 1992.

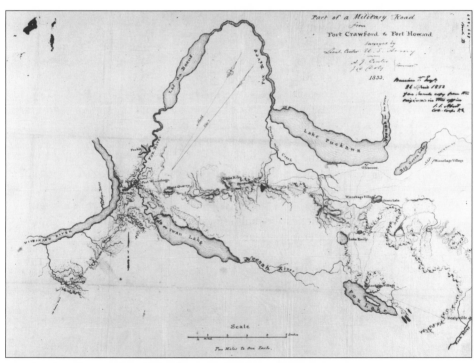

Section map of Military Road, Fort Crawford to Fort Howard, surveyed 1833.
SHSW Library Archives (X3) 39433.

Fond du Lac County

303 **FATHER CASPAR REHRL**   Erected 1991
St. John the Baptist Church, Hwy. W, Johnsburg

A priest, missionary, teacher, founder of churches and schools, and organizer of parishes, Father Rehrl was born in Salzburg, Austria, in 1809. He became a missionary to North America, arriving in the new diocese of Milwaukee in Wisconsin Territory in 1845. He traveled on foot through the Wisconsin wilderness to Johnsburg, a small community of German settlers established in 1841, where he was appointed the first resident pastor of St. John the Baptist Parish. Throughout his life, Father Rehrl energetically carried out his missionary work on this eastern Wisconsin frontier, organizing more than 15 parishes and schools, including Holy Name in Sheboygan, Holy Cross in Mount Calvary, and St. Joseph in Fond du Lac. As the number of Wisconsin parishes grew, Father Rehrl saw the need for dedicated religious women to help with education. On August 12, 1858, he founded the Sisters of St. Agnes, an order of teaching and nursing sisters whose services spread from Wisconsin to Kansas and New York. Father Rehrl died on September 3, 1881, and is buried in St. Agnes Sisters Cemetery in Fond du Lac.

Kenosha County

251 **KEMPER HALL**   Erected 1979
6501 3rd Ave., Kenosha

Kemper Hall, a boarding school for girls, dates to 1855 when St. Matthew's Episcopal Church and some dedicated Kenosha citizens signed a charter launching the Kenosha Female Seminary. In 1865, under the name of St. Claire's Hall, the school moved to this site, the home and property of U.S. Senator Charles Durkee. The name was changed to Kemper Hall in 1870 to honor Wisconsin's first Episcopal bishop, Jackson Kemper. During its 105 years of educational service, Kemper Hall achieved prominence as a young women's preparatory school.

Kenosha County

379 **GREEN BAY ETHNIC TRAIL**   Erected 1998
Hwy. 31, eastbound lane at 95th St., Kenosha

Green Bay Road was the main route of settlement and communication in 19th-century eastern Wisconsin. The road followed an ancient Indian trail network and was surveyed for use as a military road between Fort Dearborn (Chicago) and Fort Howard (Green Bay) by the United States War Department in 1835. Completed in 1840 with private funds, Green Bay Road served as the only north-south route in eastern Wisconsin for many years. Waves of European immigrants who came to Wisconsin seeking a new home traveled this route and settled along it. Eventually, about 30 different ethnic communities were established along Green Bay Road, leaving a rich cultural heritage that can be seen in their building methods, such as German "Fachwerk" and Irish fieldstone; heard in their place names like "Oostburg" and "Freistadt"; celebrated in their annual festivals such as "Holland Fest" and "Slovenian Picnic"; and observed in their unique architecture like the rural "housebarn" and the ethnic church.

Kenosha County

071 **THIRTY-SECOND DIVISION MEMORIAL HIGHWAY**   Erected 1957
Hwy. 32 at S edge of Kenosha

The 32nd Division was organized in 1917. Originally it was made up of National Guardsmen from Wisconsin and Michigan. World War I: Fought in Alsace, Aisne-Marne, Oise-Aisne and Meuse-Argonne offensives. Vanquished 23 German divisions, served in the Army of Occupation in Germany. Deactivated in 1919. World War II: One of the first to be called. Fought offensively in the Buna-Sanananda operations. Saider, Aitape, Morotai, Biak, Leyte and Luzon campaigns. 654 days in action in the Pacific theater. Served in the Army of Occupation in Japan. Deactivated in 1946. THIS HIGHWAY IS DEDICATED TO THE GALLANT MEN OF THE THIRTY-SECOND RED ARROW DIVISION WHO MADE THE SUPREME SACRIFICE IN BOTH WARS.

306 **CORDELIA A. P. HARVEY**   Erected 1991
Rest Area No. 26, I-94

Wisconsin women rallied to support the Union during the Civil War. They became nurses, hospital matrons, sanitary agents, and ministers. Cordelia A. Perrine Harvey attained national prominence for her role in promoting convalescent aid for sick and wounded soldiers. Cordelia had moved with her family to Southport (Kenosha) in 1840. She married Louis P. Harvey, who became governor in 1862. That April, Governor Harvey drowned while visiting Wisconsin troops wounded at the Battle of Shiloh in Tennessee. Mrs. Harvey thereupon dedicated herself to improving conditions for hospitalized soldiers. She criticized military hospitals for improper sanitation, urging that disabled soldiers be sent northward to medical centers near their homes where care would be better. In 1863 Cordelia Harvey met Abraham Lincoln and convinced the president to approve the establishment of recuperation hospitals in the North. The first of three such hospitals in Wisconsin opened in Madison. (The other two were in Milwaukee and Prairie du Chien.) The Harvey United States Army Hospital in Madison was redesignated the Wisconsin Soldiers' Orphans Home in 1866. It operated under Mrs. Harvey's direction until 1867, and it closed in 1874.

Cordelia Harvey.
SHSW Visual Materials Archive (X3) 21741.

Kenosha County

 THE NAME "WISCONSIN"   Erected 1994
**Tourist Area Info. Center No. 26, westbound
lane of I-94, N of I-11**

In 1673, thirty-nine years after Jean Nicolet visited the Green Bay area, Father
Jacques Marquette and Louis Jolliet set out from New France to explore the
Mississippi River. They traveled from the Straits of Mackinac between Lakes Huron
and Michigan to the Fox River at the foot of Green Bay. Two Native American
guides led them up the Fox, from which they portaged (at present day Portage) to
the river for which the state is named. Marquette and Joliet referred to the
Wisconsin River as the Miskonsing, Meskousing, Meskous and Miskous, using varia-
tions on one of the Native American names for the river. Through the years, the
spelling of Wisconsin underwent many changes. By 1800, "Ouisconsin" had
become the favorite form for both the river and the region. Finally, in 1845, the
Wisconsin territorial legislature officially endorsed "Wisconsin" as the accepted
spelling. Many interpretations of the state's name have been suggested, including
"gathering of the waters," "red earth place," "river of a thousand isles," "a good
place in which to live," and "at the great point," all of which seem appropriate
descriptions of Wisconsin's unique and varied geography.

Manitowoc County

 THE WINNEBAGO TRAIL   Erected 1978
Silver Lake Park, Hwy. 151, 0.9 mi W of I-43, just W of Manitowoc

Many modern highways follow routes marked out long ago by Indian people. The
Winnebago Trail across central Wisconsin became the general course of Highways
151 from Manitowoc to Fond du Lac, 45 from Fond du Lac to Oshkosh, 21 from
Oshkosh to Sparta, and 16 from Sparta to La Crosse. When European contact
occurred in the first half of the 1600s, the Winnebagos had their permanent village
and garden area in the Green Bay–Lake Winnebago region, ranging out seasonally
to hunt and gather wild produce. In response to the fur trade, they extended their
territorial claims and established villages throughout western Wisconsin as far north
as the headwaters of the Black River and south along the Rock River nearly to its
mouth on the Mississippi in Illinois. On occasion they crossed the Mississippi to
hunt. Over 3,000 Winnebago people still reside in their old territory in Wisconsin.

(248) MANITOWOC'S MARITIME HERITAGE   Erected 1978
Mariner's Park, S. 8th St. at the Manitowoc River, Manitowoc

In 1847 Captain Joseph Edwards built the schooner *Citizen* here, beginning an era of maritime tradition in Manitowoc which has still not ended. The *Challenge*, believed one of the first clipper ships produced on the Great Lakes, was built by one of the shipyards that lined the river banks. The *Cora A.*, launched here in 1889, was the last schooner built on the Great Lakes. During the late 1800s, the Goodrich Transportation Company played an important role in the growth of Manitowoc. Their passenger steamers brought people and goods to their docks east and west of this point. As the smaller shipyards disappeared, a new yard, the Manitowoc Shipbuilding Company, grew and prospered. They built 437 hulls in Manitowoc, including 28 submarines during World War II. By 1978 the Burger Boat Company was the only shipyard left in Manitowoc. Manitowoc's proud maritime heritage is preserved here in the Maritime Museum.

Manitowoc outer harbor at night, ca. 1900.
SHSW Visual Materials Archive (X3) 39840.

Manitowoc County

 MANITOWOC SUBMARINES   Erected 1989
Manitowoc Maritime Museum,
75 Maritime Dr., Manitowoc

At the outbreak of World War II in 1939, President Franklin D. Roosevelt called upon America to rearm. Increasing the number of submarines became a goal. Because existing shipbuilders could not meet production schedules, the U.S. Navy approached Charles C. West, president of the Manitowoc Shipbuilding Company, and requested that his firm build submarines. Government contracts led to the expansion and modernization of the Manitowoc Shipbuilding Company facilities. Workers and engineers rapidly developed innovative construction methods, including side–launching of submarines. Ultimately, the Manitowoc Shipbuilding Company employed some 7,000 workers in three shifts, seven days a week. *U.S.S. Peto*, launched in 1942, became the first of twenty-eight fleet submarines built at Manitowoc. The submarines were towed to New Orleans via the Illinois-Mississippi Waterway using a special floating dry dock. U.S.S. *Rasher,* a Manitowoc submarine, sank 99,901 tons of Japanese shipping, the second highest total for an American submarine. Four Manitowoc submarines, *Golet, Kete, Lagato*, and *Robalo*, along with 336 officers and enlisted men, were lost during the war.

Manitowoc County

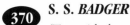

S. S. *BADGER*
(Two-sided marker)   Erected 1998
Lake Michigan Carferry Dock, 700 S. Lakeview Dr., Manitowoc

Built by the Christy Corporation of Sturgeon Bay in 1952, the S. S. *Badger* is the last of fourteen Ludington, Michigan-based car ferries still crossing Lake Michigan. Commissioned by the Chesapeake and Ohio Railroad, the S. S. *Badger,* named for the University of Wisconsin athletic teams, provided passenger and freight service between Manitowoc and Ludington. After railroad car ferry service declined, the Lake Michigan Carferry Service purchased and renovated the S. S. *Badger* in 1992. Today, the ferry transports truck freight, automobiles, and passengers.

MANITOWOC AND THE CAR FERRIES

In the first five decades of the 20th century, Lake Michigan railroad car ferry service aided national defense and the regional economy by providing a key transportation alternative to the railroad bottleneck in Chicago. At the Port of Manitowoc, where car ferries were the major cargo carriers, Manitowoc shipbuilders constructed eleven car ferries and maintained, repaired, and remodeled many more. Five of these ships were built for the Pere Marquette Line, which later evolved into the Lake Michigan Carferry Service.

Manitowoc County

THORSTEIN VEBLEN (1857-1929)   Erected 1970
Valders Memorial Park, Hwy. J, Valders

One of Wisconsin's most controversial figures, Thorstein Bunde Veblen, was born near here July 30, 1857. In 1865 the Veblen family moved to Minnesota, where Thorstein graduated from college in 1880. He was a deep thinker, usually lonely and always in debt. After receiving a Ph.D. in philosophy from Yale in 1884, Veblen taught in several colleges. He was not a popular teacher but attracted dedicated followers to his extreme social and economic ideas. In 1899, his book *The Theory of the Leisure Class* created immediate controversy. During much of his life, Veblen remained estranged from society. His pale, sick face; beard; loose-fitting clothes; shambling gait; weak voice; and desperate shyness enhanced this estrangement and deepened his loneliness. Yet the society which did not accept Veblen the man did come to value the products of his penetrating mind. His books and articles have been described as perhaps "the most considerable and creative body of social thought that America has produced."

Manitowoc County

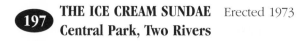

197 **THE ICE CREAM SUNDAE**   Erected 1973
Central Park, Two Rivers

In 1881, George Hallauer asked Edward C. Berner, the owner of a soda fountain at 1404 15th Street, to top a dish of ice cream with chocolate sauce, hitherto used only for ice cream sodas. The concoction cost a nickel and soon became very popular, but it was sold only on Sundays. One day a ten-year-old girl insisted she have a dish of ice cream "with that stuff on top," saying they could pretend it was Sunday. After that, the confection was sold every day in many flavors. It lost its Sunday-only association, to be called the ICE CREAM SUNDAE when a glassware salesman placed an order with his company for the long canoe-shaped dishes in which it was served, "as sundae dishes."

Manitowoc County

326 **RAWLEY POINT LIGHTHOUSE**   Erected 1995
Point Beach State Park, 5 mi. N of Two Rivers on Hwy. O

On this prominent point of land, a major threat to navigation on Lake Michigan's western shore, Rawley Point Lighthouse was erected in 1894 and is the only one of its kind on the Great Lakes. The tower is a reconstruction and enlargement of an old Chicago River lighthouse that was transported to this location. Standing at 113 feet, this soaring structure is the tallest octagonal skeletal light tower on the Great Lakes and replaced a deteriorated 1874 brick lighthouse whose keeper's quarters remain at the site. The lighthouse is designed with eight corner posts and a complex network of horizontal struts and diagonal tie rods. Rising through the center of the lighthouse is an iron stair cylinder that accesses the top lantern room and gallery. Originally equipped with a Fresnel lens and then an airport beacon light, the lighthouse was manually operated until 1980, when it became fully automated. The present optic system was installed in 1987. The light can be seen by ships 28 miles away.

MEEME POLL HOUSE Erected 1998
Pioneer Rd. and Hwy. XX, Meeme

The Meeme Poll House, the official voting place in the Town of Meeme for 83 years, was erected by Joseph Schwartz and Edmund Kolb in 1900. German immigrants and their descendants exercised their democratic right to vote in this simple wooden structure. The adjacent Meeme House (ca. 1847), originally a stagecoach inn, served as the town's polling place in the 19th century. The Meeme Poll House closed in 1983, but curtained voting booths still remain in the interior.

ROCK MILL Erected 1998
Hwy. R, 0.5 mile N of Schley Rd.

In 1847 New York millwright and speculator Pliney Pierce built this mill adjacent to the rapidly falling waters of Devils River. First constructed as a sawmill, Rock Mill was quickly converted to a gristmill after the area's available timber was depleted. Serving mostly local German, Czech, and Irish immigrant farmers, Rock Mill ground as many as 118 bags of grain a day and produced wheat, rye, and graham flour and animal feed. The mill functioned as the social center of rural life here for almost 90 years, ceasing operation in 1934.

S
O
U
T
H
E
A
S
T

Milwaukee County

328 **SINKING OF THE *LADY ELGIN*** Erected 1996
N. Water and E. Erie sts., Milwaukee

The loss of the side-wheel steamship *Lady Elgin* was one of Lake Michigan's most tragic maritime disasters. On September 8, 1860, the ship, returning to Milwaukee from Chicago, sank following a collision nine miles off Winnetka, Illinois. Milwaukee's Irish Union Guards had chartered the grand *Lady Elgin* for a special Chicago benefit trip to raise funds to purchase new weapons. Wisconsin's Governor Alexander Randall, an opponent of the federal fugitive slave law, suspected the Union Guards of disloyalty to the state because they supported the fugitive slave law. Randall ordered the unit to disband and confiscated the Guards' weapons. In defiance, Union Guards commander Garrett Barry sought to arm the unit independently from the state. Aboard the ship were more than 500 Union Guards supporters, mostly from the city's Irish Third Ward, including city officials, members of two German militia units, and the Milwaukee City Band. In the early morning hours the ship was struck amidships by an unlit, overloaded lumber schooner, the *Augusta*. At least 300 lives were lost, decimating the Irish Third Ward community.

Sinking of the Lady Elgin, Sept. 8, 1860, lithograph.
SHSW Visual Materials Archive (X3) 2309.

17

Milwaukee County

310 **PABST THEATER**   Erected 1992
144 E. Wells St., Milwaukee

Designed by Otto Strack and built by Milwaukee brewing magnate Captain
Frederick Pabst, the Pabst Theater was constructed on the site of an earlier opera
house destroyed by fire in 1895. The Pabst was completed in just six months and
opened on November 9, 1895. One of the first all-electric theaters, the Pabst also
included such innovations as air conditioning and fireproof construction. The Pabst
was home to one of the finest German theater companies in the United States and
epitomized German culture in Wisconsin while also featuring this nation's greatest
artists on its stage.

Milwaukee County

311 **THIRD WARD FIRE: 1892**   Erected 1991
200 N. Broadway, Milwaukee

On the evening of October 28, 1892, an exploding oil barrel started a small fire
in the Union Oil and Paint Company warehouse, which was located at 323 N.
Water Street. Another fire broke out in a nearby factory in the 300 block of N.
Broadway, where Commission Row is now located. Before morning, 4 persons
had died, 215 railroad cars were consumed, 440 buildings were destroyed, and
more than 1,900 people in the Irish community were left homeless. In all, the
"mountain of fire" engulfed 16 city blocks within the district. Property loss, the
greatest in Milwaukee's history, was estimated at 5 million dollars at the time.
Reconstruction began immediately. Within 30 years, predominantly Italian warehouse and manufacturing businesses had rebuilt the area, with a majority of the
buildings dating from the 1890s. Today, the magnificent buildings of the Historic
Third Ward stand as a tribute to the prominent architects who designed the structures and to those merchants who rebuilt the district as the center of dry goods
commerce in Milwaukee.

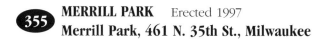

Milwaukee County

355 **MERRILL PARK**   Erected 1997
Merrill Park, 461 N. 35th St., Milwaukee

In 1879, Sherburn S. Merrill, the general manager of the Chicago, Milwaukee and St. Paul Railroad, purchased almost half a square mile in the Menomonee Valley to construct a massive railroad shop complex. By the early 1880s, the railroad company employed over 2500 workers. To provide housing for these workers, Merrill created "Merrill Park" in 1883, a housing development between 27th and 35th streets. Desiring a "respectable" neighborhood, Merrill placed deed restrictions on his property, prohibiting "intoxicating liquors" and "livery stables." New Englanders and German and English immigrants, among others, settled in the area, and the neighborhood grew with a mixture of single-family houses, duplexes, cottages, and apartments. After the disastrous Third Ward fire of 1892 many Irish families moved west to Merrill Park, and by the early twentieth century, Merrill Park became Milwaukee's premier Irish neighborhood. The community remains one of Milwaukee's most ethnically diverse.

Milwaukee County

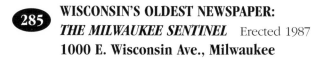

285 **WISCONSIN'S OLDEST NEWSPAPER:**
THE MILWAUKEE SENTINEL   Erected 1987
1000 E. Wisconsin Ave., Milwaukee

The Milwaukee Sentinel has chronicled the events of Milwaukee, Wisconsin, and the world longer than any other newspaper in the state. Founded as a weekly on June 27, 1837, by Solomon Juneau, Milwaukee's first mayor, the *Sentinel* was first published near this site next to Juneau's fur-trading post. On December 9, 1844, the *Sentinel* became Milwaukee's first daily newspaper. Its coverage of Wisconsin and Milwaukee news in the nineteenth century makes it an outstanding historical resource.

Milwaukee County

 **THE UNIVERSITY OF
WISCONSIN-MILWAUKEE**   Erected 1987
**Mitchell Hall, UW-Milwaukee,
N. Downer Ave.**

Milwaukee's State Normal School, which was founded in 1885 on the city's west side to train teachers, relocated in 1909 to this building, Mitchell Hall, then located on 11$^1/_2$ acres. Designed by Van Ryn and de Gelleke, expanded in 1912, and named after a distinguished Milwaukee family, Mitchell Hall continued as "Old Main" when the institution became degree-granting Milwaukee State Teachers College in 1927 and Wisconsin State College in 1951. The College merged with the University of Wisconsin's Milwaukee Extension Center in 1955 to become the University of Wisconsin-Milwaukee. The campus soon expanded to 91 acres, facilities were continuously constructed, and both undergraduate and graduate degree programs, including doctorates, grew and developed, with a student body of more than 25,000 as early as 1974. Mitchell Hall, renovated in 1977, continues to provide major classroom and office facilities.

Milwaukee County

CIVIL WAR CAMP   Erected 1989
1756 N. Prospect Ave., Milwaukee

Near here a Civil War training camp was built in August 1861. Named Camp Holton, Camp Sigel, and finally Camp Reno, its boundaries were Prospect and Bartlett avenues and Lafayette and Royall places. Six Wisconsin infantry regiments, almost 7,000 men, were mustered in and equipped for the Union army here. Two other Civil War posts, Camps Scott and Washburn, were on the city's west side.

Milwaukee County

CAPTAIN FREDERICK PABST (1836-1904)
Erected 1992

2000 W. Wisconsin Ave., Milwaukee

Of German birth, Pabst became a ship's captain in the 1850s and moved to Milwaukee in the 1860s. He later joined his father-in-law's brewery (founded 1844), which was renamed the Pabst Brewery in 1889. By the 1890s it was the world's largest lager beer brewery, and he was Milwaukee's leading citizen. The Captain's elegant Flemish Renaissance Revival mansion was designed by George Bowman Ferry and constructed on fashionable Grand Avenue 1890-93. Its pavilion housed the Pabst Brewery exhibit at the World's Columbian Exposition in 1893. Between 1908 and 1975 five Catholic archbishops resided here. In 1978 Wisconsin Heritages, Inc., purchased the property. Pabst also erected the city's first skyscraper (1891), rebuilt the Pabst Theater (1895), operated the Whitefish Bay Resort, headed the Wisconsin National Bank, and owned a local hotel and many saloons, a hops farm and street railway in Wauwatosa, and hotels and restaurants elsewhere in the nation.

Frederick Pabst House.
Courtesy of the City of Milwaukee, Carlen Hatala, photographer, 1994.

Milwaukee County

043 **ERASTUS B. WOLCOTT, M.D. (1804-1880)**   Erected 1972
Grounds of VA Hospital, 5000 W. National Ave., Milwaukee

Dr. Erastus B. Wolcott was an originator of the idea for a national soldiers' home in Milwaukee. A spirited leader in medicine, business, and government, he was state surgeon general during the Civil War and an ardent advocate for what is now the Veterans Administration Hospital at Wood. The hospital was established in 1867, and Dr. Wolcott was appointed by Congress to the national governing board. Dr. Wolcott was a founder of the State Medical Society in 1841 and the Medical Society of Milwaukee County in 1846. He made surgical history in 1861 as the first physician to remove a diseased kidney. In 1869 he married Dr. Laura J. Ross, the first woman admitted to a medical society in Wisconsin and one of the first three American woman physicians. She erected the monument to Dr. Wolcott in Milwaukee's Lake Park.

Milwaukee County

288 **NATIONAL SOLDIERS' HOME**   Erected 1989
Zablocki VA Medical Center, 5000 W. National Ave., Milwaukee

The Wisconsin Soldiers' Home Association was formed in 1864 by a coalition of women's charitable organizations led by Lydia Hewitt, Hannah Vedder, and Mrs. E. L. Buttrick of Milwaukee. The association raised funds to endow a hospital where sick and wounded Civil War soldiers could receive medical treatment and long-term domiciliary care. After securing a state appropriation of $5000, the association staged a spectacular public event known as the Soldiers' Home Fair, which opened in Milwaukee on June 29, 1865, and raised more than $110,000. The proceeds from the Soldiers' Home Fair enabled the association to purchase land and establish a hospital. In 1867, the association transferred its property and remaining funds to the federal government for the establishment of the National Asylum for Disabled Volunteer Soldiers, Northwestern Branch. Dr. Erastus B. Wolcott of Milwaukee, the state's surgeon general during the Civil War, was appointed by Congress to head the governing board of the home. In 1869, the noted architect Edward Townsend Mix designed the High Victorian Gothic structure "Old Main," now known as Building No. 2. The hospital was renamed the Clement J. Zablocki Veterans Administration Medical Center in 1985.

Milwaukee County

 BAY VIEW'S ROLLING MILL   Erected 1985
S. Superior St. and E. Russell Ave., Milwaukee

Near this site in Bay View stood the Milwaukee Iron Company rolling mill, the first major heavy industry in the region and an important producer of iron and steel for the Midwest. The mill, which opened in 1868, transformed ore from Dodge County and Lake Superior area mines into iron products, including thousands of tons of rail for the region's growing railroads. By 1885, more than 1500 people were employed at the plant, some recruited from the iron-producing districts of the British Isles, and the village of Bay View grew from a rural crossroads into an industrial community surrounding the rolling mill. On May 5, 1886, the mill was the scene of a major labor disturbance. Nearly 1500 strikers from around Milwaukee marched on the Bay View mill to dramatize their demand for an eight-hour work day. The local militia, called to the scene by Governor Jeremiah Rusk, fired on the crowd, killing seven people. The mill closed in 1929, and the buildings were demolished a decade later. But the community of Bay View remains, a neighborhood of mill workers' houses, shops, and churches.

Milwaukee County

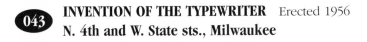

147 **MILWAUKEE DOWNER COLLEGE**   Erected 1965
N. Downer and E. Hartford aves., Milwaukee

On September 14, 1848, Mrs. William L. Parsons, the wife of a Congregational minister, opened the Milwaukee Female Seminary at the corner of Milwaukee and East Wells. Three years later it was chartered by the legislature, thus placing Wisconsin in the vanguard of education at a time when colleges for women were almost unknown. A new building was erected at 1120 North Milwaukee Street. In 1855 the Wisconsin Female College, later named Downer College, was chartered at Fox Lake. Both schools experienced financial difficulties until they merged to become Milwaukee Downer College in 1899. The two institutions combined their resources and moved in 1890 to this site, which became a new campus of forty wooded acres. When the University of Wisconsin-Milwaukee purchased this campus in 1964, Milwaukee Downer moved to Appleton to join Lawrence College and is now part of Lawrence University.

Milwaukee County

043 **INVENTION OF THE TYPEWRITER**   Erected 1956
N. 4th and W. State sts., Milwaukee

At 318 State Street, approximately 300 feet northeast of here, C. Latham Sholes perfected the first practical typewriter in September 1869. Here he worked during the summer with Carlos Glidden, Samuel W. Soule, and Matthias Schwalbach in the machine shop of C. F. Kleinsteuber. During the next six years, money for the further development of the typewriter was advanced by James Densmore, who later gained the controlling interest and sold it to E. Remington and Sons of Ilion, N.Y.

Milwaukee County

186 **SAINT MARY'S SCHOOL OF NURSING**   Erected 1972
2320 N. Lake Dr., Milwaukee

Formal nurses' training in the United States began in Boston in 1872. In 1888, the Woman's Club of Wisconsin organized the Wisconsin Training School for Nurses, patterned after the Bellevue School of Nursing in New York. In 1894, the Daughters of Charity of St. Vincent de Paul launched Wisconsin's first private hospital and organized a training school for nurses at St. Mary's Hospital, Milwaukee. The two-year curriculum was expanded to three in 1901, and a diploma was awarded upon graduation. The school, incorporated separately in 1912, became state-accredited in 1913 and nationally accredited in 1940. Affiliation with other institutions of learning began in 1924. The name was changed in 1932 to denote the transition from training to education. Rising costs and growth of college degree programs brought voluntary dissolution in 1969 after having graduated 1,913 nurses.

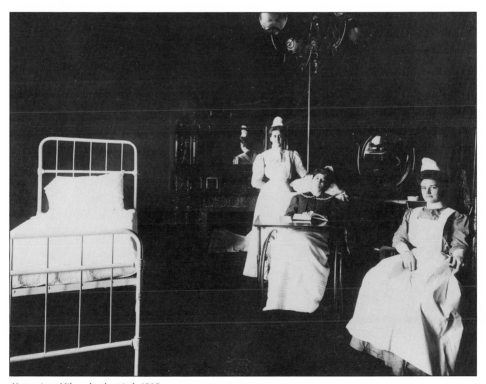

Nurses in a Milwaukee hospital, 1906.
SHSW Visual Materials Archive CF 814.

155 **SAINT JOHN'S INFIRMARY**   Erected 1966
N. Lake Dr. and E. North Ave., Milwaukee

Founded May 15, 1848, with the Sisters of Charity of St.Vincent de Paul providing direction and nursing, St. John's Infirmary offered Wisconsin's first public hospital care under the supervision of the patient's physician. (Prior institutions merely isolated the sick; no medical care was given.) St. John's original location was the southeast corner of Jackson and Wells streets. In 1855 it was moved downtown, and in 1858, it was built on this site on three acres given by the city. The name was changed to St. Mary's Hospital. It was also a Marine Hospital for Great Lakes seamen. During the Civil War, the sisters cared for as many as 110 casualties at one time. A famed chief surgeon here was Dr. Erastus B. Wolcott. His achievements included the first recorded kidney removal, on June 4, 1861.

Milwaukee County

201 **OLD NORTH POINT WATER TOWER**   Erected 1975
E. North Ave., between N. Lake Dr. and
N. Terrace Ave., Milwaukee

The 1871 Wisconsin legislature authorized the city of Milwaukee to finance and build a public water system. By 1873 the Board of Water Commissioners had constructed the old North Point Pumping Station below the bluff with intake from Lake Michigan, this tower, a reservoir a mile west, and 55 miles of water mains, delivering cheap, plentiful, pure water to Milwaukee's people and industry. This 175-foot Victorian Gothic tower, designed by Charles A. Gombert and made of cut Niagara limestone from Wauwatosa, houses a circular wrought-iron standpipe 120 feet high and four feet in diameter. Until construction of a new pumping station in 1963, the standpipe water absorbed pulsations of reciprocating steam-driven engines, and the tower prevented ice from forming in the standpipe during cold weather.

Old North Point Water Tower.
Courtesy of the City of Milwaukee.
Paul Jakubovich, photographer, 1977.

27

Milwaukee County

206 **CARL SANDBURG HALL** Erected 1975
N. Maryland and E. Hartford aves.,
UW-Milwaukee campus

Carl Sandburg (1878-1967), poet, balladeer, biographer of Lincoln, soldier in the Spanish-American War, came from Illinois to Wisconsin in December 1907 as a state organizer for the Social-Democrat Party in eastern Wisconsin. After marrying Lillian Steichen of Menomonee Falls in 1908, he traveled the state with the Debs "Red Special" presidential campaign train and worked for the Wisconsin Anti-Tuberculosis Association, Kroeger's store, and several Milwaukee newspapers before serving as secretary to Socialist Mayor Emil Seidel for nearly a year. Then he joined the *Social-Democratic Herald* and Victor Berger's *Milwaukee Leader*, while residing at 3324 North Cambridge Street. He left Milwaukee permanently in September 1912 for Chicago, where he actively involved himself in its poetic renaissance.

Milwaukee County

222 **GENERAL MITCHELL FIELD** Erected 1976
Layton Ave., E of Howell Ave., N of Mitchell Field, Milwaukee

In 1920 Thomas Hamilton established a flying field on East Layton Avenue, the field was purchased by Milwaukee County on October 29, 1926. As commercial aviation grew, the field and its operations expanded. The first scheduled passenger service began on July 1, 1927, and Thomas Hamilton started production of his all-metal passenger airplane the same year. On August 31, 1929, the Kohler line started passenger service across Lake Michigan, basing their winter operations here. On March 17, 1941, the airport was named in honor of Milwaukee's famous air-power pioneer, General William Mitchell. Other famous fliers, such as Charles Lindbergh, Lester Maitland, the Bremen fliers, Wiley Post, and Eddie Rickenbacker, visited this field. Today General Mitchell Field is the principal airport in the state, serving the metropolitan area of southeastern Wisconsin.

Milwaukee County

 MILWAUKEE INTERURBAN TERMINAL Erected 1976
231 W. Michigan St., Milwaukee

The Milwaukee Electric Railway and Light Company opened its terminal here in 1905. The first car entered this building January 1, 1905. At one time the system extended west to Madison, north to Sheboygan, and south to Kenosha. The final line was abandoned June 30, 1951. The first floor was the terminal area, with two waiting rooms and thirteen car tracks; it was the largest terminal of its kind in the United States.

Milwaukee County

 CARL FREDERICK ZEIDLER
(1908-1942) Erected 1980
300 block of W. Michigan St., Milwaukee

Milwaukee born and educated, lawyer Carl F. Zeidler became Milwaukee's 33rd mayor in April 1940, when he defeated Daniel W. Hoan, Socialist mayor since 1916. In April 1942, Zeidler left office to enter service as a U.S. Navy Lieutenant (J.G.). On the night of November 7, 1942, the merchant ship *La Salle*, on which he commanded a gunnery crew, was torpedoed off Cape Town, South Africa, with the loss of all hands.

373 BAY VIEW'S IMMIGRANTS   Erected 1998
Zillman Park, S. Kinnickinnic Ave. and E. Ward St., Milwaukee

From a quiet mid-19th-century farming community to a bustling industrial center along Kinninckinnic Avenue in only twenty years, Bay View's industrial transformation could not have occurred without the contributions of hundreds of immigrant workers who poured into the community's foundries, brickyards, machine shops, tanneries, and a glass factory, seeking employment in the last quarter of the 19th century. The first industrial workers in Bay View were recruited from Sheffield, England, for their knowledge of steel production, but over the years other immigrant workers from the British Isles, Ireland, Germany, Poland, and Italy, among others, would make Bay View one of the most ethnically diverse communities in Milwaukee.

Milwaukee tanneries.
SHSW Visual Materials Archive (X3) 41082.

Milwaukee County

255 **MACARTHUR SQUARE**   Erected 1979
Civic Center, Milwaukee

MacArthur Square was designated on September 17, 1945, to honor General of the Army Douglas MacArthur for his leadership of Allied forces in the Pacific during World War II. MacArthur, his father General Arthur MacArthur, and his grandfather Judge Arthur MacArthur were all residents of Milwaukee. Douglas lived at the Plankinton House and attended West Division High School. In 1898 he was appointed to the U. S. Military Academy by Milwaukee Congressman Theobald Otjen. Douglas MacArthur's final visit here was on April 27, 1951, when he received an honorary degree from Marquette University and spoke at this site.

Milwaukee County

334 **KILBOURNTOWN**   Erected 1998
1110 N. Old World Third St., Milwaukee

In this vicinity, Kilbourntown, one of three original Milwaukee settlements, was founded by surveyor and land speculator Byron Kilbourn in 1835. Kilbourntown's first residents were entrepreneurs from the East. In 1839, a small group of German immigrants from Pomerania arrived in Kilbourntown, heralding a major 19th-century immigration of German settlers. Concentrated in Kilbourntown, this German population helped Milwaukee become the "most German city" in the United States. By the 20th century, Kilbourntown's German population had substantially dispersed, and the area became a community of rich ethnic diversity, soon becoming the heart of downtown Milwaukee.

Milwaukee County

096 **NICHOLAS SENN, M.D. (1844-1908)**   Re-erected 1997
N. 3rd and W. Juneau sts., Milwaukee

In a laboratory under the sidewalk of his office at this site, in the 1870s, Dr. Senn conducted far-reaching experiments which led to international renown as the "great master of abdominal surgery." He was one of Wisconsin's greatest surgeons, physicians, and medical pioneers, and the 49th president of the American Medical Association. Dr. Senn was a founder of the Association of Military Surgeons of the U.S.A.

Milwaukee County

257 **GOLDA MEIR (1898-1978)**   Erected 1979
At Golda Meir Library on UW-Milwaukee campus Milwaukee

The UWM Library is named for Golda Meir. Born Goldie Mabowehz in the Ukraine, she migrated to Milwaukee in 1906, was educated at Fourth Street School and North Division High School and in present Mitchell Hall of Milwaukee Normal School (1916-17). She and husband Morris Meyerson settled in Palestine in 1921. There she helped found the Israel Labor Party, held high political and governmental posts, and eventually became prime minister (1969-74).

Milwaukee County

294 FIRST AFRICAN AMERICAN CHURCH BUILT IN WISCONSIN Erected 1990
N. 4th St. and W. Kilbourn Ave., Milwaukee

St. Mark African Methodist Episcopal Church, the first African American church built in Wisconsin, once stood on this site. The property was purchased in 1869, the year the congregation was organized. Construction on the St. Mark A.M.E. church began in November 1886, under the direction of Rev. William R. Alexander, pastor. Dedicatory services were held on April 3, 1887. The St. Mark congregation spent 43 years at this site, during which time the membership grew and the church, known as the "Friendly Church," became the center of religious, civic, and cultural affairs for the African-American community.

Milwaukee County

412 MABEL WANDA RAIMEY (1895-1986) Erected 1999
Marquette University Law School, 1103 W. Wisconsin Ave., Milwaukee

Mabel Raimey was the first African-American woman attorney in Wisconsin and the first to graduate from the University of Wisconsin-Madison (1918). She attended Marquette University Law School and was admitted to the Wisconsin Bar in 1927. An original Milwaukee Urban League board member, Raimey was also a founder of the Northside YWCA and the Epsilon Kappa Omega Chapter of the Alpha Kappa Alpha Sorority, Inc. She was a trustee of the West Allis Tabernacle Baptist Church. The Milwaukee Chapter of the National Association of Black Women Attorneys is named in her honor.

Milwaukee County

036 **FIRST MILWAUKEE CARGO PIER** Erected 1963
Foot of E. Michigan St., Milwaukee

Near here, at the foot of Huron (now Clybourn) Street, the first cargo pier in Milwaukee harbor was built by Horatio Stevens, Richard Owens, Amos Tufts, and J. G. Kendall during the winter of 1842. The first vessel to dock at North Pier was the *Cleveland,* under command of Captain M. Hazard on June 1, 1843. The pier, 1200 feet long and 44 feet wide, with a freight shed at the end and a warehouse and tollgate at the entrance, permitted the unloading of freight and passengers from large vessels which could not enter the original mouth of the Milwaukee River, south of Jones Island. Near this pier was the first Milwaukee brewery, founded in 1840. In the following years, three more lakeshore piers were built, which created lively business activity on Milwaukee's east side, known as Juneautown. The first pier was destroyed during the winter of 1846 by strong winds and ice. The same fate later overtook the other piers. A new straight cut, opened in 1857, provided access to the Milwaukee River and to the downtown inner harbor which then developed.

Milwaukee County

057 **ONEIDA STREET STATION, T.M.E.R. and L. Co.** Erected 1958
N. Edison and E. Wells sts., Milwaukee

In this station pulverized coal was first successfully burned continuously and at high efficiencies in furnaces of stationary steam boilers, November 11-15, 1919. This radical departure from conventional firing methods of the period was vigorously opposed by some engineers during its early stages. It soon met with local, national, and international acceptance, and has resulted in great benefits to mankind through reduced cost of electric power and conservation of fuel resources.

Milwaukee County

WATERTOWN PLANK ROAD Erected 1955
Miller Brewing Co., N. 40th and W. State sts., Milwaukee

Started in 1848 and completed in 1853, extended 58 miles west from Milwaukee on a course roughly paralleling State Street past the Frederick Miller Plank Road Brewery through Wauwatosa, Pewaukee, and Oconomowoc to Watertown. The $100,000 road of white-oak planks provided a route for farm products, wood, lime, and passenger vehicles. It cut round-trip travel time to three days, all at a toll of about one cent a mile.

Wisconsin plank road.
SHSW Visual Material Archives (X3) 20666.

Milwaukee County

367 **SHOREWOOD ARMORY**   Erected 1998
4145 N. Oakland Ave., Shorewood

The Shorewood Armory, once located near Capitol Drive and Oakland Avenue, was home to the cavalry unit of the Wisconsin National Guard from 1910 to 1930. Originally called the Light Horse Squadron, the cavalry drilled their horses on the thirty-acre armory grounds and the streets of Shorewood. The armory complex included military offices, the commander's house, a dormitory, a gymnasium, and a large barn with sixty-five stables. Shorewood's rapid suburban expansion forced the cavalry unit to move in 1931.

Milwaukee County

368 **SHOREWOOD HIGH SCHOOL**   Erected 1998
1701 E. Capitol Dr., Shorewood

A forerunner in secondary-school design, Shorewood High School is modeled on a university campus plan. Constructed between 1924 and 1938 by Milwaukee architects Herbst and Kuenzli, the school includes separate buildings for administration, physical education, arts and science, industrial arts, and theater arts. The splendid auditorium also serves the Shorewood community.

Milwaukee County

369 **SHOREWOOD VILLAGE HALL** Erected 1998
3930 N. Murray Ave., Shorewood

Shorewood Village Hall was built in 1908 as a four-room school to serve
Shorewood, then called East Milwaukee. In 1915 this building became the seat of
village government. The building was extensively remodeled in 1937 with Works
Progress Administration (WPA) funds, and again in 1985. It was placed on the
National Register of Historic Places in 1984.

Milwaukee County

196 **BOYHOOD HOME OF JEREMIAH CURTIN (1835-1906)** Erected 1973
8685 W. Grange Ave., Greendale

Born in Detroit of Irish immigrant parents, Curtin came to Milwaukee in 1837 to
join his mother's family, the Furlongs, and settle on a farm in Greenfield. In the
1840s the Curtins moved into this typically Irish stone house described in Curtin's
Memoirs. After his father's death, Jeremiah persevered in his love for learning and
languages and graduated from Harvard College in 1863. His command of Russian
won him a position in the U.S. legation in St. Petersburg in 1864, thus launching
his forty-year worldwide career as linguist, translator (Sienkeiwicz's *Quo Vadis*),
ethnologist, folklorist, and diplomat. He died and was buried at his wife's Vermont
home in Bristol.

280 **WISCONSIN'S LIME INDUSTRY** Erected 1986
8801 W. Grange Ave., Greendale

Lime production was an important nineteenth-century industry in southeastern Wisconsin, primarily because the region's geology provided abundant Silurian dolomite rock that was easily quarried. High-quality lime, used mainly in mortar and plaster, was produced by burning dolomite in wood-fired stone kilns. Over one million barrels of lime were produced annually in the 1880s, some shipped to surrounding states. Many of the lime manufacturers also quarried limestone used in building construction and praised for its beauty and durability. The limeworks of Trimborn Farm Park and nearby quarries represent a relatively unaltered nineteenth-century example of the lime industry. Werner Trimborn began his lime business here in 1851, and it became one of the largest in Milwaukee County. The lime industry expanded with the construction boom in Milwaukee in the 1880s but then declined, ending about 1900 due to increased fuel costs and importation of new building materials. By then, dairying had become the main business of Trimborn Farm. The Trimborn barn and kilns and neighboring Jeremiah Curtin House remain as excellent examples of the use of local stone and lime.

Wisconsin's lime industry, Trimborn Farm. SHSW Div. of Historic Preservation, Paul Jakubovich, photographer.

Milwaukee County

GREENFIELD: THE LAST TOWN IN MILWAUKEE COUNTY   Erected 1997
7325 W. Forest Ave., Greenfield

Following the end of World War II, Milwaukee's rapid urban development forced the seven rural towns of Milwaukee County into annexation or incorporation. When Greenfield incorporated as a city in 1957, the last of Milwaukee County's towns disappeared and with it ended the system of local town government Yankees brought to the area in the 1840s. Although Greenfield's original town plat of 36 square miles has been greatly reduced, this area has remained the center of civic activity for over 150 years.

Milwaukee County

MILWAUKEE COUNTY'S FIRST AIRPORT   Erected 1969
Currie Park, Wauwatosa

One of the earliest publicly owned airports in the United States was established here on July 3, 1919, by the Milwaukee County Park Commission. The nation's first commercial air transport, the Lawson Airliner, took off from this field on August 27, 1919, on a demonstration flight to New York City and Washington, D. C., and returned on November 15, 1919. This two-engine biplane, 95 feet in wingspan, carried 16 passengers and two pilots. Milwaukee's first airmail was flown from here on June 7, 1926, by the Charles Dickinson Line, operating from Chicago to St. Paul via Milwaukee and La Crosse. This airport was deactivated during November 1926 when the need for more space led the county to purchase Hamilton Airport, the site of present General Mitchell Field.

Milwaukee County

320 **WISCONSIN STATE FAIR PARK**   Erected 1993
State Park, Main Gate, S. 81st St.
and W. Greenfield Ave., West Allis

In 1892, this site became the permanent home of the Wisconsin State Fair after its purchase a year earlier by the State Agricultural Society. Until then, the fair had moved annually since the first one in Janesville in 1851. Over the years, State Fair Park has not only showcased agriculture but also military, recreational, and cultural activities. The Park housed troops and equipment for the Spanish-American War and for World Wars I and II. It has featured auto races since 1903, Green Bay Packer football games from 1934 to the 1950s, and world-class speed skating at its Olympic-sized rink since 1966. Cultural phenomena demonstrated at past fairs included cooking with gas (1859), airplane flight (1911), and television (1932). The State Fair Park Board, created in 1971, became an independent state agency in 1990. State Fair Park attracts two million visitors to hundreds of events throughout the year, including the fair, the state's oldest and largest annual event.

Milwaukee County

319 **CAMP HARVEY**   Erected 1992
State Park, Main Gate, S. 81st St. and W. Greenfield Ave., West Allis

At the outbreak of the Spanish-American War in April of 1898, President William McKinley called on the states to gather their military forces. State officials ordered the Wisconsin National Guard to report for duty at Camp Harvey, named for Wisconsin Civil War Governor Louis P. Harvey and located on the grounds of the Wisconsin State Fair Park. The Wisconsin National Guard had been established in 1879 to improve the existing militia system. The war with Spain (1898-1899) demonstrated for the first time the value of the National Guard as a reserve component of the army. In a time of crisis, the Guard units from Wisconsin and the other states could rapidly augment the small active-duty forces. Wisconsin contributed 5,469 men divided into four infantry regiments for service in the Spanish-American War. The First and Fourth Wisconsin Infantry regiments never left the United States. The Second and Third Wisconsin Infantry regiments participated in military operations in Puerto Rico, where they lost two men killed in action. A total of 132 Wisconsinites died from disease, principally typhoid fever.

Milwaukee County

 041

MEADOWMERE Erected 1955
**In triangle at S. 57th, W. Hayes Ave.,
and W. Fillmore Dr., West Allis**

This tract of land was once a part of the estate on which General William (Billy) Mitchell (1879-1936) lived as a boy. His fearless and inquisitive personality as a youth carried over into his military career when he spoke out against overwhelming odds for an adequate air force. After commanding U.S. air forces in France during World War I, he emerged as the nation's pioneer advocate of air power. He did not live to see the wisdom of his foresight, but all America now honors his great courage, heroism, and keen sense of judgment on the future of air power. This marker is erected to the memory of this great air pioneer by the West Allis Rotary Club.

General Billy Mitchell.
SHSW Visual Materials Archive (X28) 4176-E.

Ozaukee County

115 **BIRTHPLACE OF FLAG DAY** Erected 1962
Hwy. I, 0.5 mi. E of Waubeka

Here at Stony Hill School, Bernard J. Cigrand, a 19-year-old teacher, and his students held the first recognized observance of "Flag Birth Day" on June 14, 1885, with a flag ten inches high, carrying 38 stars, standing on a bottle on the teacher's desk. After thirty-one years of crusading by Dr. Cigrand, President Woodrow Wilson on June 14, 1916, proclaimed the national observance of Flag Day.

Stony Hill School, birthplace of Flag Day.
SHSW Div. of Historic Preservation, Paul Jakubovich, photographer.

Ozaukee County

359 **WASHINGTON AVENUE HISTORIC DISTRICT**
(Two-sided marker)   Erected 1997 **Doctor's Park,
Washington Ave. and Mill St., Cedarburg**

Even before Cedarburg incorporated in 1885, the community thrived with mills, shops, hotels, churches, and residences, many of which remain in Cedarburg's commercial center as part of the Washington Avenue Historic District. The district is anchored on the south by St. Francis Borgia Catholic Church and on the north by the Woolen Mill, extending about five blocks and including over 100 properties. On January 17, 1986, the Washington Avenue Historic District was listed in the National Register of Historic Places.

HISTORIC DISTRICT ARCHITECTURE

In the Washington Avenue Historic District, highly skilled masons constructed distinctive locally quarried limestone and fieldstone buildings dating from the 1840s to the early twentieth century. The district's structures were designed in Greek Revival, Italianate, Queen Anne, and vernacular architectural styles, and many were the homes and businesses of early German and Irish settlers. The architecture of the Washington Avenue Historic District illustrates every period of Cedarburg's growth and development.

ORIGIN OF CEDAR CREEK

(Two-sided marker)   Erected 1997

Columbia Rd. and Mequon Ave., Cedarburg

Dropping approximately eighty feet in two and one-half miles, Cedar Creek's falling water power provided enough energy to drive Cedarburg's many mills for over one hundred years. The creek rises from Big and Little Cedar Lakes near West Bend, flowing about fifteen miles eastward and abruptly changing course southward in the Town of Cedarburg. Blocked by dense limestone rock in the township and cutting through a narrow valley, Cedar Creek turns toward the City of Cedarburg with full force.

MILLS ON THE CREEK

Recognizing the energy potential of Cedar Creek's rapidly falling water, business speculators Frederick Hilgen and William Schroeder built a log-and-frame gristmill on the creek in 1844. Eleven years later, they replaced the wooden mill with the nearby stone Cedarburg Mill. Five stories high and massive in scale, Cedarburg Mill was built by Burchard Weber, who constructed the building in large blocks of gray limestone. The mill could produce 120 barrels of flour a day, leading to four additional mills along the creek in the mid-19th century.

Ozaukee County

INTERURBAN BRIDGE
(Two-sided marker)   Erected 1997
W62 N646 Washington Ave., Cedarburg

In 1907, the Milwaukee Northern Railway Company constructed this riveted-steel "Thru Truss Bridge" over Cedar Creek. Manufactured by Carrinage Steel and measuring 159 feet long by 12 feet wide by 20 feet high, the bridge was constructed for the company's interurban train line between Milwaukee and Sheboygan. Powered by overhead electrical lines, the interurban carried passengers and freight in and out of Cedarburg. The railway depot and servicing area once stood a few blocks away.

RIDING THE INTERURBAN

Every hour, with precise regularity, the Milwaukee Northern Railway Interurban train ran over this steel truss bridge. The trip between Milwaukee and Cedarburg took about an hour and cost less than 30 cents. In 1922 the Milwaukee Northern Railway Company was acquired by the Milwaukee Electric Railway and Light Company. The interurban line was operated until 1948. Today, the Interurban Bridge is a pedestrian walkway, and portions of the old rail bed are used as a bike path.

Ozaukee County

146 **LAST COVERED BRIDGE**   (built 1876, retired 1962) Erected 1965
**Covered Bridge Rd., 1 mi. N of Five Corners at Hwys. 60 and 143,
Cedarburg**

This bridge was built by the Town of Cedarburg on petition of neighboring farmers
to replace periodically washed-out bridges. Pine logs, cut and milled at Baraboo,
were fitted and set in place in lattice-truss construction with 3-by-10-inch planks
secured by 2-inch hardwood pins, eliminating the use of nails or bolts, and floored
by 3-inch planking. The Ozaukee County board in 1940 voted to assume the
preservation and maintenance of this bridge.

Covered Bridge, Cedarburg.
SHSW Div. of Historic Preservation, Paul Jakubovich, photographer.

Ozaukee County

290 **HISTORIC CEDARBURG**   Erected 1988
City Hall, Washington Ave., Cedarburg

The source of Cedarburg's vigor from its birth as a village in 1845 was the power-producing creek that the Irish and German immigrants found here. After building five dams and five mills, the life of the community flowed along the banks of the Cedar Creek. The historic heart of Cedarburg contains a significant group of nineteenth and early-twentieth-century buildings that embody the distinctive architectural styles and construction methods employed in the city from the 1840s to the 1920s. The diversity of the types of buildings in the downtown historic district reflects the fact that this area has served as the center of Cedarburg's social, commercial, industrial, educational, and religious activities. Despite this diversity, strong relationships exist between the buildings because of similarities in scale, style, materials, and craftsmanship. Many are constructed of locally quarried limestone or cream-colored brick. The most obvious bond between the buildings is their skillful masonry work, which gives Cedarburg its special character. While many of the early builders and masons remain anonymous, the high quality of the historic buildings serves as an enduring tribute to their skills.

Ozaukee County

332 **WISCONSIN'S GERMAN SETTLERS**   Erected 1996
Mequon City Hall, 11333 N. Cedarburg Rd., Mequon

The oldest German settlements in Wisconsin are found in the Town of Mequon. In 1839 a small group of German immigrants from Saxony settled near the Milwaukee River. They were followed that same year by about twenty immigrant families from Pomerania searching for religious freedom. They established farmsteads in the west part of the town and founded the small community of "Freystatt" or "free place," now

known as Freistadt. The first Lutheran church in Wisconsin was built there in 1840. Over the next fifty years, thousands more German immigrants settled in the surrounding area.

Log home of Christian Turck, immigrant from the German state of Nassau, ca. 1900, preserved at Old World Wisconsin.
SHSW Visual Material Archives (X3) 25839.

47

Ozaukee County

372 **WISCONSIN'S LUXEMBOURGERS**   Erected 1998
Hwys. LL and D, Belgium

Many of northeastern Ozaukee County's prosperous farms, fieldstone houses and outbuildings, and large village churches are characteristic of the Luxembourg immigrant settlement patterns in the area. Beginning in 1845, inexpensive land brought Luxembourgers to the region where they purchased land in lots of 40 acres or less, vast acreage compared to the small tilled plots in Luxembourg. By the late 19th century at least 250 Luxembourger families were living in the communities of Belgium, Fredonia, Holy Cross, Lake Church, Waubeka, Port Washington, and nearby Dacada, making this area a center of Luxembourger settlement in the United States.

Ozaukee County

376 **THE SAUKVILLE TRAILS**   Erected 1998
Triangle Park and Green Bay Rd., Saukville

An important American Indian village once stood in this vicinity near the Milwaukee River, the meeting point of two major Indian trails that led west toward the Mississippi River and north toward Green Bay. In the 1830s, Menominee, Sauk, and Potawatomi people, among others, were living here when U.S. government treaties required them to move. New settlers soon founded Saukville, and the ancient Indian trails, by this time U.S. military roads, became Decorah Road and Green Bay Road.

SOUTHEAST

Ozaukee County

380 **HISTORIC THIENSVILLE** Erected 1998
250 S. Main St., Thiensville

Although not incorporated until 1910, the Village of Thiensville became a settlement in 1842 when John Henry Thien constructed a gristmill. A German "Free Thinker," Thien disavowed organized religion and banned churches here, attracting other Free Thinkers to the settlement. By the 1880s, the village became a thriving commercial center with mills, stores, hotels, blacksmiths, and wagon makers.

Ozaukee County

085 **THE OLDEST LUTHERAN CHURCH IN WISCONSIN** Erected 1958
Freistadt and Wausaukee rds. (Hwys. F and M),
3 mi. W of Thiensville

In early October 1839, approximately 20 families settled near this site to found the colony of Freistadt. Prompted by religious persecution in the homeland, the group sought and found a religious haven in Wisconsin. The first log cabin was located southwest of the present church. The congregation immediately purchased 40 acres of land and in the spring of 1840 built the first Lutheran church in the state. The first pastor of the congregation was L.F.E. Krause (1841-1847). The Lutheran Buffalo Synod was organized here in June 1845. Since 1848 the congregation has been a member of the Lutheran Church-Missouri Synod.

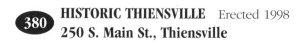

386 **CREAM – BRICK COTTAGES** Erected 1998
(Two-sided marker)
Zoological Gardens, 2131 N. Main St., Racine

Racine's rapid and diversified industrial growth after the Civil War attracted a large working population to the city. Desiring their own homes, many workers built modest cottages of similar design in wood or brick. A high concentration of the brick cottages can be found in the Northside Historic District of Cream Brick Workers' Cottages. Bounded by Goold, English, Chatham, and Erie streets, these cottages, built between 1881 and 1913, often exhibit Italianate, Queen Anne, or Colonial Revival stylistic embellishments.

CREAM BRICK

Many of Racine's historic brick buildings were made of cream brick, a local building material manufactured in the city's brickyards from 1836 to 1914. Recognized by its pale yellow color, the city's cream brick was molded from calcium and magnesium-rich clay deposits found along Lake Michigan's shore. Proving to be a durable masonry product, the local brick was used in the construction of several hundred workers' cottages.

Racine County

SOUTHSIDE HISTORIC DISTRICT   Erected 1998
(Two-sided marker)
Simonsen Park, Main and 14th sts., Racine

Extending west from Lake Michigan to Park Avenue and south from Eighth Street
to DeKoven Avenue, Racine's Southside Historic District contains one of
Wisconsin's highest concentrations of grand historic houses. Dating from 1842 to
1924, the 42-block district displays a variety of Greek Revival, Victorian period, and
Prairie School architectural styles, including designs by early pioneer-architect Lucas
Bradley and by Frank Lloyd Wright. Many of Racine's early leaders and industrial-
ists built their homes here. The Southside Historic District was listed on the
National Register of Historic Places in 1977.

SOUTHSIDE HISTORIC DISTRICT PARKS

Designated as public space as early as 1842, Racine's West Park on College Street
and East Park on Main Street remain as they were originally platted and are part
of the Southside Historic District. Notable in East Park is a granite statue of
President and Mrs. Lincoln by Chicago sculptor Frederick C. Hibbard. In 1867,
Mary Todd Lincoln visited Racine and walked often in East Park, sometimes with
her son Tad. Dedicated in 1943, the statue is rare for memorializing both the
president and his wife.

Racine County

THE SPARK   Erected 1957
Hwy. 11, W limits of Racine

In 1873 the Rev. Dr. J. W. Carhart of Racine designed and operated the first light
self-propelled highway vehicle in the United States and probably the first in the
world. He named it "the Spark." It was driven by a two-cylinder steam engine,
steered by a lever, and had a speed of five miles per hour. When his "infernal
machine" first appeared, the hideous noise created by its operation caused the people of Racine to threaten to run Carhart out of town. Carhart seems to have agreed
with the general opinion of his invention but added, "It must be remembered that
at the time there was no liquid fuel, ball bearings or rubber tires." At the 1908
International Automobile Exposition held in Paris, France, Carhart was addressed as
the "Father of Automobiles" and received a cash award and a certificate of honor
for his invention.

Racine County

129 **OLD MUSKEGO**   Erected 1963
At entrance to Norway Lutheran Church, across from Heg Park, Hwy. 36, about 5 mi. N of Waterford

Under the leadership of John Luraas, forty pioneers came to Muskego Lake from Norway in 1839, to found one of the most important settlements in Norwegian American history. After temporary setbacks, the settlement flourished here through the leadership of Even Heg, Johannes Johannsen, Soren Bache, Elling Eielsen, James Reymert, and Claus Clausen, who sent glowing reports to Norway and encouraged a large movement to this country. This settlement gave rise to the first Norwegian Lutheran congregation organized in America (1843) and published the first Norwegian American newspaper. Old Muskego became well known as a mother colony to other settlements, schools, and churches springing up on the new frontier. Countless wagonloads of newcomers stopped here before continuing west. Nearby Heg Park commemorates Colonel Hans C. Heg, one of Wisconsin's Civil War heroes.

Early Norwegian Lutheran log church in southern Wisconsin.

Interior.
SHSW Div. of Historic Preservation, Jeff Dean, photographer.

Racine County

 MORMONS IN EARLY WISCONSIN   Erected 1992
Hwys. 36 and 83, Echo Lake Park, Burlington

Among those contributing to the nation's westward expansion in the nineteenth century and to Wisconsin's early development were members of the Church of Jesus Christ of Latter-day Saints (Mormons). In 1835, Moses Smith helped establish Burlington and in 1837 organized Wisconsin's first Mormon congregation. His cabin stood across the river from here. Mormons helped develop communities in southwestern and western Wisconsin (Jenkynsville in 1837, Blanchardville in 1842, and near La Crosse in 1844-1845), where they mined lead ore and farmed, and at sites along the Black River (1841-1844), where they harvested pine and floated it down the Mississippi River to build the Mormon temple in Nauvoo, Illinois. Oliver Cowdery, second only to Joseph Smith in the church's early history, was a lawyer and newspaper editor in Elkhorn. After Smith's 1844 murder in Illinois, Wisconsin Mormons either joined the migration to Utah or formed separatist churches here. Few remained after 1850; then by 1875 Mormons re-established a growing presence in Wisconsin.

Racine County

 1888 BOHEMIAN SCHOOLHOUSE   Erected 1998
Hwy. 31 and Five Mile Rd., Caledonia

In 1850, Czech immigrants from Bohemia and Moravia, now regions in the Czech Republic, established a rural settlement between Five Mile and Seven Mile roads in Caledonia Township. This early settlement, known as "Ceska Betlemska" or Bohemian Bethlehem, later called Tabor, was a model for other Wisconsin Czech farming communities. Dedicated to preserving their cultural heritage, Tabor's immigrant families built this schoolhouse in 1888 to instruct their children in Czech language and history. Classes were held on the weekends until 1916, when the building became a community center. In 1974, the schoolhouse was acquired by the Racine County Historical Society.

Sheboygan County

163 **SHEBOYGAN INDIAN MOUND PARK**   Erected 1968
9th St. and Panther Ave., Sheboygan

Within these fifteen acres of ancient woodland and winding stream lie 18 rare Indian burial mounds, dated about 500-750 A.D. Their prehistoric builders, ancestors of the Wisconsin Woodland Indians, are called the Effigy Mound People because of their mysterious custom of burying their dead beneath mounds shaped like animals, reptiles, and birds. The 5 deer and 2 panthers here are unsurpassed. They also constructed intaglio, conical, and linear mounds, one of which, Mound 19, displays an exposed burial with artifacts. All that is known of Effigy Mound Culture comes from archeological study of such mounds. Many mound groups were found by early white settlers in southern Wisconsin, but few survive intact. These mounds were saved from destruction by the Sheboygan Area Garden Clubs through public subscription, and given to the City of Sheboygan as an archeological park. They were restored and opened to the public on June 25, 1966, dedicated to "THOSE OLDEST PEOPLE OF WISCONSIN WHOSE LOVE FOR THEIR HOMELAND KEPT IT GREEN AND BEAUTIFUL AND RICH IN NATURE'S BOUNTY. MAY WE LEARN TO PRESERVE IT HALF AS WELL."

Sheboygan County

245 **SEILS-STERLING CIRCUS**   Erected 1978
Center Ave. and N. Water St., Sheboygan

Near this site the Lindemann Brothers Circus gave its first performance in 1918. Well established by 1925, the Lindemanns adopted the name Seils-Sterling, and their circus became one of the country's greatest motorized shows. In 1937 its 29-week itinerary included stops in 10 states, but the depression of the 1930s led to the end of Seils-Sterling's travels. The final performance was in Iron Mountain, Michigan, July 4, 1938. In 1965 the Lindemann brothers–Bill, Al and Pete–were enshrined in the Circus Hall of Fame at Sarasota, Florida.

Sheboygan County

COLE HISTORIC DISTRICT   Erected 1998
Rochester Inn, 504 Water St., Sheboygan Falls

The Cole Historic District, bounded by Water, Monroe, Adams, and Michigan streets, is one of the few remaining historic districts in the state to display the early development of a Wisconsin community from the 1830s and 1840s. The district's two residences, mill house, and hotel, built between 1837 and 1848 in the Greek Revival style, were owned by pioneer settler and entrepreneur Charles D. Cole. After the construction of a Sheboygan River bridge in 1839, this area declined and Sheboygan Falls developed on the west side of the river.

Cole Historic District, Sheboygan Falls.
SHSW Div. of Historic Preservation, Paul Jakubovich, photographer.

55

389 **DOWNTOWN SHEBOYGAN FALLS**
HISTORIC DISTRICT   Erected 1998
Sheboygan River Dam, Broadway St., Sheboygan Falls

In 1835, upon finding these falls and their fine water power, Massachusetts pioneer and entrepreneur Silas Stedman decided to purchase the surrounding land for village and industrial development. The following year, Stedman platted the "Town of Rochester" and built the first sawmill at the falls. By 1849, the industrial center grew to three sawmills, a tanning mill manufactory, two flour mills, and an iron foundry. In 1850, Wisconsin legislators renamed the "Town of Rochester" to Sheboygan Falls, and the village continued to develop throughout the 19th and early 20th centuries. The Downtown Sheboygan Falls Historic District, bounded by the Sheboygan River on the east and Detroit Street on the west and including Broadway, Pine, and Monroe streets, encapsulates this history. This compact and picturesque district contains many industrial and commercial building examples in a variety of architectural styles dating from the 1840s through the early 20th century. The district was listed in the National Register of Historic Places in 1984.

.

Sheboygan County

333 **EARLY DUTCH SETTLERS**   Erected 1996
300 block of Main St., Cedar Grove

In 1847 Reverend Pieter Zonne led a group of Netherlanders, originally from the Gelderland province, to this area where a few other Dutch immigrant families had recently settled. Enticed by Zonne's energetic advertisements that "there is plenty of everything and we have sold more than $1,000 worth of fattened cattle," many additional Dutch immigrants came to the "Zonne Settlement," later named Cedar Grove. Within five years, the settlers had systematically cleared vast tracts of the forested land and more than 200 family farms were in operation.

Wisconsin immigrants (probably from the Netherlands.)
SHSW Visual Materials Archive, Classified File.

Sheboygan County

349 **HISTORIC OOSTBURG**   Erected 1997
Heritage House Triangle Park,
Center and N. 10th sts., Oostburg

The Dutch settlement of Oostburg, founded in the 1840s and named for a town in the Netherlands, was once located two miles to the southeast. In 1873, to attract the railroad to this location, local businessman Pieter Daane constructed and donated a depot to the Milwaukee, Lake Shore and Western Railroad Company. Oostburg moved here and in just three years became a thriving railroad town with a mill, grain elevator, lumber yard, post office, church, hotel, telegraph office, and various shops, including two general stores.

Sheboygan County

044 **DUTCH SETTLEMENT**   Erected 1956
Sauk Trail (old Hwy. 141) 3.75 mi. N of Cedar Grove

The names of many places and families in this vicinity reflect the origin of its early settlers. Most of the settlers of Cedar Grove and Oostburg were from the Dutch province of Zeeland, although some had lived for a time in New York before catching the westward fever in the 1840s. Here the settler cleared sufficient ground for his new home, which was raised or "logged up" with the help of neighbors. Inside, wrote Pieter Daane in 1847, "very many had nothing but a ground floor; stools sawed from logs were the only seats, a chest answered for a table." One group of about 300 immigrants headed for new homes here in 1847 met with disaster. After completing the long journey from Holland, they were within five miles of their goal when fire broke out aboard the *Phoenix* and more than 200 lives were lost.

Sheboygan County

 OLD WADE HOUSE STATE PARK Erected 1953
Hwy. 23 in the park at Greenbush,
6 mi. W of Plymouth

The Wade House, one of the earliest stagecoach inns in Wisconsin, is the major unit in this historic restoration carried out by the Kohler Foundation of Kohler, Wisconsin. Built by Sylvanus Wade between 1847 and 1851 at the total cost of $300, this "halfway house" became the most important stagecoach stop on the plank road between Sheboygan and Fond du Lac. Meetings for the discussion of Civil War issues and early railroad construction were held in the inn. The Butternut House, home of Wade's eldest daughter and son-in-law, takes its name from the timber cut on its site and used in its construction. Horses were shod and the stages repaired in the Blacksmith Shop adjoining Wade House.

Old Wade House.
SHSW Div. of Historic Preservation, Paul Jakubovich, photographer.

154 **"KISSEL"** Erected 1965
Willow Brook Park, Hwy. 60, intersection of
Sumner St. and Marine Dr., Hartford

The Kissel Motor Car Co. was located across the river from this site, manufacturing one of the world's first custom-built cars, originally called "Badger," then "Kissel Kar," and finally during World War I, "Kissel." The Kissel family's own steam car inspired brothers George and William to begin the business with a capital of $50.00, acquiring a state charter on June 5, 1906. The company, years ahead of the industry in design, produced coupes, limousines, semi-touring and semi-racer types, and trucks priced from $1,500 to $45,000. The Gold Bug, Kissel Speedster, and White Eagle Speedster models achieved international acclaim and brought celebrity purchasers to Hartford. The company reached its peak during the 1920s, having a capital stock of over $1,000,000 and producing in one year over 6,000 "Kissel" cars and trucks. Car production ceased in the late 1930s, during the Depression. The car is now a prized collector's item.

Kissel Car, 1920s.
SHSW Visual Materials Archive, Classified File.

Washington County

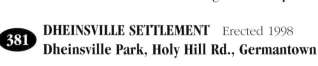

381 **DHEINSVILLE SETTLEMENT** Erected 1998
Dheinsville Park, Holy Hill Rd., Germantown

Established in 1842 by the Philip Dhein family, Dheinsville is Germantown's oldest crossroads settlement. The village contains original half-timber buildings (Fachwerk), reflecting the building construction patterns of the early pioneers who came here from the Hunsruck area of Germany. The historic commercial center is comprised of log, quarried limestone, brick, and clapboard buildings dating from early settlement through the Victorian period. An important part of eastern Wisconsin's 19th-century settlement corridor, Dheinsville preserves the built environment of pioneer life.

Dheinsville's Valentine Wolf Haus under restoration, German half-timber construction, built 1844.
Courtesy of Graff and Associates.

61

Washington County

017 **LIZARD MOUND COUNTY PARK**   Erected 1954
At the park, Hwy. A, E of Hwy. 144,
NE of West Bend

This park, named for its most outstanding mound, contains thirty-one fine examples of effigy mounds. Effigy mounds are low earthworks usually built in the shapes of birds or animals. Though used for burial purposes, a mound seldom contains more than one or two remains. From the excavations of the mounds and campsites, archeologists have gained some knowledge of the life of this prehistoric group of Wisconsin Indians. It is known that they lived in small scattered bands. They depended largely on hunting and fishing for food, though some gardening was practiced. Most of their tools and weapons were made of stone, some of wood and bone and, in rare instances, copper. Pottery vessels were used for cooking. Except for a few examples in adjoining states, effigy mounds are found only in Wisconsin.

Washington County

250 **GREAT DIVIDE**   Erected 1979
S side of Hwy. 33, 550 ft. W of jct. with Hwy. 144

You are now on the Great Divide which separates the two principal drainage areas of Wisconsin. Water falling to the west of this ridge runs down the Rock River into the "Father of Waters" and after 1,400 miles reaches the Gulf of Mexico. Water which falls to the east of the ridge drains into the Milwaukee River, then down through the Great Lakes and the St. Lawrence River 2,000 miles into the Atlantic Ocean. The elevation of the divide at this point is approximately 600 feet above Lake Michigan and 1,180 feet above sea level.

Waukesha County

160 **NASHOTAH MISSION**   Erected 1968
Nashotah House grounds, Mission Rd.
at Mill Rd., west of Delafield

Inspired by Bishop Jackson Kemper, James Lloyd Breck and his companions founded Nashotah Mission as a center for the Episcopal church's work in Wisconsin Territory. Preparation of candidates for the priesthood quickly became a major task, to meet the needs of the church on the frontier. The Blue House, built in 1842, was the community's home. In the Red Chapel, built in 1843, prayer and sacrament gave the strength and courage required for apostolic achievement.

Bishop Jackson Kemper, painting by James Reeve Stuart.
SHSW Museum Collection, negative in SHSW Visual Materials Archive,
(D489) 7067.

329 **LAPHAM PEAK** Erected 1995
Lapham Peak Unit of the Southern
Kettle Moraine State Forest, Hwy. C, Delafield

In 1870, on top of Lapham Peak, then known as Government Hill, the United States Army Signal Corps established one of its original National Weather Service signal stations. Weather data was received here from Pikes Peak, Colorado, and relayed to the United States Weather Bureau headquarters in Chicago. Lapham Peak, the highest point in Waukesha County, is named for Increase Allen Lapham (1811-1875), Wisconsin's premier 19th-century naturalist, archeologist and scholar. From this peak, Lapham recorded many weather observations for his pioneering work in meteorology, which included publishing isothermal maps of Wisconsin and working with the Smithsonian Institution as a weather observer for the Great Lakes region. Concerned with potential storm disasters to Great Lakes shipping and Wisconsin farming, Lapham proposed a state weather forecasting service in 1850. Although it was not adopted by the state, Lapham rewrote the proposal for a national weather service, which was approved by Congress on February 9, 1870. On November 8, working as the assistant to the Chief Signal Corps Officer, Lapham recorded the first published national weather forecast, calling for "high winds and falling temperatures for Chicago, Detroit and the Eastern cities."

Increase Allen Lapham, painting by Samuel Brookes.
SHSW Museum Collection, negative in SHSW Visual Materials Archive, (X3) 17916.

Waukesha County

392 **DELAFIELD FISH HATCHERY** Erected 1998
421 Main St., Delafield

Constructed in 1907, the impressive Delafield Fish Hatchery stands as a reminder of Wisconsin's dependence upon its plentiful fishing waters. In the early 20th century, Wisconsin's growing concern over lake and stream fish depletion led to a state fish hatchery program for propagating fish. The Delafield Fish Hatchery was the second hatchery built under this program. Originally comprised of 32 acres, the hatchery was designed by State Architect John T. W. Jennings. The grounds included six holding ponds, 1,430 feet of pipe line, and the hatchery building. The building is superbly constructed of fieldstone walls, split and chosen for their color and texture. Two interior concrete tanks were once used to hatch walleye-pike eggs while bass fish eggs were hatched in two ponds on the property. Fish fry (baby fish) were transported to nearby lakes and streams by electric railway. The Delafield Fish Hatchery was used until 1953 when it was converted into a research center. In 1980, the hatchery and surrounding parks were deeded by the state to the city for public recreation.

Delafield Fish Hatchery.
SHSW Div. of Historic Preservation, Paul Jakubovich, photographer.

Waukesha County

246 **ST. JOHN'S MILITARY ACADEMY**   Erected 1978
At the academy entrance, Genesee St., Delafield

St. John's, the oldest military academy in Wisconsin, was founded as a boys' prep school in 1884 when Sidney T. Smythe, a student at Nashotah House, reopened an abandoned Delafield schoolhouse for St. John's first students. Dr. Smythe graduated from Nashotah in 1886 and devoted the rest of his life to building the academy. The main campus buildings were built to complement each other in design and appearance. Of English Gothic design with serrated roofs, towers, and battlements of stone, they resemble old-time European castles. St. John's is an influential educational force in the Midwest, drawing its students from many states and foreign countries. The philosophy of the military type of education was adopted to emphasize quality, instill self-discipline, and provide team spirit and leadership qualities. This philosophy, combined with St. John's original religious intentions, represents a distinctive side of the American spirit.

Waukesha County

256 **LANNON STONE**   Erected 1979
Main St., Lannon

Commercial quarrying of Waukesha County's high grade limestone—actually dolomite—was well under way by the 1850s and became an important industry. By the early 1890s some 14 quarries were producing stone for paving and curbing, building, flagging, and other uses. As time progressed, the uniform grade, hardness, and color of the stone in the Lannon area attracted the attention of builders, and quarries advertised and received orders for "Lannon Stone." By mid-century, architects and builders had begun to use the Lannon area's colorful surface stone as veneer rather than load-bearing structural material. This use spread quickly and widely. The Village of Lannon became the center of the state's building-stone industry, and the name of the special stone from this area became synonymous with that of the village.

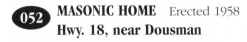

Waukesha County

052   **MASONIC HOME**   Erected 1958
Hwy. 18, near Dousman

In the fall of 1836 Elisha Edgerton and his wife Belinda came here in their wagon drawn by oxen. They cleared the land and built their farm home, with buildings recognized as a Wisconsin Premium Farm by the State Agricultural Society. Episcopal services were held in a small chapel over the carriage house for early settlers of the surrounding area. In 1865 Edgerton sold the farm to inventor-manufacturer George Washington van Brunt, who built the tall mansion in 1873 and made the Premium Farm a showplace. After van Brunt's death his children operated the farm as Springdale Resort, but the popularity of resorts dependent upon springs soon waned. Ajalon Spring still provided water for the entire installation. In 1905 Willard van Brunt, nephew of George, took over the farm, made extensive improvements, and presented it to the Masonic Grand Lodge as a home for old members.

Waukesha County

185   **CARROLL COLLEGE**   Erected 1972
Carroll College campus, Waukesha

Carroll College, chartered by the territorial legislature on January 31, 1846, is Wisconsin's oldest college. Named for Charles Carroll, signer of the Declaration of Independence, it advanced the work of Prairieville Academy, founded in 1841 in Prairieville, the town soon to be called Waukesha. Carroll College opened on September 8, 1846, with an enrollment of five men and a faculty of two. Of the latter, Professor Eleazur Root subsequently became Wisconsin's first superintendent of public instruction, and Professor John W. Sterling served as vice president of the University of Wisconsin from 1869 to 1885. On land donated by Morris D. Cutler and Charles R. Dakin, both of Waukesha, a two-story stone college building was erected in 1853. Under presidents John Adams Savage (1850-1863) and Walter Lowry Rankin (1866-1871, 1893-1903) the college grew and became firmly established as Wisconsin's pioneer college.

Winnebago County

048 **POYGAN PAYGROUNDS** Erected 1956
Poygan Shores Lane, 1 mi. N of Hwy. 110

In 1836 the Menominee Indians ceded all their lands between the Wolf and Fox Rivers to the United States government. Payment was made every October, in twenty annual installments, on these grounds. All their remaining lands were ceded in 1848 and the Menominees were offered a reservation in Minnesota, which they refused. In 1852 they moved up the Wolf River, where in 1854 they were granted eight townships, the present Keshena Reservation.

Winnebago County

226 **SAMUEL N. ROGERS SR.,**
SOLDIER OF THE AMERICAN REVOLUTION Erected 1976
Town of Winchester Cemetery, 1 mi. SW of Winchester

Born on June 3, 1760, at Branford, Connecticut, Samuel N. Rogers Sr. served several terms of enlistment with Captain Peck's Company, Col. Roger Eno's Regiment of the Connecticut militia from 1777 to 1781. Following the war, he moved to New York state, and in 1839 he moved to Walworth County, Wisconsin. In 1848, at an advanced age, he accompanied his son, Samuel N. Rogers Jr., to Winnebago County, settling in the Town of Winchester. He died at the age of ninety-two in 1852 and is buried in this cemetery. Three veterans of the War of 1812, John D. Clarke, Mayhew D. Mott, and Jacob A. Raught, are also buried here in the Winchester Township Cemetery.

Winnebago County

048 **BUTTE DES MORTS**   Erected 1955
Fritsie Park, Menasha

In 1730 the French government decided to destroy the Fox village on the shore of this lake because of the depredations of the Foxes on the fur traders. Capt. Morand came up the river with a large force of French soldiers and Menominee warriors. The soldiers were concealed under canvas until they were opposite the Indians gathered on the shore. Then they rose and fired into the crowd. The Menominees, meanwhile, attacked the village from the rear. The village was destroyed and its inhabitants slaughtered. The bodies were piled in a heap and covered with earth, forming the Hill of the Dead. In 1827 Governor Cass held a council here with the Winnebago, Chippewa, and Menominee tribes to fix their tribal boundaries. At this council Oshkosh was made chief of the Menominees.

Winnebago County

030 **WISCONSIN CENTRAL RAILROAD**   Erected 1955
Menasha Hotel, Main and Mill sts., Menasha

Wisconsin Central Railroad was formally organized in the National Hotel on this site by Judge George Reed and his associates, Feb. 4, 1871. Here the contracts were set for its construction and the first general office was located. The road secured a land grant to build a line from "Doty's Island to Lake Superior." The first train ran from Menasha to Waupaca, Oct. 2, 1871.

Winnebago County

335 **FOX-IRISH CEMETERY**   Erected 1997
9088 Clayton Ave., Town of Menasha

Near here is the "lost cemetery" of Saint Malachy Catholic Church (1849-1857), a mission church of log construction that served the local Irish community and Catholic Indians. Irish immigrants had come to Menasha to build dams, locks, and canals on the Fox-Wisconsin Waterway, later settling on land-grant farms west of Menasha.

Winnebago County

348 **EDGAR SAWYER HOUSE**   Erected 1997
Oshkosh Public Museum, 1331 Algoma Blvd., Oshkosh

Oshkosh lumberman, banker, and financier Edgar P. Sawyer hired noted local architect William Waters to design this Tudor Revival style house in 1907. Constructed of brick and limestone with parapeted gables and fluted chimneys, the house featured interior furnishings by Tiffany Studios, including art glass, bronze grilles, tapestries, light fixtures, and furniture. A city showpiece, the residence reflected Oshkosh's vast lumbering wealth. Edgar Sawyer donated his house to the City of Oshkosh in 1922, and it became the Oshkosh Public Museum in 1924.

Winnebago County

027 **KNAGGS FERRY** Erected 1955
Rainbow Park, Oshkosh

James Knaggs, who lived across the river from this point, operated a ferry here for nineteen years. In 1831 John and Juliette Kinzie, traveling on horseback from Green Bay to their Indian agency assignment at Portage, were ferried across. In the summer of 1836 Webster Stanley came by Durham boat and built a shanty. He was soon joined by Henry and John Gallup, who came on foot from Green Bay. The same year, Gov. Henry Dodge and his party crossed on their way to the Council at the Cedars, where the Menominee Indians ceded to the United States all their land between the Fox and Wolf Rivers. Later Gallup and Stanley moved across the river and settled near its mouth. This located the business center of Oshkosh. The ferry era ended with the building of float bridges at Main Street (1847) and Algoma (1850).

Winnebago County

183 **THE UNIVERSITY OF WISCONSIN-OSHKOSH** Erected 1972
UW-Oshkosh campus

Opening its doors in 1871, the University of Wisconsin-Oshkosh was then the third normal school founded by the state. Pioneering in curricular innovations, the school also established the first kindergarten at an American public normal school in 1880, and it initiated summer study in Wisconsin's teacher training system in 1893. Advancing in status, the institution attained degree-granting privileges effective in 1926 and merged with the University of Wisconsin system in its centennial year. As a school in transition, the university has enlarged upon its historic function of teacher education with broad offerings in letters and science, graduate study, business administration, nursing, and continuing education. At the threshold of its second century of service in 1972, the university continues to prepare students for the work defined by its first president, George S. Albee, as dedicated to "lifting humanity to a higher, noble life."

71

Winnebago County

211 **S. J. WITTMAN—AIRCRAFT DESIGNER, RACE PILOT, INVENTOR**
Erected 1975
Wittman Field Airport, 20th St. Rd., Oshkosh

For 38 years America's premier air race pilot, S. J. Wittman, served as manager of this airport. Since 1924 he has designed and built aircraft for which he has achieved national recognition. One of his planes (Buster) is in the Smithsonian Institution. He designed the very popular Wittman Tailwind and V-Witt Homebuilt aircraft and a commercially-used landing gear. Mr. Wittman has long been recognized as one of American's foremost air race pilots. For 50 years, 1924 to 1974, he participated in more closed-course air races than any other person in the world. He has raced in every "National Air Race" from 1928 to 1971 and still holds 2 world records. His dedication to aviation has focused worldwide attention upon Oskhosh and Winnebago County. This airport was named in his honor July 24, 1969.

Winnebago County

218 **COLES BASHFORD HOUSE**   Erected 1975
1619 Oshkosh Ave., Oshkosh

This house was once the home of Coles Bashford, who served from 1856 to 1858 as the first Republican governor of Wisconsin. It was built in 1855, a year after the Republican Party came into being as an avowed opponent to the further extension of slavery in the territories of the United States. After 1875, the house was no longer in Bashford's possession. In 1911, it became the property of trustees authorized by the will of Elizabeth Batchelder Davis to provide and maintain perpetually a home for children needing shelter and care. Now known as the Elizabeth Batchelder Davis Children's Home, the residence remains dedicated to its beneficent mission.

Markers
South Central Region

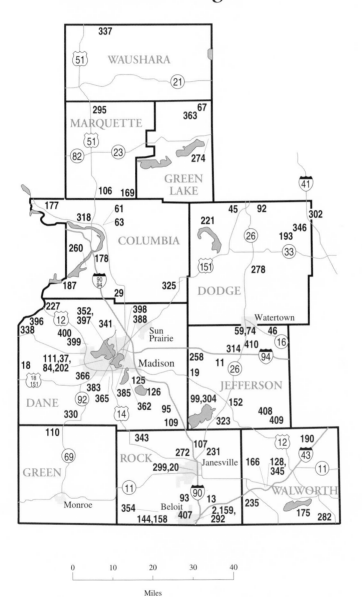

337

WAUSHARA

51

21

295

MARQUETTE

67
363

51

82   23

274

GREEN
LAKE

106   169

41

177

61
318   63

45   92   302

221

346
193

COLUMBIA

26

33

260

151

178

278

90
94

187

325

DODGE

29

227
396   352,   341
12   397

338   400
399

398
388

Watertown

59,74   46

Sun
Prairie

314   410   16

94

18   111,37,
84,202,

258
11   26

18
151

366

19

383   125
365   385   126

JEFFERSON

DANE   92

362   95

99,304   152

408
409

330

14

109

323

110

343

107
272   231

12   190
43

69

ROCK

299,20

Janesville

166   128,   11
345

GREEN

11

93   90   13
90

235

WALWORTH

Monroe

354   Beloit
144,158   407

2,159,
292

175   282

0   10   20   30   40

Miles

Columbia County

061 **FORT WINNEBAGO** Erected 1957
Hwy. 33, 0.5 mi. E of Portage

In the autumn of 1828 a permanent fort was built on this site by the First Regiment of the United States infantry under the command of Maj. David E. Twiggs, later a general in the Confederate Army. The fort was constructed primarily to control the important Fox-Wisconsin portage and to protect American traders from interference by the Winnebago Indians. Lieut. Jefferson Davis, later president of the Confederacy, served here after graduation from West Point. The fort was garrisoned until 1845 and was destroyed by fire in 1856. The only remaining portion is the restored Surgeon's Quarters on the hill across the highway. Not far from here (entrance road a half mile west on this highway) is the fully restored Indian Agency House, built in 1832 by the Government for Indian Agent John Kinzie and his bride, Juliette. Mrs. Kinzie's book *Wau-Bun* contains many interesting episodes of life at Fort Winnebago and in the surrounding community.

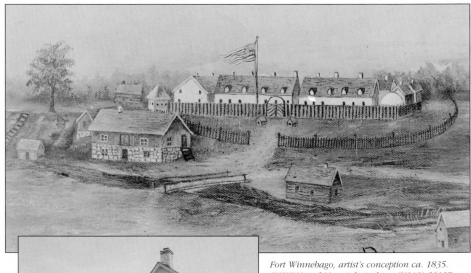

Fort Winnebago, artist's conception ca. 1835.
SHSW Visual Materials Archive, (X313) 2612E

Fort Winnebago Surgeon's Quarters.
SHSW Div. of Historic Preservation, William Guerin, photographer.

Columbia County

029 **JOHN MUIR VIEW**   Erected 1955
Hwy. 51, 0.5 mi. S of Poynette

John Muir (1838-1914), world-famous naturalist and "father of the national park system," often stopped to rest and to admire this view as he walked from his home in Marquette County to the University of Wisconsin. Muir loved the wilderness from which his parents carved a farm and home, first at Fountain Lake, later at Hickory Hill, about 20 miles north from here (south of Montello). When he left Hickory Hill to enroll at the University, Muir's love for nature was matched only by his genius for "mechanical contrivances" varying from a device to feed the horses at any designated hour to an "early rising machine" which tipped the occupant out of bed at a pre-set time. After four years in Madison, Muir left "one university for another, the Wisconsin University for the University of the Wilderness."

Columbia County

063 **MARQUETTE**   Erected 1957
Hwy. 33, 0.5 mi. E of Portage

On June 14, 1673, Jacques Marquette and Louis Jolliet started the portage (1.28 miles) from here to the Wisconsin River, which led to their discovery of the Upper Mississippi June 17, 1673, at Prairie du Chien. The expedition, in two-birch bark canoes, traveled south to the mouth of the Arkansas River and returned to St. Ignace, a trip of nearly 3000 miles. Thus a new era of exploration, settlement and commerce began for the Great Lakes region, the Mississippi Valley and the Far West. Stabilization of the fur trade followed and also the organization of numerous Indian tribes under French rule. Marquette, a talented Jesuit missionary, dedicated his life and energy ministering to the Indians. Born June 1, 1637, in Laon, France, he died near Ludington, Michigan, May 18, 1675.

Columbia County

318 **FREDERICK JACKSON TURNER**   Erected 1993
1861-1932
W. Wisconsin and Crook Sts., Portage

Considered the most important historian of the United States in the twentieth cen-
tury, Frederick Jackson Turner brought a new understanding to the meaning of the
American experience. He was born in Portage; his father was Andrew Jackson
Turner, a longtime local newspaper editor and civic activist. Young Turner left
Portage to study at the University of Wisconsin in Madison (B.A. 1884, M.A. 1888)
and Johns Hopkins University in Baltimore (Ph.D. 1890). He taught at the
University of Wisconsin (1889-1910) and at Harvard University (1910-24) and, after
a Madison stay, became senior research associate at the Huntington Library in
California (1927-32). Turner's essay on "The Significance of the Frontier in
American History," delivered in Chicago in 1893, reoriented the study of American
history toward the nation's westward migration and its consequences. For over a
half century Turner's frontier thesis, along with his own and his students' emphasis
on the history of sections of the U.S., new research resources, and environmental-
ism, defined the American character and dominated research and teaching on the
American experience.

University of Wisconsin Professor
Frederick Jackson Turner, in his office at
the Wisconsin State Historical Society
then located in the State Capitol, ca.
1892.
SHSW Visual Materials Archive, (X3)
35004.

Columbia County

 POTTERS' EMIGRATION SOCIETY Erected 1961
Hwy. CM, 5 mi. NE of Portage

Near here in 1849 Thomas Twiggs began a settlement of unemployed potters from Stafford, England. To help farmers on both sides of the Fox River reach his store and blacksmith shop at Twiggs' Landing, he operated Emancipation Ferry, named to express his hope that here they would find freedom from the poverty of the Old World.

Staffordshire Pottery Display.
SHSW Visual Materials Archive, Classified File.

Columbia County

325 **GOVERNOR JAMES TAYLOR LEWIS (1819-1904)**
(Two-sided marker)   Erected 1995
711 W. James St., Columbus

Governor James T. Lewis, the ninth Governor of Wisconsin (1864-66), led the state through the tumultuous conclusion of the Civil War. He was born in New York State and in 1845 settled in Columbus where he practiced law. In 1854-56 he built this house in the Italianate style of architecture. Lewis began his political career as a Democrat, serving in the Assembly, state Senate and as lieutenant governor. He joined the new Republican Party and was elected secretary of state in 1861 and governor, by an overwhelming majority, in 1863. Lewis served one term and returned to his large land holdings and legal profession in Columbus.

GOVERNOR LEWIS: CIVIL WAR ERA

As the last of Wisconsin's four Civil War governors, Governor Lewis made a substantial contribution to the northern cause. At a time when morale was low and money was scarce, he both met and worked to lower the state's conscription quota. Lewis, along with the four other western governors, designed the "one hundred day militia" program and convinced the War Department to continue the high bounty for new army recruits. He made extensive visits to Civil War army hospitals and camps and secured the transfer home of many of Wisconsin's sick and wounded soldiers.

Columbia County

187 **THE MERRIMAC FERRY** Erected 1973
Hwy. 113 at Wisconsin River crossing

Merrimac's first permanent settler, Chester Mattson, obtained a territorial charter in 1844 to provide ferry service across the Wisconsin River. The State Legislature of 1851 authorized a road, subsequently to become State Trunk Highway 113, to connect settlements at Madison and Baraboo via Matt's Ferry. Today, the Merrimac Ferry is the lone survivor of upwards of 500 ferries chartered by territorial and state legislatures before the turn of the century. The fee charged by early ferrymen for taking a team and wagon across the river was well earned, for their muscles provided a good share of the ferry's power until a gasoline engine was added around 1900. The ferry changed hands several times before Matt's Ferry Road was added to the state system in 1923 and Columbia and Sauk Counties took over its operation. The name Colsac is a phonetic derivation of the two county names. The State of Wisconsin assumed responsibility for the maintenance and operation of the ferry in 1933, after which the service was provided without charge.

The Merrimac ferry.
SHSW Visual Materials Archive (D485)11090.

Columbia County

THE CIRCUS Erected 1970
Rest Area No. 12, westbound lane I-90-94, 0.6 mi. E of Wisconsin River

Wisconsin has a unique heritage as the birthplace of circuses. More than a hundred had their beginnings in Wisconsin, with Delavan providing winter-quarters for twenty-six between 1847 and 1894. New York brothers Edmund and Jeremiah Mabie brought their United States Olympic Circus to Delavan in 1847, and the idea for P.T. Barnum's Asiatic Caravan was developed in Delavan by William Cameron Coup in 1871. In Baraboo the Ringling Brothers' World Greatest Shows began in 1884, followed by the five Gollmar Brothers' Circus in 1891. Each of the communities on the map was the home of at least one circus. Today, thousands of items recalling the exciting and colorful history of the circus are preserved in a vast complex 15 miles from here, at Baraboo's Circus World Museum, opened by the State Historical Society of Wisconsin in 1959.

Columbia County

KINGSLEY BEND INDIAN MOUNDS Erected 1971
Hwy. 16, 4 mi. E of Wisconsin Dells

The mounds of this group are a fairly representative sample of those built by the people of the Effigy Mound Culture between A.D. 700-1000. It has been through excavation of other burial mounds quite similar to these that archeologists have learned most of what they know about the people who built them. These people lived by hunting, fishing and gathering wild vegetable foods. They practiced little if any agriculture. There was usually only a single burial in mounds such as these, but in some mounds upwards of a dozen burials have been found. Artifacts such as flint tools and clay pots were seldom included with the burials. Archeologists have not yet accurately determined the significance of the various animal and geometric shapes in which the mounds were built.

Columbia County

 REST AREAS ON THE I-ROADS Erected 1979
**Rest Area No. 11, eastbound lane I-90-94,
0.5 mi. E of Wisconsin River**

Early roadside rest areas were rural school grounds and country churchyards with their two little houses in back. In Wisconsin, by 1920, curves were built to eliminate sharp road corners. Local garden clubs, with the American Legion and Auxiliary, began to beautify many of the resulting triangles with flowers and shrubs. Motorists used these places to relax and picnic. In 1931 the Wisconsin Legislature authorized highway beautification, and later the familiar waysides-small roadside parks at first and for many years without water or sanitation. In 1940 garden and women's clubs, the Legion, the Wisconsin Friends of Our Native Landscape and others organized the Wisconsin Roadside Council, joined by the County Highway and County Boards Association, to aid the State Highway Commission in roadside development and increasing and improving waysides. Through such initiatives Wisconsin gained the experience to become one of the very first states to provide these modern full facility I-Road rest areas you now enjoy approximately every 50 miles.
Erected 1979

Dane County

 ALBION ACADEMY Erected 1960
In park off Hwy. A, Albion

Albion Academy and Normal Institute, chartered in 1853 and opened in 1854, on land donated by Jesse Saunders, was founded and operated by the Northwestern Seventh Day Baptist Association until 1894; by Peter Hendrickson, former Beloit College professor, until 1901; and by the Synod of the Norwegian Evangelical Lutheran Church of America until 1918. Among its founders were Dr. C. R. Head, board President for forty years, and A. B. Cromwall, beloved principal during its golden era. Its objective was to afford education so inexpensive that no one need forego it. Albion Academy graduated many outstanding students, including Alva Adams, Governor of Colorado; Knute Nelson, U.S. Senator from Minnesota; and Edwin L. Greene, world famous botanist. Among its faculty were Prof. Thure Kumlien, world famous naturalist, and Prof. Rasmus B. Anderson, later U.S. Minister of Denmark. In 1928 the Town of Albion purchased the buildings and campus for a park and in 1959 conveyed the remaining building, Kumlien Hall, to the Albion Academy Historical Society for preservation as a museum.

Dane County

018 **BRIGHAM PARK**   Erected 1955
Hwy. F, 1 mi. NE of Blue Mounds

Ebenezer Brigham (1789-1861), first permanent white settler of Dane County, came here as a prospector in 1828. The inn he built became popular with travelers on the Old Military Road, and Blue Mounds became a well-known landmark. Ebenezer Brigham was a colonel in the Black Hawk War and was prominent in Wisconsin's territorial affairs and early statehood. Charles Brigham came to Blue Mounds in 1886. He became a leader in dairying and soil conservation, and in the religious, cultural and political activities of the area. This park, given to Dane County by the Brigham family, is dedicated to the memory of Charles Isley Brigham and Col. Ebenezer Brigham.

Dane County

125 **STEPHEN MOULTON BABCOCK (1843-1931)**   Erected 1963
Hwy. 51, E shore of Lake Waubesa

Stephen Moulton Babcock came to the University of Wisconsin faculty in 1887 and remained until his death in 1931. His life was filled with a great eagerness to know and a persistent desire to serve. He is best known for the perfection of the butter-fat test which bears his name. Yet great as was this development, it likely was far surpassed in significance to mankind by the solid foundation he laid for invaluable research by himself and others in the field of animal nutrition. This has repeatedly shown the importance of certain vitamins in animal and human diets. Professor Babcock won high rank among Wisconsin's and the nation's great scientists.

Dane County

126 **ROBERT MARION LA FOLLETTE SR.** **(1855-1925)**
Erected 1963
Williams Dr., La Follette County Park,
3 mi. N of Stoughton

S
O
U
T
H
C
E
N
T
R
A
L

Wisconsin's most famous political leader and greatest statesman. Born on a farm in Primrose Township, Dane County, he was the first native son and first University of Wisconsin graduate to become Wisconsin Governor. He rose from Dane County District Attorney to Congressman, Governor, and U.S. Senator. An influential fighter for reform, he viewed government as a servant, not ruler, of people. "Fighting Bob" led in establishing the Progressive movement in Wisconsin politics. He advocated much which became law-state primary elections, tax reform, railroad regulation, conservation, civil service, improved industrial standards. He advanced the "Wisconsin Idea," use of experts from the University in state service. In 1924, he was an unsuccessful Independent candidate for president. His liberal impact was nationwide.

Robert M. LaFolette Sr., "Fighting Bob."
SHSW Visual Materials
Archive (X3) 45820.

Dane County

MAIN STREET HISTORIC DISTRICT—STOUGHTON
Erected 1997
Two duplicate markers located at the Yahara River Bridge at West Main St. / City Hall at 381 E. Main St., Stoughton

This district is a collection of Victorian and early 20th-century commercial buildings, largely built between 1860 and 1910. Once southern Dane County's mercantile center, the district provided extensive retail and professional services. Extending west to the Yahara River, the district was listed on the National Register of Historic Places in 1982.

Dane County

MAZOMANIE   Erected 1996
Village Park, 39 Brodhead St., Mazomanie

In 1850, the Milwaukee and Mississippi Rail Road Company began building a line to span the lower third of Wisconsin between Milwaukee and Prairie du Chien. Chief Engineer Edward Brodhead concluded that this area's topographical features were ideal for constructing a railroad servicing station and a commercial trading village. In 1855, he platted the village and named it "Mazomanie," an Indian name he believed to mean "Iron Horse." Mazomanie developed quickly after a dam and millrace were built to harness the water power of Black Earth Creek. The new railroad village revitalized the lagging farm economy of the early settlers, who arrived in the 1840s under the auspices of the British Temperance Emigration Society. By the mid-1870s Mazomanie was a thriving commercial and industrial center of over 1100 people. The village eventually supported two flour mills, two creameries, a brewery, four blacksmith shops, a foundry, and factories which produced knitted goods, cabinets, carriages, wagons, and agricultural implements. Many of Mazomanie's 19th-century buildings remain in the village today.

Dane County

 PRIMROSE LUTHERAN CHURCH   Erected 1995
8770 Ridge Dr., Belleville

In the mid-nineteenth century, many newly arrived Norwegian immigrants in southern Wisconsin depended upon the spiritual and practical guidance of itinerant
Lutheran ministers to help them successfully adapt to the new land. One of the
most influential was evangelist Elling Eielsen, who organized a congregation of fifty
people in Primrose in 1850. Five years later, the congregation built a log church in
the community. Eielsen was a follower of Hans Nielsen Hauge, a lay preacher who
started a spiritual revival in Norway emphasizing democratic attitudes and faithful-
ness to the scriptures. In 1854 a university-trained minister of the Norwegian state
church, Pastor A. C. Preus, established a second church in Primrose called the
Primrose Norwegian Evangelical Lutheran Church which emphasized traditional
high-church principles and doctrine. The theological differences between the two
congregations became the focus of the 1856 Annual Convention of Norwegian
Lutheran Churches held in Primrose and heightened existing divisions within
Norwegian American Lutheranism. The Primrose congregations, however, recon-
ciled in 1915, and the present Primrose Lutheran Church joins the 1881 bell tower
of the Norwegian Evangelical Lutheran Church with the 1894 Hauge Church,
moved to this location in 1941.

S O U T H C E N T R A L

*Norwegian Lutheran Sunday School
Picnic, Dane County, ca. 1875.
SHSW Visual Materials Archive,
Andreas Dahl Collection (D31) 689.*

Dane County

037 **STATE HISTORICAL SOCIETY**   Erected 1955
816 State St., Madison

Dedicated to the conservation, advancement and dissemination of the American heritage, the Society was founded in 1846, chartered in 1853. Legislative support, the first bestowed in any state, began in 1854; the Society became a state agency in 1949. Under Lyman Copeland Draper (1854-1886) the library achieved preeminence; research, publication and a modern museum were begun. Local societies followed in 1895. The Society became the state archives in 1907. The quarterly magazine was launched in 1917, historical markers in 1942, school services in 1947, regional depositories for local research in 1951, the operation of historic sites in 1952. Dedicated in l900, rededicated in 1955, this building has long been a mecca for the student of American and Wisconsin history and a center for the greater public appreciation of the basic dynamics of the American experiment.

Dane County

084 **9XM-WHA, "THE OLDEST STATION IN THE NATION"**   Erected 1958
Vilas Communication Hall, North Park St., UW-Madison campus

On this campus, pioneer research and experimentation in "wireless" led to successful transmissions of voice and music in 1917, and the beginning of broadcasting on a scheduled basis in 1919. Experimental station 9XM transmitted telegraphic signals from Science Hall until 1917 when it was moved to Sterling Hall. In that year Professor Earle M. Terry and students built and operated a "wireless telephone" transmitter. In 1918, during World War I, when other stations were ordered silenced, 9XM operated under special authorization to continue its telephonic exchange with U.S. Navy stations on the Great Lakes. After the war, programs were directed to the general public. The WHA letters replaced the 9XM call on January 13, 1922. Thus the University of Wisconsin station, under the calls of 9XM and WHA, has been in existence longer than any other.

Dane County

CAMP RANDALL   Erected 1961
near the E end of Monroe St. in Camp Randall Memorial Park, UW-Madison Campus

From these historic grounds went forth Wisconsin's sons to fight for the preservation of the nation in the American Civil War 1861-1865. More than 70,000 men trained for service within the boundaries of this camp, named after Alexander W. Randall, a wartime governor. Originally comprising 53 $1/2$ acres and owned by the estate of William D. Bruen, the track was leased to the State Agricultural Society in 1859. When war came in April 1861, the land was turned over to the state as a military training rendezvous and Camp Randall became the state's largest staging point. A hospital and a stockade for Confederate prisoners of war were also located here. Purchased by the state in 1893, the land was deeded to the University of Wisconsin. Since that time, a portion of the grounds has been used as an athletic field. As a memorial to Wisconsin's Civil War soldiers, a small segment of the land was set aside as a park and the Memorial Arch was completed in 1912.

Dane County

NORTH HALL   Erected 1974
Bascom Hill, UW-Madison campus, Madison

The first building erected by the University of Wisconsin–Madison was North Hall, opened as North Dormitory for men on Sept. 17, 1851. It was built of Madison sandstone at a cost of $19,000. Initially, the first three floors housed from 50 to 65 students; the fourth floor was divided into six public rooms for lectures, recitations, and study. The building was first heated by two hot-air furnaces. As an economy measure during the war (1865), stoves were placed in each room, and students were required to provide their own fuel, often a tree from nearby Bascom Woods. A mess hall was set up in the dormitory for those who wanted board at cost, about 80 cents a week. Sanitary conveniences were primitive; the students hauled their water from a nearby well, and the bad condition of the outdoor privies was the subject of lengthy discussions by both faculty and regents. In 1884 North Hall became an office and classroom faculty, and since has been occupied by various University departments and for a time by the U.S. Weather Bureau. It was designated a Registered Historic Landmark in 1966.

Dane County

383 **PECK CABIN**   Erected 1998
General Executive Facility, 125 S. Webster, Madison

Once located here, Peck Cabin—Madison's first residence, business and post office—was built by entrepreneurs Ebenezer and Roseline Peck in 1837. Constructing their cabin with adjoining additions near the new territorial capitol site, the Pecks opened their building as a public house and provided food, drink and lodging to visitors and new arrivals. On July 4th 1837, the Pecks hosted the Capitol cornerstone-laying celebration. Robert Ream assumed the business in 1838, and the cabin remained important to Madison's early development but was demolished in 1857.

Eben Peck's Cabin, painting by Isabella A. Denzel, ca. 1893, based upon pioneer recollections..
SHSW Museum Collections, negative in SHSW Visual Materials Archive, Oversize 5-5413.

Dane County

341 **YAHARA RIVER PARKWAY**   Erected 1996
501 S. Thornton Ave., Madison

In January 1903, the leader of Madison's park development and president of the Madison Park and Pleasure Drive Association, John M. Olin, presented a grand development plan for the Yahara River to city leaders. The plan called for deepening, widening and straightening the river between lakes Mendota and Monona and creating a parkway. In only six months and with contributions from many Madison citizens, Olin and the Park and Pleasure Drive Association raised the money and secured the land to begin construction. The Yahara River Parkway was designed by renowned landscape architect Ossian Cole Simonds, who fostered a regional style of landscape architecture known as the "Prairie School." Using native Midwestern plants such as hawthorne, dogwood, and crabapple, Simonds created a naturalistic landscape for the parkway. As part of the design, several bridges were erected or reconstructed, and a lock was built at the Mendota outlet for boat passage between the lakes. The parkway was completed in 1906.

S O U T H C E N T R A L

Dane County

352 **CERAMIC ARTS STUDIO OF MADISON**   Erected 1997
8-12 N. Blount St., Madison

Once located at this site on North Blount Street, the Ceramic Arts Studio of Madison operated from 1940 until its closing in 1956. Founded by Lawrence Rabbitt and Reuben Sand, the company was one of the largest manufacturers of figurines in the world and distributed up to 500,000 pieces annually. The vases, figurines, and salt-and-pepper sets, designed chiefly by Betty Harrington, were known nationally for their great originality and consistently high standards of manufacture.

Dane County

398 **THIRD LAKE PASSAGE**   Erected 1998
Olbrich Park, 3330 Atwood Ave., Madison

On July 20th, during the Black Hawk War of 1832, Black Hawk led about 700 Sac, Fox and Kickapoo Indians past this point and through the "Third Lake Passage," the juncture of the Yahara River and Lake Monona. By sunset, the military also reached the passage but abandoned their chase at nightfall to camp in this vicinity.

Ma-ka-tai-me-she-kia-kaik, Black Hawk (Black Sparrow Hawk).
SHSW Visual Materials Archive (X3) 14313.

90

Dane County

397 **TRAGEDY OF WAR**   Erected 1998
415 E. Wilson St., Madison

On July 21, 1832, during the Black Hawk War, the U. S. Militia "passed through the narrows of the four lakes," Madison's Isthmus, in pursuit of Sac Indian leader Black Hawk and his band. Near this location, the Militia shot and scalped an old Sac warrior awaiting his death upon his wife's freshly dug grave.

Dane County

388 **NATHANIEL DEAN (1817-1880)**   Erected 1998
(Two-sided marker)
4718 Monona Dr., Madison

As an early Regent of the University of Wisconsin, State Assemblyman and Madison area landowner and businessman, Nathaniel Dean was influential in campus, Capitol and city construction activities. He was also instrumental in the town of Blooming Grove's growth and donated land for the original Town Hall and the Commonwealth Cemetery. Nathaniel and Harriet Dean built this Madison Landmark and National Register listed farm house in 1856 on their country estate of 508 acres, which produced grain crops and livestock.

DEAN HOUSE

This simple flat-roofed cream brick structure with wood cornice and dentils was built by the Dean family as their country home. After 1871, the house was used by tenant farmers and in the 1920's as the Monona Golf Course clubhouse, serving in this capacity for 50 years. The Historic Blooming Grove Historical Society began restoration of the Dean House in 1972. The house serves as a center for cultural events and local history study and as a living testament to the pioneer spirit.

Dane County

THE OUTLET MOUND   Erected 1998
Indian Mound Park, 6200 Block of Ridgewood Ave., Monona

The largest of nineteen conical, oval and linear mounds once located in this vicinity, the Outlet Mound was constructed as a burial place by Woodland Indians about 2,000 years ago. It was saved from destruction by the Wisconsin Archeological Society and local citizens in 1944 and donated to the City of Monona.

Dane County

THE McCOY FARMHOUSE   Erected 1998
2915 Syene Rd., Fitchburg

Located on one of Dane County's earliest and most successful tobacco farms, the cream brick-Italianate McCoy Farmhouse was built by Benjamin Brown in 1861. Tobacco growing began here in 1853 and boomed during the Civil War when Southern tobacco became unavailable in the North. In 1949, microbiologist Elizabeth McCoy, renown for her work in bacteria toxins and botulism, purchased the property. After her death in 1978, the farmhouse was named in her honor and listed on the National Register of Historic Places.

Dane County

366 **JOHN MANN HOUSE**   Erected 1998
Quivey's Grove, 6261 Nesbitt Road, Fitchburg

Once the centerpiece of a 130 acre farm, this stone house and adjacent outbuildings were built by New York native John Mann in 1856. Of classical proportions, the vernacular Mann House displays a mixture of Greek Revival and Italianate architectural styles. Set amid a walnut grove, the house is constructed of locally quarried sandstone. One of Dane County's outstanding examples of sandstone construction, the Mann House became Quivey's Grove Restaurant in 1980 and is listed on the National Register of Historic Places.

Dane County

399 **PHEASANT BRANCH ENCAMPMENT**   Erected 1998
Branch Creek Conservancy Park, Pheasant Branch Rd., Middleton

On the night of July 20th, during the Black Hawk War of 1832, Sac Indian leader Black Hawk and his followers camped near this location. Desperate for food and frightened by the approaching military, the Indians fled northwest towards the Wisconsin River the next morning.

S
O
U
T
H
C
E
N
T
R
A
L

93

Dane County

396 **BATTLE OF WISCONSIN HEIGHTS** Erected 1998
Black Hawk Unit, Lower Wisconsin State Riverway, Hwy. 78, 2 mi. S of Sauk City

On July 21, 1832, during a persistent rainstorm, the 65-year old Sac Indian leader, Black Hawk, led 60 of his Sac and Fox and Kickapoo warriors in a holding action against 700 United States militia at this location. The conflict, known as the Battle of Wisconsin Heights, was the turning point in the Black Hawk War. Here commanders General James D. Henry and Colonel Henry Dodge and their troops overtook Black Hawk and his followers after pursuing them for weeks over the marshy areas and rough terrain of south central Wisconsin. Yet because of Black Hawk's superb military strategy, the steady rain and nightfall, approximately 700 Indians, including children and the aged, escaped down or across the Wisconsin River about one mile west of here. Their success was short-lived. The war ended just 12 days later at the *Battle of Bad Axe* when many of Black Hawk's followers drowned or were slain in their attempt to cross the Mississippi River.

Battle of Wisconsin Heights, painting by Brookes and Stephenson.
SHSW Museum Collection, negative in SHSW Visual Materials Archive (X3) 38410.

Dane County

 INDIAN LAKE PASSAGE   Erected 1997
**In parking lot, Indian Lake County Park, Hwy. 19,
1 mi E of Marxville**

On July 21, 1832, during the Black Hawk war, Sac Indian leader Black Hawk and his band left Pheasant Branch, west of Madison, retreating ahead of the military forces commanded by Colonels Ewing and Dodge. The band fled north following a route past the west end of Indian Lake and turned westward down the broad valley now bisected by Highway 12. The military, despite rain and exhausted horses, managed to catch up to Black Hawk's warriors late that afternoon at the Heights overlooking the Wisconsin River.

Dodge County

 AUTO RACE-GREEN BAY TO MADISON   Erected 1956
Hwys. 26 and 67, City Utility Property, Waupun

In 1875 the Wisconsin Legislature offered a prize of $10,000 to the citizen of this state who could produce a machine "which shall be a cheap and practical substitute for the use of horses and other animals on the highway and farm." Such machine was to perform a journey of at least 200 miles, "Propelled by its own internal power, at the average rate of at least five miles per hour, working time." By July, 1878, two steampowered vehicles were ready to run the prescribed course from Green Bay to Madison. This highway was on the route of the "race" which was interrupted along the way to demonstrate the comparative pulling capacity of the machines. The entry sponsored by an Oshkosh group completed the trip in about 33 hours, but the other broke down and returned to Green Bay.

Dodge County

BERNARD R. "BUNNY" BERIGAN (1908-1942)
Erected 1996
Adams Spring Park, Spring Street (Hwy. 33), Fox Lake

This was the hometown of famed jazz trumpeter and band leader, Bunny Berigan. As a child he played in the Fox Lake Juvenile Band directed by his grandfather, John C. Schlitzberg. In his early teens, he began his professional career with the Merrill Owen dance band at Beaver Dam. A few years later in Madison, he was in demand for campus dances. Beginning in 1930, he became the featured soloist for such band leaders as Paul Whiteman, Benny Goodman, and the Dorsey brothers. Singers Bing Crosby and the Boswell Sisters were among those who recorded with him. With his own orchestra in 1937, he recorded his most popular hit and theme song, "I Can't Get Started With You." Jazz great Louis Armstrong predicted Berigan would be the trumpeter most likely to succeed him in the affection of music lovers, but Berigan's life and music came to an untimely end at age of 33 in New York City. He is buried in St. Mary's Cemetery south of Fox Lake.

Dodge County

SOLOMON JUNEAU HOUSE   Erected 1997
Hwy. 175, Theresa

Born in 1793, Solomon Juneau, a French Canadian agent for the American Fur Company and founder of the City of Milwaukee, established one of his outlying trading posts in this vicinity along the east branch of the Rock River in the early 1830s. He named it "Theresa" in honor of his mother. In 1847, after helping to develop Milwaukee and serving as mayor, Juneau turned his attention to the pretty spot near the Rock River where he had a trading post and constructed this Greek Revival house, which he and his wife Josette called their "summer retreat." In 1848, Juneau platted the Village of Theresa, opened a general store and soon constructed a dam for his grist and sawmill. In 1852, the Juneau family moved permanently to Theresa. Josette died in 1855 and Solomon Juneau died a year later. The Juneau House is the last remaining home of Solomon Juneau. It was moved 200 feet from its original location and is maintained by the Theresa Historical Society as a house museum.

Dodge County

302 **WORLD WAR II**   Erected 1991
Rest Area No. 64, northbound lane Hwy. 41

More than 330,000 Wisconsin residents, including 9,000 women, served in the armed forces between December 7, 1941, and the surrender of Japan on September 2, 1945. They participated in every theater of war and in virtually every major campaign; from Wake Island to New Guinea, from France and Romania to Burma and Okinawa. Approximately 8,000 perished. Another 13,000 were wounded in combat. Fifteen earned the nation's highest award for valor, the Medal of Honor. On the home front, Wisconsin contributed its share and more to Allied victory. Despite shortages of feed, fertilizer, new machinery, and labor, state farmers delivered record amounts of agricultural products. Wisconsin's industries responded similarly, producing automotive components, marine engines, ammunition, aircraft parts, uniforms, footgear, even ocean-going vessels such as frigates, minesweepers, cargo ships, and submarines. And on farms and in factories throughout the state, women and schoolchildren took the place of men in uniform. World War II was truly a "people's war."

Dodge County

193 **WISCONSIN'S FIRST IRON SMELTER**   Erected 1973
Hwys. 28 and 67, on Main Street, Mayville

Mayville was founded in 1845 by Alvin and William Forster and Chester and S.P. May. Iron ore was discovered by these men approximately four miles south of Mayville. A quantity of the ore was taken to the nearest iron smelter in Mishawaka, Indiana, in 1846. In 1847 Judge Alonzo Kinyon promoted a company chartered as the Wisconsin Iron Company. Construction of the first furnace was started at Mayville in 1848 approximately 500 feet southwest of this marker. In 1849 the furnace cast its first molten iron, yielding about 12 tons per day, using charcoal from native hardwoods for fuel. The industry prospered for 79 years, modernizing with the times to an eventual 800 tons of iron per day capacity. It once occupied this entire marker area as well as adjacent acreage. Due to curtailed demand for pig iron, the plant closed permanently in 1928. The last owner was the Mayville Iron Company.

Dodge County

278 **ADRIAN "ADDIE" JOSS**   Erected 1986
Addie Joss Park, Juneau

Tall and lanky, Wisconsin native Adrian "Addie" Joss became one of baseball's greatest pitchers, praised for his terrific speed and accurate control. Born in nearby Woodland on April 12, 1880, his family moved here to Juneau in 1886, where he played second base for the high-school team. He attended Watertown's Sacred Heart Academy and played baseball in the Wisconsin State League before joining the Cleveland "Naps" of the American League in 1902. Famous for his "hip pocket" delivery, Joss pitched a perfect game against the White Sox in 1908 and a no-hitter in 1910. He had a career record of 160 wins and 97 losses, winning 20 or more games in four successive seasons with a total of 45 shutouts. His career was cut short when he died suddenly of meningitis in 1911 after his ninth season. The day after his funeral, a Cleveland newspaper wrote: "Addie Joss still lives! His body may be molding into dust-but his spirit remains a potent, living thing in the sphere where his name won an honorable place." He was elected to baseball's Hall of Fame in 1978.

Green County

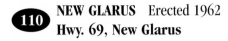

NEW GLARUS Erected 1962
Hwy. 69, New Glarus

In 1845 the Emigration society of the Canton of Glarus, Switzerland, sent Nicholas Duerst and Fridolin Streiff to the United States to purchase land for a Swiss settlement. They were joined in August by 108 settlers who began their homesteads on 1280 acres of farm and timber land bordering the Little Sugar River. The first years were hard and it was not until April, 1850, that the town was organized. Then New Glarus began to prosper; in 1851 the first store opened, in 1853 the first hotel and in 1870 the first cheese factory. By 1892 the population had increased to 600. The culture of Old Glarus has not been forgotten; the Swiss German dialect is still spoken and the traditional holidays are observed.

House with Swiss ornamentation, built 1855 in Green County, photograph ca. 1928.
SHSW Visual Materials Archive (X3) 40121.

SOUTHCENTRAL

Green Lake County

067 **UPPER FOX RIVER**   Erected 1957
Riverside Park, Berlin

On these banks of the Upper Fox River June 7, 1673, explorers Marquette and
Jolliet visited the Mouscouten Indian Tribe that lived here. For many years traders
and missionaries camped here while visiting the Indians. In 1846 Nathan Strong, a
Flourierite, was commissioned by the Federal Government to select a site for a
bridge to reach the timberland to the north. Strong selected this location and
founded Strong's Landing. Settlers of English descent arrived in 1847, followed by
immigrants from Poland and Germany. In 1857, a Community Charter was authorized and the name Berlin was chosen. Until 1890 the Fox River played an important role in transportation. Steamboats carried freight and passengers on the Upper
Fox from Lake Winnebago to the Wisconsin River Canal at Portage. Excursion
boats continued to use the river until 1920 when dredging was discontinued.

Green Lake County

363 **LUCY SMITH MORRIS (1850-1935)**   Erected 1998
Nathan Strong Park, East Huron St. (Hwy. 116), Berlin

Before women achieved the right to vote, clubs often served as women's political
and cultural forums. Foreseeing the political power of a statewide alliance of
women, Lucy Smith Morris organized Wisconsin's women's clubs into one coalition
in 1896. Serving as the first president of the "Wisconsin Federation of Woman's
Clubs," Morris used her influence to garner support for civic causes and social
reform. Known as "the little mother of the Federation," Morris helped to found 100
community libraries her first year in office. From a wealthy family, Morris was an
active local club woman and a strong supporter of women's suffrage bringing Julia
Ward Howe, Elizabeth Cady Stanton, and Susan B. Anthony to speak in Berlin.
These leaders of the women's suffrage movement were guests at the Morris home,
which still stands at 209 East Park Avenue. In the 20th century, Morris helped to
organize Wisconsin's League of Women Voters.

Jefferson County

 LAKE RIPLEY Erected 1955
**By the lake in Lake Ripley Park, N off
Hwy. 12, just E of Cambridge**

As a boy Ole Evenrude (1877-1934) lived near Cambridge. His father hoped to keep him on the farm, and when Ole built a sailboat like he had seen in a picture-book his father destroyed it. Ole found a secret place in the woods and built another. Here on Lake Ripley as his father watched from the shore, Ole sailed the well-built craft with all the instinctive skill of his Viking ancestors. Soon afterward he set out for the city to work as a mechanic. In 1908 he invented the outboard motor and founded a new American industry.

Jefferson County

 DRUMLINS Erected 1979
Rest Area No. 13, eastbound lane I-94, 1 mi. E of Lake Mills

This is glaciated country. Here as you approach the western edge of Wisconsin's kettle moraine, you see many land features created by glacial ice some 15,000 years ago. Among the most interesting of these are long oval hills known as drum-lins. Wisconsin is world-famous for its drumlins and there are numerous good specimens between Madison and Milwaukee. Drumlins look like eggs sliced in half lengthwise and laid on the surface in large groupings in line with the direction of ice movement. Their steeper, higher ends indicate the "up-ice" direction. Here they have a north-south alignment; closer to Milwaukee they lie more nearly east-west. Geologists do not know exactly how drumlins were formed but do know that they are composed of glacially transported soils and gravels and were formed at the bottom of the ice. Look for these unique reminders of the Great Ice Age as you continue eastward.

Jefferson County

011 **AZTALAN STATE PARK**   Erected 1964
on Hwy. Q, S off Hwy. B, 3 mi. E of Lake Mills

Indians of more advanced culture than surrounding tribes occupied a village on this site around the year 1500. They were strangers to this region, and their cannibalism made them unsatisfactory neighbors. The strength of their stockade walls proves they lived in a hostile world. The original village had a population of about 500. The area enclosed by the stockade contained about 21 acres, and within the stockade were cornfields as well as houses and temples. Eventually the village was destroyed by other local Indian tribes, leaving no known survivors of the Aztalan people.

Aztalan State Park.
SHSW Div. of Historic Preservation.

102

Jefferson County

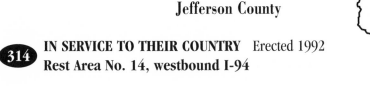

314 **IN SERVICE TO THEIR COUNTRY** Erected 1992
Rest Area No. 14, westbound I-94

Wisconsin contributed significantly to the military activities of the United States
since it became a state in 1848. During the Civil War, for instance, Wisconsin made
a major contribution to support the Union. About 50 percent of Wisconsin's adult
male population served in the Civil War, a percentage exceeded only by the service
of state citizens during World War II, when more than 80 percent of Wisconsin's
adult male population served in the military. Moreover, the mobilization of
Wisconsin's domestic economy during 1941-1945 added tens of thousands of
women and teenagers to the numbers of state citizens who assisted in the
American war effort.

Military Action	Wisconsin Residents in Service	Deaths
Civil War (1861-1865)	91,379	12,216
Spanish-American War (1898-1899)	5,469	134
Mexican Border Service (1916)	4,168	0
World War I (1917-1918)	122,215	3,932
World War II (1941- 1945)	332,200	7,980
Korean War (1950-1953)	132,000	801
Vietnam War (1958-1975)	165,400	1,238
Lebanon and Grenada (1982-1983)	400	4
Panama (1989-1990)	520	0
Persian Gulf (1990-1992)	10,400	12

S O U T H C E N T R A L

059 OCTAGON HOUSE   Erected 1957
919 Charles St., Watertown

This eight-sided, five-story house of solid brick construction was built in the early 1850's by pioneer John Richards. It is the best example in Wisconsin of an unusual architectural design which was in vogue briefly before the Civil War. It was claimed to be Wisconsin's largest single family residence when its 57 rooms, closets and halls were completed. Most interesting feature is the cantilever spiral staircase.

Richard's Octagon House, 1870.
SHSW Visual Materials Archive (X3) 23168.

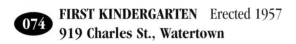 **FIRST KINDERGARTEN** Erected 1957
919 Charles St., Watertown

The first kindergarten in the United States was founded by Margarethe Meyer Schurz in this building in 1856. Moved to the present site and restored in 1956 by the Watertown Historical Society

Margarethe Meyer Schurz.
SHSW Visual Materials Archive (X3) 48032.

SOUTHCENTRAL

Jefferson County

410   **TRAIL DISCOVERY**   Erected 1998
One Main St. (at bridge) Watertown

On July 18th, during the Black Hawk War of 1832, Little Thunder—a Ho-Chunk (Winnebago) Indian guide to the U.S. Militia—discovered Black Hawk's Band crossed the Rock River in this vicinity. After receiving the news, Gen. James D. Henry and Col. Henry Dodge and the militia also crossed the river and followed the band's trail west.

Jefferson County

046   **HIGHWAY MARKING**   Erected 1956
7 mi. SE of Watertown, Hwy. 16

In the old days when both automobiles and roads were few in number, it was easy for those who had cars to get far enough away from home to get lost. While there were some "trails" such as the Cannon Ball Trail and the Yellowstone Trail (marked by daubs of yellow paint on the convenient object along the roadside) the long-distance traveler was usually guided by such natural features as hills, boulders, creeks and rivers, or by man-made landmarks (bridges, barns, schoolhouses, etc.). In 1917 the Wisconsin Highway Commission engineers recommended and inaugurated, with the Legislature's authorization, the first statewide system of identifying highways by number. This highway was designated State Trunk Highway 19 (later U.S. 16) and was the first to be marked and signed by numerals. The now familiar number system was later adopted by all other states and many foreign countries.

Jefferson County

152 **FORT KOSHKONONG**   Erected 1966
400 block Milwaukee Ave. E., Fort Atkinson

"Whilst lying here we have thrown up a stockade work flanked by four block houses for the security of our supplies and the accommodation of the sick," wrote General Henry Atkinson of this spot in his army report to General Winfield Scott on July 17, 1832. Atkinson with more than 4,000 frontier soldiers had followed Black Hawk and his British Band up the Rock River in an attempt to end the Black Hawk War. After an unproductive sortie east up Bark River, Atkinson returned and built Fort Koshkonong, later known as Fort Atkinson. The fort, constructed of oak logs eight feet tall, was abandoned when the army pursued and defeated Black Hawk at the Battle of Bad Axe in August 1832. Thus ended the Sauks' last hard fight against continued encroachment of the white men into their tribal lands. In September of 1836, Dwight Foster arrived and erected the first cabin in what is now Fort Atkinson on this site. He and other settlers used logs from the stockade to build cabins, river rafts and for firewood. By 1840 little of the fort remained.

*General Henry Atkinson, 1832,
artist unknown.
SHSW Visual Materials Archive (X3)
20944.*

Jefferson County

 409 **BLACK HAWK WAR ENCAMPMENT**   Erected 1998
**Southern Kettle Moraine State Forest at Bald Bluff Overlook,
Hwy. H, 1.5 mi. S of Palmyra**

During the Black Hawk War of 1832, General Atkinson camped near this location on two occasions. On July 7th, Atkinson led his entire militia, including future President's Abraham Lincoln and Zachary Taylor here. On July 19th, Atkinson returned briefly with a smaller contingent, but left soon after he heard that Generals' Henry and Dodge has located Black Hawk's trail.

Jefferson County

 408 **BLACK HAWK WAR ENCAMPMENT**
"Burnt Village"   Erected 1998
Burnt Village County Park, Hwy. N, 2 mi. SE of Ft. Atkinson

A large Ho-Chunk (Winnebago) village dating from the 1700s once stood in this vicinity. Just before the 1832 Black Hawk War, the village was burned during an intratribal battle. On July 6th and 8th, the United States Military camped at this site in their pursuit of Black Hawk and named this place Burnt Village.

Jefferson County

099 **PANTHER INTAGLIO**   Erected 1960
Hwy. 106, W city limits, Fort Atkinson

Discovered in 1850 by Increase A. Lapham, this is the only known intaglio effigy mound in the World. It was excavated for ceremonial purposes by American Indians of the Effigy Mound culture about 1000 A.D. A part of the tail has been covered. Of ten other recorded intaglios, all now destroyed, eight were similar in representing the panther; and two represented bears.

Jefferson County

323 **LAKE KOSHKONONG EFFIGY MOUNDS**   Erected 1994
Koshkonong Mounds Rd., Jefferson County Indian Mounds and Trail Park, near Fort Atkinson

Between AD 650 and 1200, groups of Native Americans throughout the southern half of Wisconsin and portions of adjacent states built earthen mounds of various shapes and sizes, including mounds shaped like animals, today called effigy mounds. The 11 mounds preserved here in the Jefferson County Indian Mounds and Trail Park were part of a larger group of 72 mounds and include symmetrical and animal shapes, resembling birds, turtles, or lizards, and perhaps spiritual figures. A remnant of an ancient trail is also visible in the park. The people who built effigy mounds hunted and collected food, often returning to the same locations seasonally. They lived in semi-permanent villages, used the bow and arrow, and made and used pottery. Mounds likely served ceremonial, spiritual and practical purposes, perhaps marking territories and designating special gathering places. Mounds often, but not always, contain burials. The Lake Koshkonong area once had 23 effigy mound groups, composed of about 500 individual mounds.

304 **LORINE NIEDECKER** Erected 1991
**Blackhawk Island Rd., Town of Sumner,
near Fort Atkinson**

Fish
      fowl
            flood
      Water lily mud
My life
in the leaves and on water
My mother and I
           born
in swale and swamp and sworn
to water

Lorine Niedecker (1903-70) lived on Black Hawk Island most of her life and celebrated the sights and sounds of this place in poems ranked among the 20th Century's finest. She lived first in the log sided house and later in the house near the river from 1947-70.

Nobody, nothing   than time
  ever gave me   unless light
    greater thing   and silence
                which if intense
                 makes sound

Lorine Niedecker.
Courtesy of Bonnie Roub and the Dwight Foster Public Library, Ft. Atkinson.

Marquette County

169 **JOHN MUIR COUNTRY**   Erected 1969
Hwy. 22, 8 mi. S of Montello

It was over this road that John Muir traveled to such early settlements as Kingston and Pardeeville. Muir was eleven when he came here from Scotland with his father, brother and sister in 1849. His mother arrived with her other children after a home had been carved out of the wilderness. They settled west of here at "Fountain Lake," at what is now John Muir Memorial Park. Here, surrounded by the beauties of nature, Muir began his love of wild animals, flowers, trees and waters. Later, the family moved five miles east to the Hickory Hill Farm. Muir's early education began at home. His mechanical skill was demonstrated by many ingenious inventions. He entered the University of Wisconsin but left without completing his studies to travel throughout the West on foot. While hiking through the Sierra Nevadas, he found his real inspiration and life work. His many and persistent articles and letters persuaded Congress to pass the National Park Act in 1890. This was the beginning of a formal national park movement. "Everybody needs beauty as well as bread; places to play in and places to pray in, where nature may heal and cheer, and give strength to body and soul alike."... John Muir.

S O U T H C E N T R A L

John Muir, 1908.
SHSW Visual Materials Archive (X96)
9731.

Marquette County

295 **KOREAN WAR**   Erected 1990
Rest Area No. 82, Hwy. 51, 4 mi. N of Westfield

On June 25, 1950, Communist North Korea invaded the Republic of Korea. Backed by Soviet Russia, the North Koreans quickly overran most of the peninsula. South Korea appealed to the United States for assistance, and President Harry Truman immediately ordered General Douglas MacArthur to commit U.S. troops. The United Nations condemned North Korean aggression and solicited military aid from member nations. Following a series of defeats, General MacArthur launched a daring amphibious landing at Inchon in September 1950 and advanced northward to the Yalu River. Then Communist China massively intervened, and the Allied forces retreated southward. The fighting eventually stabilized along the 38th Parallel, the original boundary between North and South Korea. After a long, bloody stalemate and protracted negotiations, an armistice was signed on July 27, 1953. The Korean War—or "police action" as it was called—cost 33,629 Americans killed in action and another 103,000 wounded. More than 132,000 Wisconsinites were involved in this "forgotten war," of whom 801 were killed in action and 4,286 were wounded. Another 111 were captured, and 84 remain listed as missing in action.

Rock County

272 **ROCK RIVER INDUSTRY**   Erected 1982
Rest Area No. 17, I-90 eastbound lane

Flowing through rich agricultural land, the Rock River provided needed water power for local Wisconsin industries. Among the earliest in the 1840's were flour and lumber mills, followed in the 1850's by woolen and paper mills and, later, cotton mills. Efficient farming was provided for with the manufacture of plows, reapers, twine binders, windmills, and platform and wagon scales for weighing grain. Farm wagons, carriages, sleighs and cutters, as well as furniture, were also early products of Rock River industry. So too were processed meats, churns and other dairy equipment for the farm. By the turn of the century, the early gasoline engine, motorized vehicles, machine tools and precision instruments were among familiar products of the valley, as were the electric brake and clutch. In more recent times, such Rock River industrial products as fountain pens, diesel engines, automobiles and paper-making machinery have become worldwide in their markets.

Rock County

 WISCONSIN'S TOBACCO LAND Erected 1961
Hwy 51, 0.5 mi. S of Edgerton

Wisconsin's first commercial tobacco was raised in Dane and Rock counties by cousins Orrin and Ralph Pomeroy in 1854. Grown as a cash crop to supplement dairy income, Wisconsin tobacco is used as a binder in making cigars. Because of the large amount of hand labor, the areas planted are small, usually two to five acres. In late April the seed is sown in the steam-sterilized soil of long white muslin-covered seedbeds, and transplanting to the field is done by machine in June. The plants are cut and speared on lath in August and are hung in the long unpainted sheds to cure for two to three months. "Case Weather" (fog or rain) in late fall conditions the leaf so that it can be stripped from the stalks and bailed for market. About 100 miles to the northwest, in Vernon and surrounding counties, tobacco production began in the 1880's and is an important crop today.

Southern Wisconsin Tobacco Farm, ca. 1930.
SHSW Visual Materials Archive (W63) 15678.

Rock County

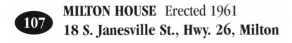

VILLAGE OF COOKSVILLE   Erected 1996
(two-sided marker)
11204 N. Church St., Cooksville

Cooksville consists of two villages: Cooksville platted in 1842 and Waucoma platted in 1846. John and Daniel Cook settled here in 1840, establishing Cooksville on the Badfish Creek, where a sawmill was soon constructed. Dr. John Porter of Massachusetts laid out Waucoma east of Cooksville. The two villages were settled by people from New England, New York, the British Isles, and, later, Norway. But the village, known as Cooksville because of the post office's location, was by-passed by railroads in the 1860s, becoming "the town that time forgot."

VILLAGE OF WAUCOMA

The Village of Waucoma was established in 1846 by Dr. John Porter, who purchased land next to Cooksville from his Massachusetts friend, Senator Daniel Webster. Waucoma was laid out around a public square. Soon Greek Revival and Gothic Revival style houses, some of locally fired brick, were built by Yankee settlers, along with blacksmith shops, general stores, a hotel, a door and sash factory, a schoolhouse, and two churches. Listed in the National Register of Historic Places in 1973, Cooksville is known as "a wee bit of New England in Wisconsin."

Rock County

MILTON HOUSE   Erected 1961
18 S. Janesville St., Hwy. 26, Milton

Erected in 1844 by Joseph Goodrich, this frontier inn is constructed of grout-a mixture of gravel, lime and water. An important stagecoach stop and transfer point, it was also a pre-Civil War station in the underground railroad, and is still connected by a secret escape tunnel to the old log cabin. In 1948 the Goodrich family donated the inn to the Milton Historical Society for a museum.

Rock County

 STORRS LAKE, MILTON   Erected 1976
Jct. of Hwy. 26 and Storrs Road, Milton

On July 1, 1832, here beside Storrs Lake, Brigadier General Henry Atkinson and 4,500 soldiers camped overnight in their pursuit of Black Hawk, Sac Indian chief, who was fleeing northward up the east side of Rock River with 400 warriors and 1200 women and children. In a diary dated July 1, 1832, Lt. Albert Sidney Johnston wrote: "After marching 23 miles (from Turtle Village) this day, we camped by a small lake, and had to drink the water, which was very bad, but it was all that could be found. Here General Atkinson had, on this night, breastworks thrown up, which was easily done, as we encamped in thick timber...(July 2). This morning the army proceeded almost directly north towards Lake Koshkonong." Among Captain Early's mounted scouts was the 23 year old Abraham Lincoln, finishing his third 30 day enlistment. General Atkinson's Army of the Frontier had entered Wisconsin at Turtle Village (Beloit) where it camped on June 30. It then moved north through the Prairie Road to this lake east of Milton. On July 2, the army moved north again and camped on Otter Creek about two miles east of Lake Koshkonong, before entering Jefferson County. At Cold Spring, on July 10, Lincoln was mustered out, his horse was stolen, and he returned by foot and canoe to New Salem, Ill.

Rock County

THE MEDAL OF HONOR   Erected 1990
Rest Area-Tourist Info. Center, westbound lane I-90

The Medal of Honor is the highest decoration for bravery awarded to members of the armed forces of the United States It is bestowed by the President, in the name of Congress, only for a deed of supreme valor and self-sacrifice distinguished by "gallantry and intrepidity at risk of life above and beyond the call of duty." More often than not, the Medal of Honor is awarded posthumously. President Abraham Lincoln approved the creation of the Medal of Honor in 1862, and during the Civil War some 1,527 Union soldiers and sailors earned it. In all, 3,394 Medals have been awarded. Wisconsin citizens received 62, including the special Medal of Honor awarded by Congress to Milwaukee-born advocate of air power General William C. "Billy" Mitchell. Wisconsin citizens have received the Medal of Honor in the following conflicts: Civil War, 21; Frontier Wars, 7; Spanish American War, 1; Philippine Insurrection, 1; Boxer Rebellion, 1; Mexican Campaign, 2; World War I, 2; World War II, 15; Korea, 5; Vietnam, 6.

Rock County

354 **HOW-BECKMAN MILL**   Erected 1997
Beckman Mill County Park, Hwy. H, Newark Township

Constructed in 1868 by William How, the How-Beckman grist mill stands along Raccoon Creek where a distillery and sawmill were once located. In 1882 the Beckman family purchased the property. German-born August Beckman operated the turbine-powered mill followed by his sons Henry and Charles. Reaching peak production in the early twentieth century, the mill was enlarged in the 1920s and served as the local commercial and social center. Milling operations ceased in 1954. The How-Beckman Mill was listed on the National Register of Historic Places in 1977.

Rock County

 JEFFERSON PRAIRIE SETTLEMENT   Erected 1951
Hwy. 140, 4 mi. S of Clinton

Ole Knutson Nattestad, first Norwegian settler in Wisconsin, came to Clinton Township, July 1, 1838. In his native Numedal, Nattestad had been a farmer, peddler, and blacksmith. In 1836 he and his brother Ansten visited Stavanger and there heard for the first time about America. Early the next year they secured passage to Massachusetts and a few months later worked their way to Chicago. In the spring of 1838 Ansten returned to Norway while Ole explored northward, eventually reaching Clinton Township. Ansten organized more than a hundred emigrants and led them to Wisconsin the following year. Some joined Ole Nattestad on Jefferson Prairie; others went west to Rock Prairie (Luther Valley). Although the groups organized different church congregations and were separated by settlers of different nationality, they are usually regarded jointly as the first Norwegian settlement in Wisconsin, and the fourth in America.

093 **ROUTE OF ABRAHAM LINCOLN–1832 AND 1859**
Erected 1959
Hwy. 51, 3.8 mi. S of Janesville

Twice in his lifetime Abraham Lincoln is known to have traveled within sight of the Rock River east of this marker. Lincoln passed this way July 2, 1832, as a private in a mounted company of Illinois militia accompanying forces under General Henry Atkinson during the Black Hawk War. On October 1, 1859, Lincoln again passed this way after delivering a political address in Hanchett's Hall at the invitation of the Beloit Republican Club. He spoke the same evening in Janesville and spent the weekend as a guest in the home of William M. Tallman. While following the Prairie Road between Beloit and Janesville in 1859 Lincoln pointed out to his companions the route taken by the army in pursuit of Black Hawk's band.

S
O
U
T
H
C
E
N
T
R
A
L

A young Abraham Lincoln, ca.1846, probably 37 years old, photograph taken about 5 years after the Black Hawk War.
SHSW Visual Materials Archive, Lincoln File N 17464.

117

Rock County

013 **HOME OF GOVERNOR HARVEY** Erected 1953
Hwy. J, Shopiere

Louis Powell Harvey lived here 1851-1859. He was a leader in business, education, journalism, and politics. Soon after his inauguration, Gov. Harvey led a relief expedition of Wisconsin troops who had just fought their first major battle and suffered big losses in the Battle of Shiloh. While boarding a steamboat, he fell into the Tennessee River and drowned. His wife, Cordelia Perrine Harvey, founded Harvey Hospital for wounded soldiers in Madison, and was known as the "Wisconsin Angel."

Rock County

020 **FIRST STATE FAIR OCTOBER 1-2, 1851** Erected 1954
in Courthouse Park on South Atwood Ave., behind Courthouse, Janesville

Thirteen counties were represented at the first state fair sponsored by the Wisconsin Agricultural Society. Entries included horses, cattle, sheep, swine, farming implements, dairy products, flour and corn meal, domestic manufactures, needle work, fruits, vegetables and flowers. Highlights of the occasion were the plowing matches and an address by John W. Lathrop, Chancellor of the University of Wisconsin. The fairgrounds contained 6 acres, and about 10,000 people attended.

Rock County

 BELOIT COLLEGE Erected 1967
Beloit College Campus, Beloit

Chartered by the Territorial Legislature of Wisconsin on February 2, 1846, Beloit College has had an uninterrupted life of service since its first class assembled on November 4, 1847. The main college grounds, and this first building, Middle College, were the generous gifts in money, materials, land, and labor of the pioneer citizens of Beloit, resolved to have a college in this then-Western frontier.

SOUTHCENTRAL

Beloit College at the time of the Civil War. The campus building is Middle College.
SHSW Visual Materials Archive Classified File.

Rock County

299 JANESVILLE TANK COMPANY Erected 1992
Rock County Historical Society, 10 S. High St., Janesville

During the 1930s, the Janesville National Guard armory was the headquarters for the 32nd Tank Company, a unit of Wisconsin's famed 32nd Division, which had been reorganized after World War I and equipped with light tanks. In November 1940, as part of the mobilization ordered by President Franklin D. Roosevelt, the unit was melded with three other Midwestern National Guard units and redesignated Company A of the 192nd Tank Battalion. Within a year, the Janesville tank company had been trained and dispatched to the Philippine Islands. Following the outbreak of war on December 7, 1941, members of Company A became the first of 330,000 Wisconsin residents to engage the enemy. During a harrowing four-month defense of the Bataan Peninsula, short of supplies and devoid of air cover, the Janesville tank unit fought bravely alongside other American and Filipino forces until surrendering on April 9, 1942. As prisoners of war, the Janesville men participated in the infamous Bataan Death March. Of the original ninety-nine members of the unit, only thirty-five survived imprisonment by the Japanese.

Rock County

144 WISCONSIN'S FIRST AVIATOR Erected 1964
at Hwy. 81 and Cranston Road, near the fire station, Beloit

The nation's first commercially built "aeroplane" was assembled and flown here November 4, 1909, by Arthur P. Warner, Wisconsin's first pilot. Self-taught, Warner was the 11th American to pilot a powered aircraft and first in the U.S. to buy an aircraft for business use. Built by Glen H. Curtiss, the biplane was "sister" to the aircraft in which Curtiss won the Bennett trophy race in Rheims, France, August 29, 1909. Inventor and manufacturer, Warner used the aircraft in research and to publicize his automotive products. He developed the automobile speedometer, automotive and machine tool accessories, and built the first electric power plant in Beloit. For his contributions to the aviation and automotive industries, Warner was posthumously elected to the Wisconsin Industrial Hall of Fame in 1962.

Rock County

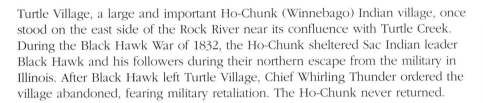

S
O
U
T
H
C
E
N
T
R
A
L

 BLACK HAWK AT TURTLE VILLAGE
(Two-sided marker)   Erected 1998
Corner of Public Ave. and State St., in Heritage Park,
along Rock River walkway, Beloit

Turtle Village, a large and important Ho-Chunk (Winnebago) Indian village, once stood on the east side of the Rock River near its confluence with Turtle Creek. During the Black Hawk War of 1832, the Ho-Chunk sheltered Sac Indian leader Black Hawk and his followers during their northern escape from the military in Illinois. After Black Hawk left Turtle Village, Chief Whirling Thunder ordered the village abandoned, fearing military retaliation. The Ho-Chunk never returned.

THE U.S. MILITARY AT TURTLE VILLAGE

In this vicinity, during the Black Hawk War of 1832, Sac Indian leader Black Hawk and his followers left Illinois and entered the Michigan Territory (now Wisconsin), seeking refuge with the Ho-Chunk Indians at Turtle Village. On July 1, 1832, more than five weeks after Black Hawk left Turtle Village and continued his northern retreat up the Rock River, General Henry Atkinson and his troops arrived here, only to find an abandoned Indian settlement with extensive gardens and fields of grain.

Rock County

 BLACK HAWK WAR   Erected 1968
Rest Area, Tourist Info Center No. 22, westbound lane I-90, S of Beloit

In the spring of 1831, the Sauk Indians led by Chief Keokuk left their ancestral home near the mouth of the Rock River and moved across the Mississippi, to fulfill the terms of a treaty signed in 1804. On April 6, 1832, a dissatisfied faction led by Black Hawk returned with 400 warriors and 1200 women, children and old men. Why he risked this return to "my towns, my cornfields, and the homes of my people" in the face of certain opposition is not clear, but Black Hawk probably hoped that other Indians would join him in resisting further white settlement. When this hope failed and the Illinois militia was called up, Black Hawk sent messengers to negotiate for peaceable removal across the Mississippi. One of his messengers was shot by the excited and poorly-disciplined militia and the war was on. The Indians briefly took the offensive and scalping parties attacked isolated communities of white settlers. The exact route taken by Black Hawk as he retreated through southern Wisconsin toward the Mississippi is difficult to trace, because both pursued and pursuers were traveling unfamiliar terrain and their later accounts varied. Major engagements took place at Wisconsin Heights and at the Bad Axe, where the war ended August 2, 1832.

Walworth County

DELAVAN'S HISTORIC BRICK STREET   Erected 1996
Tower Park, Walworth Ave., Delavan

Dusty and rutted in dry spells, muddy and miserable in wet, Delavan's main street, Walworth Avenue, remained unpaved from the 1830s until the second decade of the 20th century. In 1911, Delavan's City Council voted to pave the three block central business district of Walworth Avenue and chose brick as the preferred paving material. The city contracted with the Birdsall-Griffith Company of Racine to install the street at a cost of $19,198.18. A workforce of thirty laborers graded the street, poured the concrete base and installed a two inch layer of sand. A crew of skilled Italian immigrant workers then laid the bricks in a running bond pattern along the street and in a herringbone pattern at the intersections. Paved in vitrified brick, a durable waterproof material resistant to wear, the street was completed in 1913 and hailed as a great transportation improvement. Delavan's brick street has been in continuous use since its installation and remains one of the last and best examples of brick paved roadway in the State of Wisconsin. The street was listed in the National Register of Historic Places in 1995.

Walworth County

 DELAVAN'S CIRCUS COLONY Erected 1963
Horton Park, Hwy. 11, Delavan

S O U T H C E N T R A L

In 1847 two New York brothers, Edmund and Jeremiah Mabie, toured Wisconsin with their United States Olympic Circus. The circus stopped over in Delavan and the brothers took time off to hunt prairie chicken near Delavan Lake. They liked the area so well that they purchased 400 acres of land and established winter quarters for the circus here. Because this circus was the largest and most profitable in existence, circus performers and other show personnel flocked to Delavan. Twenty-six circuses winter-quartered here between 1847 and 1894, including Harry Buckley's National Circus and Roman Hippodrome, W. C. Cour-Dan Castello's Egyptian Caravan, Holland and McMahon World's Circus. The colorful days of the circus era in Delavan ended with the E. G. Holland and Co. Railroad shows. In 1871 the idea for forming the P.T. Barnum Circus was developed in Delavan by W. S. Coup, who also was first to put a large circus on rails and introduced the second and third ring to the performance. Delavan reached its peak as a "circus town" during the 1870's. About seventy members of the "circus colony" are buried in Spring Grove and St. Andrew's cemeteries.

Walworth County

 WISCONSIN'S FIRST SCHOOL FOR THE DEAF Erected 1969
Grounds of State School for the Deaf, Hwy. 11, Delavan

In 1839 Ebenezer Cheseboro emigrated to Wisconsin from New York and settled in the town of Darien, two miles west of Delavan on the Janesville road. Due to the lack of a school for his deaf daughter, Ariadna, a teacher of the deaf was hired to come to the home. Two years later the school, then numbering eight pupils, had to be discontinued for lack of funds. A petition for the establishment and maintenance of a school for deaf children was then sent to the State Legislature. On April 19, 1852, a bill was passed incorporating a school for the deaf to be located in Walworth County. Soon after, Franklin K. Phoenix, the son of one of the founders of Delavan, donated twelve acres of land to be used as the school site. The grounds are called "Phoenix Green" in his honor. The school now comprises thirty-five acres of land and is supported by the State of Wisconsin for the education of its hearing impaired children. On October 20, 1962 dedication ceremonies were held for a Vocational Rehabilitation Center for the Deaf, which provides services at this site for eligible adult deaf persons.

Walworth County

190 **EAST TROY RAILROAD**   Erected 1973
2002 Church St., East Troy

The East Troy Railroad is the last vestige of Wisconsin's once broad network of electric interurban railways. Concentrated in the southeastern quarter of the State, this network once totaled approximately 385 miles of track. Most of the interurban railway mileage in Wisconsin was built between 1890 and 1910; the last interurban passenger in the State was carried in 1963 by the North Shore Line. The East Troy Interurban Line, formerly a part of The Milwaukee Electric Railway and Light Company, carried passengers between East Troy and Milwaukee from 1907 until 1939. Since 1939 the six mile line has existed as a railroad freight connection for the Village of East Troy.

Walworth County

235 **ALLEN FAMILY**   Erected 1976
Village Park, Allen Grove, on Hwy. X, 3 mi. SW of Darien

Philip Allen, a Revolutionary War veteran, and his children: Philip Jr., Harvey, Sidney, Pliny, Asa Keyes, and Persis, came from New York in May, 1845, to settle in Allen Grove. Sixty-five Allens traveled by canal boat, steamboat, and overland from Kenosha bringing with them material to build four houses, carpenters to build them, a minister, Bibles and hymnals. The Allens organized the Congregational church here in 1845. They established a preparatory school for Beloit College in 1856. Philip Junior became the first postmaster in 1846. Philip Allen Sr. is buried in Mt. Philip Cemetery, west of here.

Walworth County

175 **WISCONSIN'S FIRST 4-H CLUB** Erected 1996
Hwy. BB, 3.5 mi. S of Lake Geneva

The Linn Junior Farmers Club was the first 4-H Club organized in Wisconsin. Mrs. May Hatch, local community leader, and Thomas L. Bewick, newly appointed State Boys and Girls Club Leader at the University of Wisconsin organized the club here on the Hatch farm, October 30, 1914. This club was started five months after Congress passed the Smith-Lever Act which created the Cooperative Extension Service whereby federal, state and county governments participate in the county agent system. Four boys and three girls attended the first meeting of the club. Membership grew to 21 during the year with projects in livestock, crops, gardening, canning, cooking and sewing. During this period, similar boys' and girls' clubs were beginning in other states. The movement grew rapidly, and the variety of projects with appeal to rural and urban youth increased. By 1970, four million urban and rural members were participating annually in the nation, and 4-H had spread to 84 countries of the World.

Walworth County

282 **FIRST SWEDISH SETTLERS IN WISCONSIN** Erected 1988
Veterans Memorial Park, Hwy. 12, Genoa City

Carl Friman (1781-1862) emigrated from Sweden with five sons in 1838 and purchased 80 acres near Genoa City. The Friman family members were recognized as the first Swedes to settle permanently in Wisconsin. Returning to his homeland, Friman corresponded regularly with his sons who remained here. Their letters from Wisconsin appeared in Swedish newspapers, stimulating interest in opportunities and conditions in America. The Friman family was in the vanguard of the 19th century Swedish immigration to the United States. By 1900 over 1.1 million persons of Swedish birth or descent resided in the United States, and nearly 49,000 individuals born in Sweden lived in Wisconsin. Carl Friman's son, Adolph (1826-1871), owned numerous town lots in Genoa City, where he became a successful businessman. Freeman Street in Genoa City is named in his honor, and he is buried in Hillside Cemetery. Carl's son, Wilhelm (1823-1911) also owned land that was incorporated into this community. The other sons lived for a time in this area before moving west.

Waushara County

337 **SIR HENRY SOLOMAN WELLCOME**   Erected 1996
(1853-1936)
Hwy. J, 2 mi. S of Almond

Sir Henry Soloman Wellcome, key figure in the development of pharmaceutics and the promotion of medical research, was born to Yankee settlers on a hardscrabble farm in the vicinity of Almond, Wisconsin, where he spent the first eight years of his life. Wellcome moved to Minnesota with his family in 1861 and was later educated in pharmacy schools in Chicago and Philadelphia. In 1880 he went to London, England, where he and Silas Mainville Burroughs formed a business partnership creating Burroughs Wellcome and Company to manufacture and market a new, compressed form of American medicine: pills. Sir Henry later established the Wellcome Chemical and Physiological laboratories, among the first medical research institutes in the pharmaceutical industry. Eventually, Wellcome researchers helped discover new treatments for diseases such as diphtheria, yellow fever, malaria, leprosy, and sleeping sickness. Wellcome's collection of rare medical manuscripts form the basis for the Wellcome Institute for the History of Medicine in London. A naturalized British citizen, Sir Henry was knighted in 1932. The Wellcome Trust, established in England after Sir Henry's death in 1936, is recognized as one of the world's great benefactors of medical research and the Burroughs Wellcome Fund in the United States has supported medical research since 1955.

Markers
Southwest Region

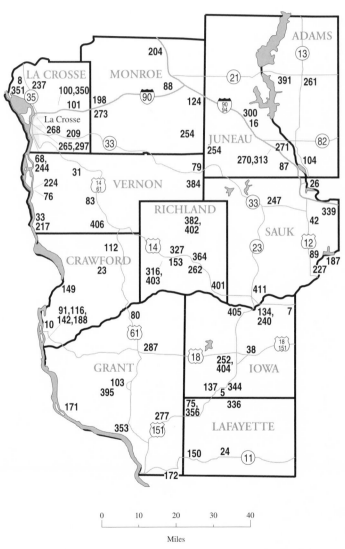

ADAMS

204

13

LA CROSSE   MONROE

8

237

351   100,350

35

101   198   88

La Crosse   273   90

268   209

265,297   33

21

391   261

124

90
94

300
16

82

JUNEAU

254

271   104

270,313   87

68,
244

31

224

76   83

14
61

VERNON

254

79

384

26

33   247

42   339

33
217   406

112

CRAWFORD

23

149

91,116,
142,188

10

RICHLAND

382,
402

14   327

153   364

316,   262

403

401

SAUK

23

12

89   187

227

411

405   134,
240   7

80

61

287

18

18

252,
404

38

18
151

GRANT

103

395

171

277

353   151

137   344

5

IOWA

75,
356   336

LAFAYETTE

150   24   11

172

0   10   20   30   40

Miles

SOUTHWEST

Adams County

261   **ROCHE-A-CRI STATE PARK**   Erected 1976
at the Park, Hwy. 13, 3 mi. N of Friendship

This prominent butte, perhaps the steepest hill in Wisconsin, was called La Roche-a-Cri by 17th and 18th century French voyageurs. Rising 300 feet above the surrounding plain, this landmark undoubtedly guided Indians and early pioneers. Indians of an undetermined cultural group left rock carvings, called petroglyphs, at places on Roche-a-Cri. Like many similar formations on Wisconsin's sandy Central Plain, this butte is composed of Cambrian sandstone about 500,000,000 years old. The flat plain is the old bed of Glacial Lake Wisconsin, which covered 1,800 square miles of central Wisconsin some 15,000 years ago. The buttes were islands in that immense lake. The State Highway Commission purchased nearby land for a roadside park in 1937 and ten years later conveyed it to the Wisconsin Conservation Department. Roche-a-Cri State Park was established in 1948 and now contains over 400 acres. It is listed in the National Register of Historic Places.

Adams County

391   **SITE OF THE FIRST NORWEGIAN LUTHERAN CHURCH OF THE ROCHE-A-CRI**   Erected 1998
South Arkdale Cemetery, 1801 Cypress Ave., Strongs Prairie

In 1850, a group of Norwegian settlers from Koshkonong, the foremost Norwegian settlement colony in the United States at the time, left their southern Wisconsin home and migrated north, settling here in "Roch-a-Cree" or Roche-a-Cri. Imbued with pioneer spirit and a firm faith in Lutheranism, these settlers homesteaded and became successful farmers, growing potatoes as the their staple crop. In 1853, the Rev. H. A. Preus, a university-trained minister of the Norwegian state church, visited Roche-a-Cri and organized "The Norwegian Evangelical Lutheran Church of Roche-a-Cri" with a membership of about thirty individuals who held services in their homes. By 1859, the community and congregation had outgrown these meeting places and built a log church at this site. This structure was destroyed by fire and in 1868 a frame church was erected one mile north of this location. The old church cemetery remains here, however, and is known as the South Arkdale Cemetery.

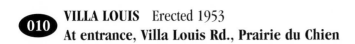

Crawford County

010 **VILLA LOUIS**   Erected 1953
At entrance, Villa Louis Rd., Prairie du Chien

On the site of old Fort Crawford, Col. Hercules Louis Dousman, important agent in John J. Astor's fur company, built his "house on the Mound" in 1843. Later it was named Villa Louis. Today this luxurious mansion appears much as it did in the days when it was a brilliant center of social activity, even while the pioneers lived side by side with the Indians.

Crawford County

142 **WAR OF 1812**   Erected 1964
On the grounds of Villa Louis, Prairie du Chien

Although Prairie du Chien belonged to the United States after the American Revolution, its pioneer residents were tied by trade, tradition and family to the French-British community at Mackinac and to the St. Lawrence River ports. During the War of 1812, Gov. William Clark of Missouri recognized the strategic importance of Prairie du Chien's location, and sent about 150 soldiers to build a fort here. When it was dedicated June 19, 1814, the American flag was raised for the first time over a Wisconsin fort. Pro-British residents alerted the British at Mackinac and a force of 150 militia and 400 Indians was quickly sent to Prairie du Chien. Fort Shelby was compelled to surrender on July 20 and was re-named Fort McKay by the British. When the war ended, the British burned the fort and withdrew to Mackinac. The Americans began construction of another fort July 3, 1816, and named it Fort Crawford. This reconstructed blockhouse marks one corner of the first Fort Crawford.

SOUTHWEST

Crawford County

116 **PRAIRIE DU CHIEN**   Erected 1962
Tourist Info. Center at Mississippi River Bridge, Prairie du Chien

In prehistoric times water from melting glaciers cut a wide valley between the bluffs of the Mississippi River to form a broad flood plain. On it French explorers, traders and missionaries found a large and well-established Fox Indian village. The chief's name was Alim in Indian, Chien in French, and dog in English. Jonathan Carver visited the village in 1766 and called it "Dog Plain" but the residents preferred the French "Prairie du Chien". Another traveler, who could trade and fight better than he could spell, was Peter Pond. In 1773 Pond visited Prairie du Chien and wrote: "This Plane is a Very Handsum one. The Plane is verey Smooth hear. All the traders and all the Indians of Several tribes Meat fall and Spring." The United States Government negotiated three important treaties with the Indians here in 1825, 1829 and 1830. Most important was the council that opened August 5, 1825. In a conference that lasted fourteen days, leaders of most of the Indian tribes of the Old Northwest met with William Clark and Lewis Cass to establish territorial boundaries for each tribe.

Confluence of the Mississippi River and the Wisconsin River.
SHSW Div. of Historic Preservation.

Crawford County

MUSEUM OF MEDICAL PROGRESS
Erected 1960
Beaumont and Rice Sts., Prairie du Chien

The Second Fort Crawford Military Hospital was built here in 1831. In 1934 this portion of it was restored with original stone as a memorial to William Beaumont, M.D. (1785-1853), pioneer military surgeon. Among prominent military personnel stationed at Fort Crawford were Zachary Taylor, later President of the United States, and Jefferson Davis, President of the Confederacy. The Museum of Medical Progress has been established by the Charitable, Educational and Scientific Foundation of the State Medical Society and is operated by the State Historical Society of Wisconsin.

Fort Crawford, Prairie du Chien, 1840.
SHSW Visual Materials Archive (X313) 2618.

PERE MARQUETTE AND SIEUR JOLLIET
Erected 1973
Tourist Info. Center at Mississippi River Bridge, Prairie du Chien

In 1673, Louis Jolliet, Canadian fur-trader and explorer, and Father Jacques Marquette, French Jesuit Missionary, with five French Canadian boatmen, were the first white men to enter the upper Mississippi River. Indians directed them to the Great River via the Fox-Wisconsin waterway from the present site of Green Bay to Prairie du Chien. The Frenchmen entered the Mississippi River June 17, 1673. Descending the river until July 16, the explorers turned back at the Arkansas River because they anticipated possible danger ahead from the Spanish and Indians. Returning North, the expedition pioneered what is now the Illinois-Des Plaines-Chicago River passage to Lake Michigan. Marquette and Jolliet were back at the mouth of the Fox River by the end of September. The trip had taken them over 2,000 miles through country never before seen by white men.

"Marquette and Joliet Discover the Mississippi," from Young Folks History of America, *1886. SHSW Visual Materials Archive (X3) 47169.*

Crawford County

 RAFTING ON THE MISSISSIPPI Erected 1965
Hwy. 35, 1.2 mi. S of Lynxville

After 1837 the vast timber resources of northern Wisconsin were eagerly sought by settlers moving into the mid-Mississippi valley. By 1847 there were more than thirty sawmills on the Wisconsin, Chippewa, and St. Croix river systems, cutting largely Wisconsin white pine. During long winter months, logging crews felled and stacked logs on the frozen rivers. Spring thaws flushed the logs down the stream toward the Mississippi River. Here logs were caught, sorted, scaled, and rafted. Between 1837 and 1901 more than forty million board feet of logs floated down the Great River to sawmills. The largest log raft on the Mississippi was assembled at Lynxville in 1896. It was 270 feet wide and 1550 feet long, containing two and one-fourth million board feet of lumber. The largest lumber raft on the river originated on Lake St. Croix in 1901. Somewhat smaller in size, 270 feet wide and 1450 feet long, it carried more lumber-nine million board feet. The last rafting of lumber on the Mississippi came in 1915, ending a rich, exciting, and colorful era in the history of Wisconsin and the Great River.

Log raft on the Mississippi River.
SHSW Visual Materials Archive (X32) 6320.

Crawford County

SOLDIERS GROVE ORIGIN   Erected 1998
406 **Soldiers Grove Park, Mill and Main sts., Soldiers Grove**

In late July, during the Black Hawk War of 1832, Sac Indian leader Black Hawk led his starving followers through this area in their escape from the General Henry Atkinson and his military forces. After Black Hawk's brilliant delaying tactics at the Battle of Wisconsin Heights, he fled with his band towards the Mississippi River. On August 1st, in their pursuit of Black Hawk, about 1,300 United States army and militia, including notable future leaders, Col. Zachary Taylor, Col. Henry Dodge and Albert Sidney Johnson, encamped in this vicinity, known then as Pine Grove Village. Weary from their trek through the rugged terrain of western Wisconsin, the soldiers rested; their exhausted and hungry horses, who were unable to find food for days in the jagged terrain, foraged in the grass here. Because this military encampment became widely known throughout the territory, Pine Grove Village was renamed Soldiers Grove.

Zachary Taylor, future President of the United States.
Visual Materials Archive (X3) 51352.

134

Crawford County

112 **JAMES DAVIDSON**   Erected 1961
Hwy. 61, 0.5 mi. S of Soldiers Grove

Product of a small American community, James O. Davidson's life illustrates the romance of citizenship in a democracy. Born 1854 in Norway, where he received little formal education, he emigrated in 1872 and was a farmer and tailor before coming in 1877 to Soldiers Grove. A leading merchant here for twenty-three years, "Yim" was village president, village treasurer, assemblyman, state treasurer and lieutenant-governor before he attained the governorship, 1906-1911. As governor, he introduced the law providing for bank examiners and promoted legislation giving the railroad commission jurisdiction over most public utilities. He was visionary and popular without being spectacular. He had strong convictions, cool judgment and keen administrative ability. He died December 16, 1922, and was buried in Forest Hill Cemetery, Madison.

Crawford County

023 **GAYS MILLS APPLE ORCHARDS**   Erected 1955
Hwy. 171, 0.5 mi. E of Gays Mills

Farmers in this area learned early that the land on both sides of the Kickapoo River offered excellent conditions for apple growing. In 1905, John Hays and Ben Twining collected apples from eight or ten farmers around Gays Mills for exhibit at the State Fair. The exhibit won first prize, then went on to capture first honors in a national apple show in New York. This experience prompted the Wisconsin State Horticultural Society to urge a project of "trial orchards" around the state to interest growers in commercial production. The Society examined a site on High Ridge and planted five acres with five recommended varieties. By 1911, the orchard had grown so vigorously that an organization was formed in Gays Mills to promote the selling of orchards. Today more than a thousand acres here produce apples nationally known for their color and flavor.

Grant County

353   VILLAGE OF POTOSI   Erected 1996
114-108 S. Main St., Potosi

One of Wisconsin's early mining communities, Potosi was settled in 1829 after lead ore was found near St. John Mine. Named for the silver mining city of "Potosi" in Bolivia, South America, the village began as three separate settlements and developed along the steep walls of the narrow valley, incorporating in 1841. Located on the Grant River feeding into the Mississippi, Potosi quickly became a leading shipping port for lead ore and a supplier for in land miners. Potosi was one of the largest communities in the Wisconsin Territory, but its early boom was short-lived: by the late 1840s its port, filled with river silt, no longer accommodated large vessels, and the promise of gold in California drew many area miners further west. However, Potosi's mining industry was revived in the later half of the 19th century when zinc, a by-product of lead mining, was produced. The Potosi Brewery, built by Gabriel Hail in 1855, remained an important industry for over a hundred years.

Miners in Southwest Wisconsin.
SHSW Visual Materials Archive (X3) 20770.

Grant County

 FIRST STATE NORMAL SCHOOL   Erected 1985
Rountree Hall, UW-Platteville

Wisconsin's first college devoted wholly to training teachers, the Platteville Normal School, opened here on October 9, 1866, in Rountree Hall, which since 1853 had housed its predecessor, the Platteville Academy. The Academy (1842-1866) had functioned largely as a private high school, preparing students for college and teaching. When in 1865 the legislature authorized the state to establish "normal" schools for the training of teachers, many cities offered proposals. Platteville Academy's trustees provided Rountree Hall, the community raised money, and Platteville Normal School opened with a 5-member faculty and 60 students. Two years later, General Ulysses S. Grant participated in the dedication of a new wing. Rountree Hall became the home of the Wisconsin Mining Trade School in 1907, and the Normal School moved to an adjacent site. In 1925, normal schools were converted to state teachers colleges and empowered to grant bachelor's degrees. In 1959, the Wisconsin State College Platteville and the Wisconsin Institute of Technology merged and in 1971 became the University of Wisconsin-Platteville.

Grant County

 THE POINT OF BEGINNING   Erected 1969
Hwy. 80 at the WI–IL State Line, S of Hazel Green

Late in 1831, when Wisconsin was still in Michigan Territory, at a point 45 chains (2,970 feet) east of here, Lucius Lyon, United States Commissioner on the survey of the Wisconsin-Illinois border, built a mound six feet square at the base and six feet high to mark the intersection of the border and the 4th principal meridian. From this point all Wisconsin public land surveys began, including sixteen townships in Southwestern Wisconsin which Lyon surveyed in 1832 and 1833. Lyon was completing these surveys which opened Wisconsin to legal settlement by white men when he was nominated Michigan Territory's delegate to Congress. The mound he built on this border disappeared long ago but every surveyor's monument in the state, the borders of all townships and counties, the locations of villages and cities, the position of roads, lakes and streams-all were determined and mapped from lines and distances measured from this point of beginning.

Grant County

171 **DENNISTON HOUSE**   Erected 1969
Denniston House grounds, 117 E. Front St., Cassville

When Wisconsin Territory was established by Congress in 1836, more than a dozen communities eagerly sought to become the capital. Daniels, Denniston, and Company of New York offered this building free if Cassville were chosen. When the Legislature selected Madison, Denniston's dream ended in bankruptcy. Nelson Dewey arrived in Cassville in 1836 and worked for the Denniston firm. Later, Dewey acquired vast properties here including this building which he opened as "Denniston House" in 1854. It has been in continuous operation as a hotel ever since. Dewey's plantation home "Stonefield" is preserved in Nelson Dewey State Park about one mile upriver from here.

Grant County

103 **NELSON DEWEY—FIRST GOVERNOR OF WISCONSIN**   Erected 1961
Cemetery, 1 block W of Hwys. 61, 35, and 81, Lancaster

When Nelson Dewey left his parents' home at Hamilton, New York, at the age of 23, he traveled by stagecoach, steamer, sailing vessel, horseback, and on foot to reach Wisconsin. The trip took four weeks and Dewey arrived in Cassville in June of 1836, about two weeks before Wisconsin was officially established as a territory. He soon became interested and active in politics and when Grant County was organized the next year, he became its first Register of Deeds and moved to Lancaster. Next he entered the Territorial Legislature and when Wisconsin became the thirtieth state in 1848, Dewey was elected its first governor. Because of his election to such high office at the age of 35, many people expected him to continue in a political career but he disliked politics and returned to Grant County. In 1854 he began to acquire land at Cassville and developed a 2000-acre plantation which he called "Stonefield," today preserved in Nelson Dewey State Park. He died July 20, 1889, and his was the last burial in this cemetery.

138

Grant County

 THE GIDEONS Erected 1958
Hwy. 61, 0.3 mi. S of Boscobel

"AND THEY STOOD EVERY MAN IN HIS PLACE ROUND ABOUT THE CAMP."
JUDGES 7:21 One night in September, 1898 two salesmen, John H. Nicholson and
Samuel E. Hill, shared room 19 in the Central Hotel, Boscobel. They wondered if
some organization could not be started for the mutual help and recognition of
Christian travelers. A chance meeting of the two on May 31, 1899, in Beaver Dam
led to plans for an organizational meeting held July 1 in Janesville. They were
joined by William J. Knights who suggested the name "The Gideons" from the
Book of Judges. Hill was chosen first President. By 1948 (the Fiftieth Anniversary)
the Gideons Commercial Travelers' Association of America had become world-wide
and had distributed over 15 ½ million Bibles, Psalms and New Testaments to
hotels, the armed forces and to young people.

Central Hotel, Boscobel.
SHSW Div. of Historic Preservation, James Potter, photographer.

Grant County

287 THE "DINKY"   Erected 1989
620 Lincoln Ave., Fennimore

Fennimore's narrow gauge train, affectionately known as the "Dinky," operated from 1878 to 1926, far longer than most 3-foot gauge lines in Wisconsin. At a nearly depot, standard and narrow gauge trains exchanged their passengers and freight. Trains ran daily between Fennimore and Woodman by way of Werley, Anderson Mills and Conley Cut, meandering 16 miles through the Green River Valley and serving as a key link to other railroads. The line was famous for a horseshoe curve that made it possible to climb the steep slope from the valley to the ridge west of Fennimore. The "Dinky" was noted for its versatility, carrying farmers, fishermen, salesmen and school children, as well as the U.S. mail, milk, livestock and other freight. The narrow gauge line was a remnant of a larger, 92-mile system in southwestern Wisconsin purchased by the Chicago and North Western in 1880. All except the Fennimore–Woodman line were converted in 1882 to standard gauge. Narrow gauge tracks once were scattered across the country, as railroad builders looked for economy in construction and equipment costs to reach remote areas. At the peak of narrow gauge operations, the state had 150 miles, some used in logging operations in northern Wisconsin, now all abandoned.

Iowa County

344 HISTORIC MINERAL POINT   Erected 1996
Water Tower Park, Hwy. 151, Mineral Point

In the 1820s, after hearing reports of abundant lead in the area, prospective miners with "lead fever" began pouring into southwestern Wisconsin. Finding ore just beneath the surface, miners set up "diggings" and soon established Mineral Point. It quickly became the regional center for land sales and government. In 1836, the Territory's first governor, Henry Dodge, was inaugurated here and served his first term out of Mineral Point. Immigrant Cornish miners brought advanced hard-rock and deep mining skills and a distinctive stone building tradition to the area. The lead industry waned in the 1860s, but zinc mining developed in the 1880s and flourished into the early 20th century. After new technology slowed the demand for lead and zinc, Mineral Point's industrial focus changed to agriculture. The 1930s marked the birth of Mineral Point's preservation movement, but it did not develop on a large scale until the 1960s when artists, craftspeople, and preservationists began to restore many of the old mining town's limestone buildings. In 1971 Mineral Point was listed as Wisconsin's first historic district in the National Register of Historic Places.

Grant County

 PLEASANT RIDGE   Erected 1998
AFRICAN AMERICAN COMMUNITY
Hwy. 35 and Slabtown Rd., 5 mi. W of Lancaster

A significant chapter in Wisconsin's history occurred between the mid 19th century, when a group of African Americans settled Pleasant Ridge, the first African American farming community in the state, and the mid 20th century, when the last descendent of the early land-owning families died. About 1850, the Shepard family began the farming community, near here, on land purchased from William Horner, who brought the Shepards from Virginia as freed slaves. In the early 1860s, two fugitive slaves joined the Shepards, and over the next decade the Pleasant Ridge community became a welcoming home to many ex-slaves. Several African American men from Pleasant Ridge served with the Union Army during the Civil War. The local church and school played central roles in the community. But the late 1880s, the population declined, in part because the emphasis placed on education led many of the young to seek opportunities elsewhere. On the landscape today, only the Pleasant Ridge Cemetery remains as a reminder of this early African American community.

S O U T H W E S T

Pleasant Ridge School.
Courtesy of the Grant County Historical Society, negative in SHSW Visual Materials Archive.

Iowa County

005 **SHAKE RAG** Erected 1951
114 Shake Rag St., Mineral Point

In the 1830's tin miners from Cornwall, England, started coming to S.W. Wisconsin to work the newly discovered lead ore deposits. In certain localities they built their stone cottages similar to the ones of their homeland. Shake Rag, the greatest concentration of these homes, was so named because at mealtime the shaking of rags by the womenfolk would summon the men from the mines of the opposite hill.

Pendarvis, Mineral Point Historic District.
SHSW Div. of Historic Preservation, Jeff Dean, photographer.

142

Iowa County

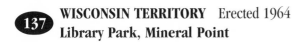

137 **WISCONSIN TERRITORY**   Erected 1964
Library Park, Mineral Point

On July 4, 1836, here in Mineral Point, Col. Henry Dodge took the oath of office to become the first Governor of the newly created Territory of Wisconsin. This Territory, previously attached to Michigan, embraced the vast and important area of what is now the states of Wisconsin, Iowa, Minnesota and portions of North and South Dakota.

Iowa County

038 **OLD MILITARY ROAD**   Erected 1955
Hwy. YZ, 4 mi. E of Dodgeville

You are traveling the route of the Old Military Road, built in 1835-36 to connect Fort Crawford at Prairie du Chien and Fort Howard at Green Bay, via Fort Winnebago at "the Portage" between the Fox-Wisconsin rivers. The section from Prairie du Chien to Fort Winnebago was built by soldiers from Fort Crawford, under the command of Colonel (later President) Zachary Taylor. The road was crudely constructed: two rods in width, with corduroy over the marshy places. Describing his travels over this road in March, 1855, Herbert Quick wrote, "here we went, oxen, cows, mules, horses; coaches, carriages, bluejeans, corduroys, rags, taters, silks, satin, caps, tall hats, poverty, riches; speculators, missionaries, land-hunters, merchants-a nation on wheels, an empire in the commotion and pangs of birth."

DODGE'S GROVE AND FORT UNION
Erected 1998
Hwy. Y, 3 mi. S of Dodgeville

Arriving in Dodgeville in 1827, Henry Dodge, later renowned as a Black Hawk War military leader, territorial governor and state senator, began his Wisconsin career as a miner. In circa 1830, Dodge established living quarters and a large two-furnace smelting and mining operation at this site, a few miles south of Dodgeville. Bringing his family, slaves and about 200 miners to work at this location, Dodge constructed many log dwellings and a stockade, later known as Fort Union during the Black Hawk War.

Henry Dodge, painting by William Cogswell.
SHSW Museum Collection, negative in Visual Materials Archive (W65) 20428.

Iowa County

 SHOT TOWER Erected 1977
Tower Hill State Park, Hwy. C, S of Hwy. 14

Twenty years before Wisconsin became a state, the discovery of vast lead deposits brought a population boom to this area. Green Bay merchant Daniel Whitney organized the Wisconsin Shot Company to build a shot tower on this site. T. B. Shaunce dug out the shafts with pick and gad and removed the earth in buckets. The history of the shot tower is told in detailed exhibits within the tower house. Men like Daniel Whitney, T.B. Shaunce and others worked with humble tools and crude methods, but their ideas and principles provided the foundation for the highly sophisticated procedures to today's manufacturing engineers.

Shot Tower at Helena on the Wisconsin River.
SHSW Visual Materials Archive (X3) 31710.

SOUTHWEST

Iowa County

134 **FRANK LLOYD WRIGHT** Erected 1963
Hwy 14, E of Wisconsin River, near Spring Green

Frank Lloyd Wright, Wisconsin-born, world-renowned architect, lived and worked in Wyoming Valley, 6 miles southwest of here, at Taliesin, his home and school for apprentices. In the practice of "organic" or natural architecture, he sought to blend structure with site, to create harmonious surroundings for the occupants, to bring the outdoors indoors, and to use materials naturally. Among Wright's many innovations were the pre-fabricated house, gravity heat, indirect lighting, concrete block as an effective building material, and revolutionary engineering concepts such as the earthquake-proof structure. Shortly before his death in 1959 at the age of 90, he designed a mile-high office building. Colorful non-conformist, believer in beauty, and champion of democracy, he scorned all criticism. "Early in life," he said, "I had to choose between honest arrogance and hypocritical humility. I chose the former and have seen no reason to change."

Frank Lloyd Wright.
Courtesy of De Longe Studios,
Madison, negative in SHSW Visual
Materials Archive (X3) 19838.

Iowa County

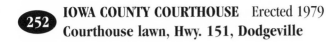

252 **IOWA COUNTY COURTHOUSE** Erected 1979
Courthouse lawn, Hwy. 151, Dodgeville

This is the oldest courthouse in Wisconsin. Construction started June 11, 1859. It was dedicated in 1861, enlarged in 1894 and again in 1927. In 1937 the Doric Columns, pediment and cupola were restored exactly as the 1859 original. In 1969 the interior was completely renovated to better utilize space. It is Iowa County's fourth courthouse. The first three were located in Mineral Point, the county seat from 1829 to 1861. The design is Greek Revival and the material is native Galena limestone quarried north of Dodgeville and cut to precision by local Cornish stone-masons.

Iowa County

405 **MILITARY RIVER CROSSING** Erected 1998
Frank Lloyd Wright Visitor Center, Hwy. C, Spring Green

In this vicinity, during the Black Hawk War of 1832, General Henry Atkinson and approximately 1,000 soldiers crossed the Wisconsin River in pursuit of Sac Indian leader Black Hawk and his followers. On July 26th, at the old abandoned Village of Helena, the soldiers dismantled the village's buildings to make rafts for the crossing.

SOUTHWEST

Iowa County

007 **VILLAGE OF DOVER** Erected 1953
Hwy. 14, 3 mi. E of Arena

Beginning in 1844, nearly 700 settlers were brought into this area by the British Temperance and Emigration Society, organized the previous year in Liverpool, England. By 1850 Dover boasted a hotel, post office, cooper, blacksmith, shoemaker, wagon shop and stores. When the railroad chose Mazomanie for a depot site and made no stop in Dover, Doverites moved their houses into Mazomanie and Dover faded away to become a ghost town. A local boy who made good was John Appleby, inventor of the knotter on the grain binder. The idea came to Appleby as he watched the monotonously regular movement of his mother's hands in knitting. In 1867 he successfully demonstrated his revolutionary "contraption" in a wheatfield east of the cemetery.

Juneau County

270 **THE WISCONSIN RIVER** Erected 1982
Rest Area No. 9, eastbound lane I-90-94

From its source at Lac Vieux Desert to the Mississippi River at Prairie du Chien, the Wisconsin River descends 1,071 feet in 430 miles. Twenty-six power dams utilize 640 feet of the fall of the river to produce an annual average of one billion kilowatt hours of electrical energy. The Wisconsin Valley Improvement Company, created after passage of state enabling legislation in 1907, operates a system of 21 reservoir dams in the upper valley designed to store water during high flow periods for use in the downstream power dams during periods of low flow. The reservoir system, in addition to enhancing power production, diminishes flood damage and enriches the recreational potential of the valley. The system of private development and management under state regulation, made possible by the 1907 legislation, is unique and has enabled the Wisconsin River to earn the title "The Nation's Hardest-Working River."

148

Juneau County

087 **HOP RAISING**   Erected 1959
in village park Hwy. HH, Lyndon Station

"Keep hopping, hoeing and hoping" said an editorial in 1867 when hops were selling for 50 cents a pound, pickers by the thousands worked in the fields, merchants were selling silks, laces, paisley shawls and grand pianos, and farmers were building new larger homes and driving carriages drawn by "blooded" horses. Introduced to Wisconsin in 1852 by Jesse Cottingham, hop culture reached its peak in 1866-67 when this area was called "the greatest primary hop district in the United States." Competition and crop disease brought the short-lived prosperity to an end in 1868 when farmers were eager to dispose of their hops at 15 cents a pound. In August during the boom period the land was canopied by clusters of yellowish-green hops growing up the hop-poles. At harvest time young people from all over the state arrived to do the picking. Working hours were long but singing helped to pass the time. Popular songs of the day were "Barbara Allen," "Billy Boy," "Lorena" and "Listen to the Mocking Bird."

Beaumont Hop House, for drying and storing hops.
SHSW Div. of Historic Preservation, photographer, Paul Jakubovich.

149

Juneau County

THE IRON BRIGADE   Erected 1992
Rest Area No. 9, eastbound I-90-94, near Mauston

The Iron Brigade became one of the most celebrated units of the Civil War (1861-1865). Of its five regiments, three came from Wisconsin: the Second, Sixth, and Seventh Wisconsin Volunteer Infantry. (The other two regiments were the Nineteenth Indiana and the Twenty-fourth Michigan.) Together, these units ranked among the most gallant and effective of the 3,559 regiments of the Union army. The Iron Brigade earned its nickname during its first campaign at South Mountain in northern Virginia during the fall of 1862. It thereafter fought in all major campaigns of the Army of the Potomac, the Union's principal force in the eastern theater of war. The battles of Second Manassas, Antietam, Gettysburg, and Spottsylvania were recorded on the Iron Brigade's colors. Iron Brigade casualties ranked among the highest of the war. The Twenty-fourth Michigan, for example, sustained casualties of 80 percent at Gettysburg, higher than any other Union regiment in the battle. The Second Wisconsin suffered the greatest percentage of loss of the entire Union army, and during the course of the war, the Seventh Wisconsin had more men killed in battle than any other Union regiment.

Officers of the Iron Brigade: Rufus King, John C. Starkweather and George B. Bingham.
SHSW Visual Materials Archive (X3)7930.

150

Juneau County

016 **CASTLE ROCK**   Erected 1967
Hwy. C, 0.5 mi. E of Camp Douglas

You are standing on what was once the bottom of a glacial lake in which castle rock, the buttress rising before you, was an island. This wayside is part of Camp Williams, the Wisconsin State Military Reservation, acquired in 1900. It is the birthplace of the world famous 32nd "Red Arrow" Division, named "Les Terribles" by the French in World War I, which thrust through the Japanese lines from Buna, New Guinea, to Manila, P.L., in World War II. You are standing on ground carved by millennia of rushing water, ice, and wind and hallowed by men who trained here to fight and die for their country.

Juneau County

300 **WISCONSIN MILITARY RESERVATION**   Erected 1991
Camp Williams, off I-94

Following the Civil War, state officials reorganized the Wisconsin Militia and in 1879 renamed it the Wisconsin National Guard. Adjutant General Chandler P. Chapman of Madison, a veteran of the famed Iron Brigade, purchased 440 acres near the Village of Camp Douglas, which was used for rifle practice beginning in 1888. Chapman transferred the land to the State shortly thereafter. The original tract was enlarged and became known as the Wisconsin Military Reservation. National Guard training camps were conducted at the Military Reservation, and within a few years Wisconsin troops had earned a national reputation for marksmanship and other soldiering skills. Four regiments of the Guard were rapidly mobilized for duty at the outbreak of the Spanish-American War (1898), demonstrating the efficiency of the state's training program. Guard units mobilized on the grounds during both World Wars. In 1927 the Wisconsin Military Reservation was renamed Camp Williams in honor of Lt. Col. Charles R. Williams, the training camp's Quartermaster who is buried on the site. Hundreds of thousands of Guard members have been trained on the installation since 1900. In 1957 the state legislature ordered the portion of the Reservation used by the Air National Guard to be named Volk Field in honor of Lt. Jerome A. Volk, the first Wisconsin fighter pilot killed in action during the Korean Conflict.

THE SAND COUNTIES—ALDO LEOPOLD TERRITORY
Erected 1983
Rest Area No. 10, I-90-94 westbound lane

"There are some who can live without wild things, and some who cannot." For those who cannot, Aldo Leopold's *A Sand County Almanac* helps reveal the unsuspected natural riches hidden in these sand counties of Wisconsin. At the core of Aldo Leopold's writing is the concept of a land ethic in which love and respect for the land are the guiding principles. He believed that public conservation efforts had little chance of success unless private individuals felt a strong personal responsibility for the health of the land. In 1935, driven to action by this philosophy, Leopold purchased a sand county farm "worn out and then abandoned by our bigger-and-better society" and "selected for its lack of goodness and its lack of highway." There the Leopold family spent twelve years of time and effort changing their 80 acres of desolation into a showpiece of native Wisconsin habitat complete with abundant wildlife and restored natural landscape. In so doing, Aldo Leopold left us an inspiring example of the land ethic in action.

Aldo Leopold.
SHSW Visual Materials Archive (X3) 23600.

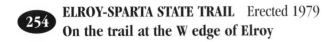

Juneau County

254 **ELROY-SPARTA STATE TRAIL**   Erected 1979
On the trail at the W edge of Elroy

This 32 mile state trail was formerly the mainline of the Chicago and North Western Railway. The conversion from "rail to trail" represented a new concept in recreational development. Utilizing the abandoned railbed, it was the first trail of its kind in the United States to be designated a National Recreation Trail by the United States Department of Interior. The trail is primarily used for bicycling, hiking and snowmobiling. Passing through scenic areas, it links the communities of Elroy, Kendall, Wilton, Norwalk and Sparta. Added attractions are its three tunnels, the longest being 3,833 feet. Train service began in 1873 as steam locomotives hauled grain, livestock and passengers. Rail service ended in 1964. The trail was established by the Department of Natural Resources in 1965 and opened to the public in 1967.

La Crosse County

273 **THE DRIFTLESS AREA**   Erected 1983
Rest Area No. 15, eastbound lane I-90

Several times during the ice ages, glaciers flowed out of Canada, sometimes reaching as far south as the Ohio and Missouri Rivers. During recent glaciations, southwestern Wisconsin was untouched because the glaciers were diverted to the east or west by the highlands of north-central Wisconsin and northwestern Michigan. Here, in the Driftless Area, you see a rugged landscape with deep valleys and rocky crags. Much of the Midwest would look like this today if it had not been glaciated, but the ice sheets smoothed those areas by eroding away the crags and filling in the valleys. The Driftless Area was never completely surrounded by ice, and the glaciers reached only its eastern edge during the last glacial episode. At that time, about 15,000 years ago, the Wisconsin River was dammed by the glacier, and the sediment deposited in glacial Lake Wisconsin forms the flats between Tomah, Wisconsin Dells and Wisconsin Rapids. Then the Driftless Area was treeless and had a tundra climate.

La Crosse County

 THE VALLEY VIEW SITE   Erected 1981
Hwy. 16 at entrance to Valley View Mall shopping center, just N of Medary

This is the location of a village occupied between 1000 and 1200 by the Oneota, ancestors of the Winnebago and Ioway. The village site was chosen by the Oneota to make the best use of the area for farming, fishing, hunting, transportation, and defense. The village was surrounded by a stockade and inhabited by 50 to 100 people. It was excavated in 1978 by archaeologists and students from the University of Wisconsin-La Crosse.

La Crosse County

 MAJOR GENERAL C. C. WASHBURN   Erected 1990
Rest Area No. 31, I-94, French Island, La Crosse

Cadwallader Colden Washburn was born in Maine in 1818. He settled in Mineral Point, Wisconsin, in 1839 and served in Congress before moving to La Crosse. When the Civil War broke out, Washburn organized the Second Wisconsin Volunteer Cavalry Regiment and became its colonel. Washburn's ability and political influence marked him for advancement. He served with distinction throughout the war. He commanded the Military District of Western Tennessee by 1865, and he was one of only two Wisconsinites to attain the rank of major general. Washburn returned to Congress in 1866 and became governor in 1871. Washburn advocated moderate reforms such as government control of telegraphs, regulation of railroads, and support for libraries. Washburn retired from politics in 1874 to attend to his business and philanthropic interests. He donated an observatory to the University of Wisconsin, funded the establishment of a public library in La Crosse, and with his Madison residence ("Edgewood") endowed a Catholic Girls' school. His flour-milling concern in Minneapolis eventually became General Mills. Washburn died in 1882 and is buried in La Crosse.

La Crosse County

 THE COULEE REGION Erected 1975
Bishop's View Overlook, Hwy 33, 5 mi.
E of La Crosse

Coulee is a term derived from the French verb "couler", meaning to flow. The area before you and in the entire coulee region of west central Wisconsin has been dissected by water erosion into a series of narrow ridges separated by steep sided valleys called coulees. Fertile soils are farmed on the bottom and sides of coulees. The narrow ridges, often protected with woodlands, are capped by erosion resistant dolomite bedrock which commonly overlies sandstone. During formation of the coulees, erosion cut through the dolomite and removed the underlying weaker sandstone thereby creating the valleys. To the north and south of this marker you can view several coulees and intervening ridges and note that State Highway 33 is situated on one of the dolomite-capped ridges. The Wisconsin novelist, Hamlin Garland, was a native of this area and wrote about pioneer life in the coulee region.

La Crosse County

 RED CLOUD PARK Erected 1957
Red Cloud Park, La Crosse

This park, on the site of a Winnebago village, commemorates an heroic descendant of those people, Corporal Mitchell Red Cloud, Jr. Fighting in Korea in 1950 as a member of the 34th Army division, Corporal Red Cloud bravely held off an enemy attack with machine gun fire until his death, thereby saving the lives of many of his comrades. Posthumously he was awarded the Congressional Medal of Honor. Part of this area once was owned by "Buffalo Bill" Cody, famous frontier scout, and his friend White Beaver (Dr. Frank Powell), who served four terms as mayor of La Crosse in the 1880's and 1890's. Dr. Powell received the name White Beaver from Sioux Chief Rocky Bear for saving the life of his daughter. He was made chief Medicine Man of the Winnebago Nation in 1876 after successfully treating Chief Wee-Noo-Sheik.

La Crosse County

 SPENCE PARK   Erected 1978
Corner of Front and State Sts., La Crosse

Because of its fertile soil and lush woodlands on the river shores, the Winnebago Indians settled in this area in 1772. Sixty years later they ceded these lands to the U.S. Government. In 1842, Nathan Myrick, the first white settler in La Crosse, built his log cabin and trading post on this site. It was designated a public boat landing in 1851. This was the most strategic Mississippi River port on the western boundary of Wisconsin. Boats traveling north and south docked here, and wagons traveling west crossed the river on ferries from this place. La Crosse thus became known as the Gateway City. The Indians made this a neutral ground and met on the prairie east of here only in peace, and competed in athletic contests. Their most notable game was lacrosse, from which the city derived its name. In 1903 the city named this park for Thomas H. Spence, a pioneer businessman and civic leader who gave this land to the people.

La Crosse County

 THE UPPER MISSISSIPPI   Erected 1980
Rest Area, Tourist Info Center No. 31, I-90, French Island, La Crosse

From Lake Itasca, Minnesota, to Cairo, Illinois, the upper Mississippi River flows through America's heartland for over 1100 miles. Its currents have borne the Indian's canoe, the explorer's dugout, and the trader's packet. Jacques Marquette, Louis Jolliet, and Zebulon Pike tested its strength. Mark Twain gave it life in literature. Paddle-wheelers by the hundreds ferried lesser known passengers over its waters during the halcyon days of steamboating in the 19th century. Into the Great River pour the St. Croix, Chippewa, Black, Wisconsin, Rock, Illinois, Missouri, and Ohio. Along its banks have flourished St. Paul, Winona, La Crosse, Davenport, Keokuk, Quincy, and St. Louis. For a time diminished in importance by the railroads, the Great River came back into its own in the 20th century through dredging and damming. The present nine-foot channel and a series of locks and dams allow 300-foot barges to transport coal, cement, grain, and other products vital to the region's economic well being. Imposing in size and beauty, violent and muddy in floodstage, calm and serene on a summer morn, the Great River sustains life and livelihood within itself, along its banks, and upward in the hinterlands east and west.

La Crosse County

101 **HAMLIN GARLAND** Erected 1960
Hwy. 16, 1 mi. NE of West Salem

Gifted author of this region, Hamlin Garland was born at West Salem September 14, 1860, and died March 4, 1940. His ashes rest in the Garland family plot in Neshonoc cemetery, heart of the Coulee Country immortalized in his books: *"Trailmakers of the Middle Border," "A Son of the Middle Border," "A Daughter of the Middle Border,"* and *"Backtrailers from the Middle Border."* These biographical novels depict the pioneer life of his forefathers, the Garlands and McClintocks, tell of his boyhood on the farm in Green's Coulee near Onalaska and the increasing hardships endured by his family as they moved westward. He describes his life in the East as a struggling young author and the recognition and success which came to him. Garland was elected to the American Academy of Arts and Letters in 1918, and in 1920 his book *"A Daughter of the Middle Border,"* was awarded the Pulitzer Prize as the best biography of the year. In 1893 Garland provided a home for his aging parents in West Salem, a study for himself where he continued to write, and a summer home for his wife and small daughters.

Hamlin Garland.
SHSW Visual Materials Archive
(X3)32275.

La Crosse County

100 **HAMLIN GARLAND**   Erected 1960
Neshonoc Cemetery, West Salem

"A Son of the Middle Border" is buried here with his wife and pioneer parents.

La Crosse County

390 **VILLAGE OF NESHONOC**   Erected 1997
Swarthout Lakeside Park, Hwy. 16, West Salem

The nearby limestone grist mill and dam are the remnants of what once was a mid-19th century village located at this site. Vermont millwright and speculator Monroe Palmer purchased fifteen acres of land on the La Crosse River and constructed the dam and mill in 1852. Three years later, Palmer hired a surveyor to plat a village of eighteen blocks and 147 lots, which he called "Neshonoc," after the Ho-Chunk name for this place. Neshonoc was considered for the La Crosse County seat and a La Crosse and Milwaukee Railroad Company station, and soon businesses, a church, a school, and homes sprang up. The forward thinking Palmer and his brother, Dr. Horace Palmer, built two innovative Octagon houses near the river. But in 1858, the railroad bypassed Neshonoc, laying its line closer to the nearby Village of West Salem. Many residents of Neshonoc moved their homes and businesses there, and by the 1890s Neshonoc had almost disappeared from the landscape.

La Crosse County

THE McGILVRAY "SEVEN BRIDGES ROAD"
Erected 1997
McGilvray Road Access,
Van Loon State Wildlife Area, Hwy. XX

In the early 1850s Scottish immigrant Alexander McGilvray established a small settlement and ferry service, both known as "McGilvray's Ferry," along the Black River. For the next forty years the ferry made seasonal river crossings despite frequent log jams. Local citizens repeatedly petitioned for a more dependable means to cross the river, and in 1892 La Crosse County erected the first in a series of wooden bridges on McGilvray Road. Unfortunately, the river's marshy waters and frequent floods soon rotted the wood. From 1905 through 1908, the La Crosse Bridge and Steel Company erected a series of steel bridges. Designed and patented by Charles M. Horton, these bowstring arch truss bridges incorporated "hook clips" instead of rivets to fasten and strengthen structural members. Five of these rare bowstring truss bridges are found on McGilvray Road and are listed on the National Register of Historic Places. In 1975 the bridges became part of the Van Loon Wildlife Area. In 1997 an additional historic truss bridge was moved to this location.

S
O
U
T
H
W
E
S
T

Truss bridge on the McGilvray "Seven Bridges Road."
SHSW Div. of Historic Preservation, photographer, James Potter.

LaCrosse County

237 **LUTHER COLLEGE** Erected 1977
Halfway Creek Lutheran Church, off Hwys D and W, 2.5 mi. E. of Holmen

The first college founded by Norwegian Lutheran pioneer immigrants in the United States opened in the parsonage of Halfway Creek Lutheran Congregation, Sept. 1, 1861. Teachers were Laur Larsen and F. A. Schmidt, who also served as pastors for area immigrants. Enrollment was 16. The parsonage was destroyed by fire in 1865. The site and a marker are one-half mile west of Halfway Creek Lutheran Church on Knutson Road, near Halfway Creek Cemetery. The College moved to Decorah, Iowa, in 1862 where it continues.

Lafayette County

BELMONT-WISCONSIN TERRITORY 1836
Erected 1957
First Capitol State Park, Hwy. G, 4 mi. NW of Belmont

When Gov. Henry Dodge addressed the joint session of the Legislature here on Oct. 25, 1836, the Territory of Wisconsin included all of present-day Wisconsin, Minnesota, Iowa, and part of the two Dakotas. The population was about equally divided east and west of the Mississippi. There was so much criticism of Gov. Dodge's choice of Belmont as the Territorial capital that he immediately offered to accept any location decided upon by a majority of the representatives. A bitter contest developed, with the Dubuque and Burlington (Iowa) delegations finally joining the eastern Wisconsin group to move the capital for one year to Burlington and thence permanently to Madison. The briefly-booming village of Belmont quickly declined. When the railroad by-passed it about two miles to the southeast many of the residents moved their buildings to "new" Belmont.

SOUTHWEST

Wisconsin Territorial Capitol before restoration in 1924.
SHSW Visual Materials Archive (G5) 1176.

Lafayette County

356 **1998 WISCONSIN ASSEMBLY (Sesquicentennial marker)**
Erected 1998
First Capitol State Park, Hwy. G, 4 mi. NW of Belmont

On January 14, 1998, the Wisconsin Assembly met at the First Capitol in Belmont in honor of the Sesquicentennial of Statehood. The Territorial Legislature held its first session here in 1836, and convened for two more sessions in what is now Burlington, Iowa, during 1837 and 1838. In November of 1838, the legislature moved to Madison, where subsequent sessions have been held. Members of the 1998 Assembly include:

SPEAKER Scott R. Jensen
SPEAKER PRO TEMPORE Stephen J. Freese
CHIEF CLERK Charles R. Sanders

John H. Ainsworth	Suzanne Jeskewitz	Cloyd A. Porter
Sheryl Albers	DuWayne G. Johnsrud	Rosemary Potter
Tammy Baldwin	Dean R. Kaufert	Mike Powers
James R. Baumgart	Neal J. Kedzie	Marty Reynolds
Spencer Black	Carol Kelso	Antonio R. Riley
Peter E. Bock	Judith Klusman	Judy Biros Robson
Frank Boyle	Rob Kreibich	John J. Ryba
David A. Brandemuehl	James E. Kreuser	Chuck Schafer
Tim Carpenter	Shirley Krug	Marlin D. Schneider
G. Spencer Coggs	Peggy Krusick	Lorraine M. Seratti
David A. Cullen	Walter J. Kunicki	Rick Skindrud
John P. Dobyns	John La Fave	Thomas J. Springer
Robert M. Dueholm	Bonnie L. Ladwig	Anthony J. Staskunas
Marc C. Duff	Frank G. Lasee	John P. Steinbrink
Steven M. Foti	Mary A. Lazich	Tom Sykora
John G. Gard	John W. Lehman	David M. Travis
Robert G. Goetsch	Michael A. Lehman	Robert L. Turner
Mark A. Green	Barbara J. Linton	Gregg Underheim
Barbara Gronemus	William D. Lorge	Frank H. Urban
Glenn Grothman	Mark Meyer	William N. Vander Loop
Scott L. Gunderson	Johnnie Morris-Tatum	Daniel P.Vrakas
Eugene Hahn	William M. Murat	Scott K. Walker
Joseph W. Handrick	Terry M. Musser	David W. Ward
Doris I. Hanson	Stephen L. Nass	Sheldon A. Wasserman
Sheila E. Harsdorf	Barbara Notestein	Steve Wieckert
Donald W. Hasenohrl	Luther S. Olsen	A. Polly Williams
Tom Hebl	Alvin R. Ott Jr.	Wayne W. Wood
Timothy T. Hoven	Clifford Otte	Leon D. Young
Gregory B. Huber	Thomas D. Ourada	Rebecca Young
Mary Hubler	Carol Owens	Bob Ziegelbauer
Michael D. Huebsch	Jeffrey T. Plale	Robert K. Zukowski
David E. Hutchison	Joe Plouff	

Lafayette County

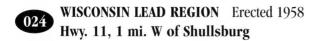

024 **WISCONSIN LEAD REGION** Erected 1958
Hwy. 11, 1 mi. W of Shullsburg

Grant, Iowa and Lafayette counties were once the center of a lead-mining boom.
Indians had sold lead to early traders, but there were few white miners here in
1820. Mining brought in a large part of the 37,000 population credited to the three
counties in 1850. Prospecting was done by practical men with little aid from miner-
alogical experts. Their tools were the shovel, pick, gad or crowbar, hand drill, and
blasting powder. Mines were lighted by candles set in gobs of fireclay which
would stick to any part of the rock wall. Some of the miners spent the winters in
caves or hurriedly prepared dug-outs and were nicknamed "Badgers". Many of the
once thriving mining centers are now ghost towns, only their refuse dumps and
pockmarked land bearing the evidence of the mining days.

Map of lead mines on the Upper Mississippi River by R. W. Chandler, 1829.
SHSW Library Archives (X3) 40370

163

150 FATHER SAMUEL MAZZUCHELLI Erected 1966
Hwy. 11, 1 mi. W of Benton

In 1835 Father Samuel Mazzuchelli, Dominican missionary, came to the lead region from the Green Bay-Mackinac frontier. One year later he addressed the opening session of the territorial legislature. Soon he was establishing schools and preparing teachers for the children of the settlers. In 1847 he formed Wisconsin's first teaching sisterhood, the Sinsiniawa Dominican Sisters. At Benton he founded St. Clara Academy and taught science with the earliest laboratory instruments. To the Irish miners, this American from Italy was "Father Matthew Kelly." To settlers of many creeds, he was civic leader and friend, builder of the city of man and the city of God. At his death in 1864, Father Mazzuchelli was interred in the cemetery of St. Patrick's Church in Benton, one of the twenty churches he designed and built in the upper Mississippi Valley.

Father Samuel Mazzuchelli.
SHSW Visual Materials Archive (X3) 1522.

St. Augustine Church, New Diggings, built in 1844 by Father Mazzuchelli.
SHSW Div. of Historic Preservation, photographer, James Potter.

164

Lafayette County

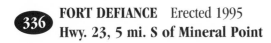

336 **FORT DEFIANCE** Erected 1995
Hwy. 23, 5 mi. S of Mineral Point

Fort Defiance was one of the last garrisoned stockade forts constructed in territorial Wisconsin. Located in the booming lead mining region, an area of early settlement, the fort was built by local settlers in 1832 when developing tensions over Indian land rights erupted in the Black Hawk War. Although Fort Defiance did not undergo attack, it did have a garrison of about forty militia men who were said to be among the best drilled in the territory. The fort stood on the hill about 300 yards east of here and was enclosed by a sharply pointed palisade of heavy timbers set face to face, creating an almost impenetrable wall except for the musket loopholes. Measuring 80 feet wide by 120 feet long and 18 feet high, Fort Defiance had two blockhouses located at opposite corners of the stockade. Within the walls were two buildings used to accommodate the garrison and the families of settlers in case of a siege. There are no visible remains left of Fort Defiance.

Monroe County

088 **TOMAH** Erected 1959
in park on Hwy. 12, Tomah

When this site was selected for a settlement in 1855, one of its founders read in an old history of the state that the Menominee Chief Tomah had at one time gathered his tribe in this vicinity for a conference. He suggested the name "Tomah" for the new village, and his choice was adopted. The chief's name was Thomas Carron, "Tomah" being the French pronunciation for Thomas. He was born in 1752 in the old king's village opposite Green Bay. A man of magnificent appearance, six feet tall, with dark eyes and handsome features, he was firm, peaceable, conciliatory, and sincerely loved by the red and white men of his time.

Monroe County

124 **MESAS AND BUTTES**   Erected 1963
Hwy. 12, 4 mi. W of Camp Douglas

This is Mill Bluff, one of many isolated and rocky castle-like hills which rise abruptly from the surrounding plain. This formation is properly called a mesa (Spanish for "table") if large and butte if small. Mesas and buttes in this driftless area escaped glacial activity and have a capping on top hard enough to resist weathering. Erosion by wind and water eventually wears away the soft sides until the weight of the overhanging cap causes it to fall. The mounds decrease in size until the capping is all removed. Then the mound becomes a conical hill, gradually blending with the plain. Mill Bluff received its name from a sawmill operated here in the early days of settlement.

Monroe County

198 **COULEE COUNTRY**   Erected 1973
Rest Area No. 16, westbound lane 1-90, 5 mi. E of Bangor

From the hills all around, rugged valleys collect for rivers that feed the mighty Mississippi. The early French called such a valley a coulee. These many valleys, large and small, still are known as coulees, a regional name for a regional landscape. Here the glaciers never came. The great ice sheets grinding out of the north sometimes passed to the west, other times to the east, to plane the land, carve out the Great Lakes, and leave deep deposits of gravel and other sediment everywhere but in coulee country. Coulee views along the Mississippi are proudly compared with the Palisades of the Hudson and the hills along the Rhine. Coulee Country is world known through the writings of Hamlin Garland, 1860-1940, a native son.

Monroe County

 ELROY-SPARTA STATE TRAIL   Erected 1979
at the Kendall Depot, N. Railroad St.,
Hwy. 71, Kendall

This 32 mile state trail was formerly the mainline of the Chicago and North Western Railway. The conversion from "rail to trail" represented a new concept in recreational development. Utilizing the abandoned railbed, it was the first trail of its kind in the United States to be designated a National Recreation Trail by the United States Department of Interior. The trail is primarily used for bicycling, hiking and snowmobiling. Passing through scenic areas, it links the communities of Elroy, Kendall, Wilton, Norwalk and Sparta. Added attractions are its three tunnels, the longest being 3,833 feet. Train service began in 1873 as steam locomotives hauled grain, livestock and passengers. Rail service ended in 1964. The trail was established by the Department of Natural Resources in 1965 and opened to the public in 1967.

Richland County

 THE PURSUIT WEST   Erected 1998
Wayside, Hwy. 14, 1 mi. E of Gotham, Buena Vista Township

During the Black Hawk War of 1832, Black Hawk and his band fled down the Wisconsin River after the July 21st Battle of Wisconsin Heights. Two miles west of here, where the Pine River flows into the Wisconsin, the band left the Wisconsin River and headed north up the Pine River Valley.

Richland County

ADA JAMES (1876-1952)   Erected 1998
Krouskop Park, 400 W. Sixth St. (Hwy. 140) Richland Center

Born in Richland Center, Ada James was an important suffrage leader, campaigning throughout Wisconsin in support of women's right to vote. In 1919, James mobilized her father, a state legislator, to deliver Wisconsin's ratification papers to Washington, D. C., making Wisconsin the first state in the Nation to ratify the Nineteenth Amendment.

Ada James, center, and suffragists on the campaign trail.
SHSW Visual Materials Archive, Classified File.

Richland County

262 **BIRTHPLACE OF GTE**   Erected 1980
Krouskop Park, Hwy. 14, Richland Center

General Telephone and Electronics Corporation, among the world's largest businesses and a leader in telecommunications, is headquartered in Stamford, Connecticut but was born in Richland Center. Officially founded in 1918 when John F. O'Connell and Sigurd L. Odegard purchased the Richland Center Telephone Company, the firm today called GTE grew rapidly and has telephone operations in 31 states. Designated Commonwealth Telephone in 1920 and Associated Telephone Utilities in 1926, the company became General Telephone Corporation in 1935. The name General Telephone and Electronics was adopted in 1958 to more accurately reflect corporate diversification.

Richland County

327 **BOAZ MASTODON**   Erected 1995
Hwy. 14, 5 mi. W of Richland Center, Boaz

In 1897, after a severe rainstorm in Richland County, farm boys Chris, Harry, Clyde and Verne Dosch found large bones sticking out of an eroded bank on a tributary of Mill Creek near Boaz. The bones were later identified as those of the extinct American Mastodon, a large, hairy animal, nine feet tall and weighing eight tons, related to modern elephants. This was the first recorded discovery of mastodon bones in Wisconsin. Mastodons lived in North America from Florida to Alaska during cool, wet times dominated by spruce forests. They had moved into Wisconsin after the last glacial retreat about 13,000 years ago and lived here for the next 4,000 years when they became extinct. A fluted quartzite spear point found near the bones suggests that humans also arrived in Wisconsin shortly after the glacial retreat and may have hunted these animals for food. The assembled Boaz Mastodon skeleton is on exhibit at the Geology Museum, University of Wisconsin-Madison.

Richland County

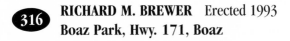

RURAL ELECTRIFICATION   Erected 1965
Hwy. 14, 5 mi. W of Richland Center, Boaz

This farm was the first in Wisconsin to obtain central station electric power from a rural electric cooperative. The farm home was constructed and wired for electric service by James Hanold in 1917. The Richland Cooperative Electric Association, incorporated January 8, 1936, energized the first section of its rural electric system built into this area and connected this farm to its lines on May 7, 1937. Load funds, available to all electric power suppliers to aid in electrifying rural America, were obtained from the rural Electrification Administration, created by executive order of President Franklin D. Roosevelt on May 11, 1935, and continued as an agency of our federal government by Act of Congress, May 20, 1936.

Richland County

RICHARD M. BREWER   Erected 1993
Boaz Park, Hwy. 171, Boaz

 One of the most colorful incidents in the violent history of the American West during the late 1800s, the Lincoln County War in New Mexico involved a Boaz man named Richard M. Brewer. Born February 19, 1850, "Dick" Brewer came to Richland County with his family in 1854, then like thousands of other Wisconsinites he left to seek his fortune even farther west. By 1870, he was a rancher in New Mexico, where he also worked as foreman on John H. Tunstall's ranch. The murder of Tunstall on February 18, 1878, by rival cattlemen launched the Lincoln County War. Brewer, loyal to Tunstall, led a group called the Regulators to arrest Tunstall's murderers. Among the Regulators deputized by Brewer was his friend, William Bonney, who became better known as Billy the Kid. Brewer lost his life in a shoot-out on April 4, 1878, and he became a legend both in Boaz and New Mexico.

Richland County

403 **OCOOCH MOUNTAINS** Erected 1998
Boaz Park, Hwy. 171, Boaz

During the Black Hawk War of 1832, Black Hawk's band and the pursuing military ventured into this unknown terrain of steep ridges and valleys. Following nearby Mill Creek, some of the band headed over these rugged hills known as the Ocooch Mountains. Along the way, many Indians died from exhaustion, starvation and battle wounds.

Richland County

382 **ROCKBRIDGE** Erected 1998
Pier County Park, Hwy. 80, 8 miles N of Richland Center

One of the largest natural bridges in Wisconsin, Rockbridge is 20 feet wide and 10 feet high. Archaeological investigations have revealed that the bridge's sandstone overhang was once used as a shelter by Native Americans. Through the efforts of local citizens, Rockbridge was made a public park in the early 1920s. The West Branch of Pine River flows under Rockbridge, joining the Pine River a few hundred feet to the east. Long ago, however, the West Branch of the Pine River flowed south in its own river valley on the other side of this sandstone ridge. Like most rivers, the West Branch of the Pine River and the Pine River shifted back and forth, gradually scouring away, grain by grain, their sandstone river bottoms. Eventually these rivers undercut their valleys along the east and west sides of the sandstone ridge and created the cliff overhang and natural bridge opening here. Spilling under Rockbridge, the West Branch of the Pine River merges with the Pine River to flow south towards the Wisconsin River.

S O U T H W E S T

Richland County

TROOP ENCAMPMENT   Erected 1998
Pier County Park, Hwy. 80, 8 miles N of Richland Center

According to local tradition, on the night of July 29, 1832, during the Black Hawk War, General Atkinson's troops camped at this location. The next day, the troops proceeded up the West Branch of the Pine River, only to abandon their supply wagon in this rough terrain.

Sauk County

DAWN MANOR—SITE OF THE LOST CITY OF NEWPORT
Erected 1955
Hwy. A, 1.5 mi. S of Wisconsin Dells

Here on the Wisconsin River, the village of Newport was begun in 1853, planned for a population of 10,000. Assuming that the Milwaukee and La Crosse Railroad would cross the river here, over 2,000 settlers quickly came to Newport, causing a lively land boom. When the bridge and dam were ultimately located a mile upstream after an alleged secret moonlight survey, Newport was almost completely deserted in favor of Kilbourn City (today Wisconsin Dells). Only Dawn Manor, with its servant quarters, remains. Dawn Manor was completed in 1855 by Capt. Abraham Vanderpoel, friend of Lincoln and signer of the Wisconsin Constitution. The home is built of Potsdam sandstone, white mahogany and white pine, put together with brass screws and wooden pegs. Dawn Manor housed the art collection of George Raab, one of Wisconsin's famous artists.

Sauk County

 RINGLING BROTHERS CIRCUS Erected 1956
Hwy. 12, 1.5 mi. S of Baraboo

"The Greatest Show on Earth" was born and grew to maturity in Baraboo, just north of here. When the five Ringling brothers gave the first performance of their "Great Double Shows, Circus and Caravan" May 19, 1884, the main tent was 45 by 90 feet. There was no band wagon, no menagerie. The menagerie was started in 1886, with a hyena advertised as the "Hideous Hyena Striata Gigantium, the Mammoth, Midnight Marauding, Man-Eating Monstrosity." After traveling in horse-drawn wagons for six seasons, the circus became the "Ringling Bros. United Monster Railroad Show." Until 1918 the circus wintered in Baraboo, where many of the winter quarters still stand. From humble beginnings, a little hall room show became the mightiest and most spectacular organization in the entertainment world.

The Ringling Brothers.
Courtesy of the SHSW Circus World Museum.

Sauk County

089 **THE BARABOO RANGE**   Erected 1958
Hwy. 12, 5 mi. NW of Sauk City

The rugged range of hills which can be seen to the north of here is among the oldest visible physical features on the earth. The hard quartzite rock that forms them was deposited as sand in a shallow sea which once covered this region. Although deposited horizontally, the layers were warped until they were tilted fifteen degrees at Devils Lake and vertically at Rock Springs. The gorges which may be seen at these places were eroded by rivers millions of years ago. The Wisconsin River once flowed through the Devils Lake Gorge. Glaciers brought debris which blocked the river, leaving the lake after melting. Exploration for iron ore began in 1887, and in 1900 ore was found and mining operations started. By 1925 the cost of mining had become too high to compete with other sources and mining in the district ceased after producing 643,030 tons of ore.

Sauk County

247 **CLARE A. BRIGGS—CARTOONIST**   Erected 1978
Reedsburg Area Historical Park, Hwys. 23 and 33,
3 mi. E of Reedsburg

Clare A. Briggs was born in Reedsburg on August 5, 1875 to Mr. and Mrs. William Pardee Briggs. At an early age Briggs became a sketch artist, and in 1896 he accepted a job as an illustrator with the St. Louis Globe-Democrat. After working for several newspapers, he gained national recognition as a cartoonist with the New York Herald Tribune. Briggs is best remembered for such titles as "The Days of Real Sport," "When a Feller Needs a Friend" and "Ain't it a Grand and Glorious Feeling?" His most popular cartoons depicted his boyhood in Reedsburg and made the town's "Old Swimming Hole" and his childhood friend "Skinny" famous. He died January 3, 1930, and according to his request his ashes were scattered over New York Harbor. The keen observation and gentle humor of Briggs are evident in his cartoons and make his work just as enjoyable today as when it first appeared.

Sauk County

104 **WISCONSIN DELLS** Erected 1961
Hwy. 16, 0.1 mi. W of Wisconsin Dells

The Indians believed that many ages ago the Great Spirit, in the form of a snake, created the Dells when it forced its huge body through a narrow opening in the rocks. Geological studies, however, show that the Dells were formed some fifteen thousand years ago after a glacier turned the Wisconsin River into a new channel through the center of a sandstone plain. French-Canadian traders used their work "dalles," meaning a trough or narrow passage, to describe this section of the Wisconsin River. Wind, weather and the river have combined to create the seven miles of chasms, cliffs, pillars and columns which form part of the many scenic features of the world-famous Dells.

*Lone Rock, Wisconsin Dells, photograph by H. H. Bennett, ca. 1908.
SHSW Visual Materials Archive (X3) 29719.*

Sauk County

339 **THE LOWER NARROWS** Erected 1996
Hwy. 33 at County U, 5 mi. E of Baraboo

This large gap, called the Lower Narrows, is one of three major gorges that cut through the 50 mile circumference of the Baraboo Range. These gorges were created by rivers more than 500 million years ago and then buried by sediments in a vast sea over the next 150 million years. Wind, water and glacial erosion have once again exposed the gorges. The Baraboo River now flows through the Upper Narrows gorge near Rock Springs, entering a basin surrounded by the Baraboo Range, and exits here at the Lower Narrows. Notable for its ancient rock formations, the Lower Narrows features vertically-tilted Precambrian pink Baraboo quartzite rock ribs on both walls of the gorge. Red rhyolite rock, over 1.5 billion years old, is visible on the northeast flank of the Lower Narrows along Highway 33. Devil's Lake, in the longest and deepest gorge of the Baraboo Range, was formed when the gap was blocked by glacial debris 15,000 years ago. Of the Baraboo Range, geologist and president of the University of Wisconsin, Charles R. Van Hise commented: "I know of no other region in Wisconsin which illustrates so many principles of the science of geology."

Sauk County

227 **AUGUST W. DERLETH** Erected 1976
Derleth Park, Water St., Sauk City

Born February 24, 1909, in Sauk City, August Derleth lived virtually his entire life in his native "Sac Prairie." He began writing at the age of thirteen and had over 150 books to his credit at the time of his death on July 4, 1971. Versatile as he was prolific, Derleth is best known for his regional literature that includes historical novels, biographies, short stories, journals and poetry. He lived his own life in the spirit of Thoreau and believed that life in Sac Prairie is representative of what can be found in the small towns across the country, indeed that Sac Prairie is a microcosm that mirrors universal truths. August Derleth was also a noted editor, publisher and lecturer. In 1939 he founded Arkham House Publishers and saw it achieve an international reputation under his directorship. He was the recipient of many honors and awards including a Guggenheim Fellowship and the Governor's Award for service to the creative arts.

Sauk County

 WESTERN ESCAPE   Erected 1998
**Lower Wisconsin Riverway, Hwy 14, 2 mi
E of Spring Green**

On July 22, during the Black Hawk War of 1832, Sac Indian leader Black Hawk
and about 700 followers escaped down the Wisconsin River after the Battle of
Wisconsin Heights. Traveling the river in hastily built canoes and rafts or on foot
along the river, the Indians managed to stay ahead of the pursuing military. On
July 26th to the 28th at the old abandoned Village of Helena, about 3 miles west of
here, the military crossed the Wisconsin River in their search for Black Hawk.

Vernon County

DAMS ON THE MISSISSIPPI   Erected 1958
Hwy. 35, Genoa

Lock and Dam No. 8 at Genoa, 679.2 miles above the mouth of the Ohio River, is
set on a foundation of sand, gravel and broken rock. It has a 110-foot-wide cham-
ber and an 11-foot lift from the lower to the upper pool. Construction of the dam
cost $6,702,500 and affected 18,591 acres of land. In May 1937, the battery of fif-
teen gates closed and the Genoa Dam opened for navigation. This dam is one of
26 locks and dams built by the United States Government to improve transportation from Minneapolis to the mouth of the Missouri River. The project, approved by
Congressional Act on August 30, 1935, was largely completed by 1938. In the next
fifteen years river traffic increased from 458 to 2,636 million tons.

384 **AFRICAN AMERICAN SETTLERS OF CHEYENNE VALLEY**
Erected 1997
Hillsboro Lake Park, 300 Water Ave. at Hwys. 33, 80, and 82, Hillsboro

The Cheyenne Valley near Hillsboro was Wisconsin's largest rural African American settlement in the 19th century. The State's early defiance of the 1850 Fugitive slave Act and the later demise of the slavery system after the Civil War encouraged freed slaves to settle in Wisconsin. Nearly 150 African American settlers, with the assistance of the Quaker religious order, came to Hillsboro, where they successfully farmed. Many settlers became landowners and a few, like Thomas Shivers who was born on a Tennessee plantation, owned large acreages. The African American settlers socialized well with neighboring European immigrants, establishing among the State's first integrated schools, churches and sporting teams. Thomas Shivers' son, Alga Shivers, was a notable builder, designing and constructing many of Vernon County's round barns in the early 20th century. The advent of the automobile, and other elements of change led to the gradual decline of the rural African American population.

Samuel Arms family of the Cheyenne Valley African-American Settlement.
SHSW Visual Materials Archive (X3) 36023.

Vernon County

224 **WISCONSIN'S FIRST NUCLEAR—FUELED ELECTRIC GENERATING STATION** Erected 1976
In power plant parking lot, W side of Hwy. 35, Genoa

Dairyland Power Cooperative, in April of 1961, was designated by the Joint Congressional Atomic Energy Commission as eligible to construct and operate a nuclear-fueled electric power plant as a research and development pilot installation. On June 8, 1962, the Atomic Energy commission entered into a contract with the Allis Chalmers Company of Milwaukee for the fabrication of a 50-megawatt facility, now identified as the La Crosse Boiling Water Reactor (LACBWR), and with Dairyland Power Cooperative for its eventual operation. Construction began in May of 1963. On July 11, 1967, at 7:39 in the evening, the reactor achieved its first self-sustaining chain reaction, which ushered Wisconsin into the nuclear age. Operation at full power level was attained on August 1, 1969. After several modifications and numerous tests, it was declared operational for commercial use on February 1, 1971, with a firm capacity of 50 megawatts. Dairyland Power Cooperative acquired full ownership of this nuclear-fueled electric generation facility by its purchase from the Atomic Energy Commission in August of 1973.

Vernon County

079 **ADMIRAL MARC A. MITSCHER, U.S. NAVY** Erected 1958
Hwy. 33, 0.1 mi. W of Hillsboro

Admiral Marc A. Mitscher, U.S. Navy, pioneer in naval aviation and commander of Naval Air Task Force 58, famed for its destruction of Japanese sea power in World War II, was born in Hillsboro, January 26, 1887. A 1910 graduate of the U.S. Naval Academy and the Naval Flying School, he served with dedicated purpose and distinguished achievement in a career that proved the effectiveness of naval aircraft carriers. As the result of his brilliant leadership, his indomitable fighting spirit, and his many conspicuous firsts in naval aviation, he was awarded many high decorations by the U.S. and foreign governments. Admiral Mitscher died Feb. 3, 1947, and lies in the hallowed ground of Arlington National Cemetery, always remembered and highly respected by all men of naval aviation.

Vernon County

031 **NATION'S FIRST WATERSHED PROJECT**   Erected 1955
Hwy. 14, 0.5 mi. W of Coon Valley

This point is near the center of the 90,000 acre Coon Creek Watershed, the nation's first large-scale demonstration of soil and water conservation. This area was selected for this purpose by the U.S. Soil Conservation Service (then Soil Erosion Service) in October, 1933. Technicians of the SCS and the University of Wisconsin pooled their knowledge with experiences of local farm leaders to establish a pattern of land use now prevalent throughout the Midwest. Planned practices in effect include improvement of woodlands, wildlife habitat and pastures, better rotations and fertilization, strip cropping, terracing and gully and stream bank erosion control. The outcome is a tribute to the wisdom, courage and foresight of the farm families who adopted the modern methods of conservation farming illustrated here.

Vernon County

083 **GOVERNOR RUSK**   Erected 1958
Hwy. 14, 0.5 mi. N of Viroqua

Jeremiah McLain Rusk, who owned and lived on this farm, was born June 17, 1830, in Deerfield, Ohio. In 1853 he moved to Viroqua. He served with distinction in the Civil War and in the United States Congress. As Governor (1882-1889) Rusk gained national prominence for his support of striking railroad workers. Later in May, 1886, he was widely acclaimed for suppressing the Milwaukee riots and for his statement "I seen my duty and done it." As the first United States Secretary of Agriculture (1889-1893) Rusk sought to promote the interests of the farmer by encouraging scientific research, inspection of meat exports and eradication of horse and cattle disease. Weighing about 250 pounds and 6'3" tall, with gray hair and flowing beard, "Uncle Jerry" Rusk was a colorful personality who won the respect and admiration of people in all walks of life.

Vernon County

 BATTLE OF BAD AXE   Erected 1955
Hwy. 35, 2.5 mi. N of DeSoto

After holding off his pursuers at the Battle of Wisconsin Heights (about 1¹/₂ miles east of present Sauk City), Black Hawk led his people over unfamiliar country toward the Mississippi. In the meantime, the Army alerted Ft. Crawford at Prairie du Chien. When the Indians reached the Mississippi, they found an armed steamboat blocking escape. The Battle of Bad Axe, fought near here Aug. 1-2, 1832, ended the Black Hawk War. Driven into the water by their pursuers, the Indians-warriors, old people, women, and children, were shot down or drowned as they tried to escape. Black Hawk succeeded in getting away but was soon taken prisoner. Later, when asked about his ill-fated venture, he said simply "Rock River was a beautiful country; I loved my towns, my cornfields, and the home of my people. I fought for it."

Black Hawk, painting by Robert Sully. SHSW Museum Collection, negative in Visual Materials Archive (X32) 8781.

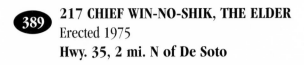

217 CHIEF WIN-NO-SHIK, THE ELDER
Erected 1975
Hwy. 35, 2 mi. N of De Soto

Win-no-shik, the Elder, was a notable chief of the Winnebago. On a treaty signed February 27, 1855, at Washington, D. C., his signature reads "Wau-kon-chaw-koo-haw, or the Coming Thunder, or Win-no-shik." Win-no-shik was promoted to the rank of chief when quite young and was always popular with his people. Historians have written that he was of medium-size, handsome, and "always carried a pipe, especially at council meetings. As a man, he was modest, kind and courteous: as a chief, dignified, firm and just in the exercise of his authority." In 1829, Win-no-shik was head chief of the larger Winnebago village at La Crosse. When the Winnebago moved to Iowa, he was made head chief of the tribe and remained chief of his own band. After Win-no-shik's death, his brother, young Winneshiek, or Short Wing, and his son, Little Winneshiek, or Striking Tree, moved back to Wisconsin, near Black River Falls, where his descendants still live.

Markers
Northwest Region

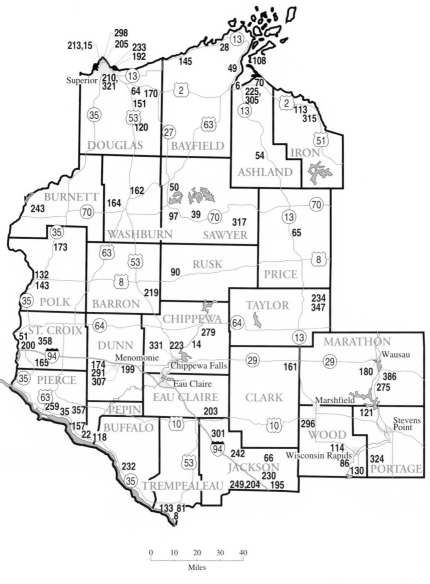

298
213,15   205   233
                  192
                        145   28   13
                                              108
Superior 210,   49
          321   13   6   70
              64 170   225,
              151   305   2   113
                                  13   315
          35   53
                120   27   63   51
                                              54
      DOUGLAS   BAYFIELD   IRON
                                  ASHLAND
                        50
          162
    BURNETT   164   97   39   70
    243   70   317   13
                                              65
          35
              173
          63   RUSK   8
              53   90
    132   PRICE
    143   35   219
              BARRON   234
    35   POLK   TAYLOR   347
              64   CHIPPEWA
    51   ST. CROIX   279   64
    200   358   DUNN   331   223   14   13   MARATHON
          94   Wausau
    165   174   Menomonie   29   161   29   180
    35   PIERCE   291   199   Chippewa Falls   386
              307   Eau Claire   Marshfield   275
    63   EAU CLAIRE   CLARK   121
    259   35   357   203   Stevens
          PEPIN   Point
    157   BUFFALO   10   10   296
    22   118   301   WOOD   114
              232   94   242   66   Wisconsin Rapids   86   324
          53   JACKSON   130   PORTAGE
    35   TREMPEALEAU   230
              249,204   195
          133   81
              8

0   10   20   30   40
          Miles

Ashland County

305 **FLEET ADMIRAL WILLIAM D. LEAHY** Erected 1991
Bay View Park, Hwy. 2, east of jct. with Hwy. 13, Ashland

William Daniel Leahy was born in Iowa in 1875, and his family soon moved to Wisconsin. He graduated from Ashland High School in 1892 and for the rest of his life considered Ashland his home town. Leahy graduated from the Naval Academy and served in the Spanish-American War. He planned naval operations for U.S. interventions in Nicaragua (1912), Haiti (1916), and Mexico (1916). During World War I, he became friendly with Assistant Secretary of the Navy, Franklin D. Roosevelt. Leahy was made chief of the Bureau of Ordinance in 1927, rear admiral in 1930, and chief of naval operations in 1937. During the darkest hours of World War II in 1942, President Roosevelt appointed Leahy chief of staff to the commander-in-chief. Leahy's tact and resourcefulness made him a valuable aide in military and diplomatic undertakings, including the inter-Allied conferences at Tehran, Yalta, and Potsdam. Admiral Leahy became the first American sailor, and the only Wisconsinite, to attain the five-star rank of Fleet Admiral. He died in 1959 and is buried in Arlington National Cemetery.

Ashland County

006 **RADISSON-GROSEILLIERS FORT** Erected 1951
in park on Hwy. 2, at W limits of Ashland

A crude structure of boughs of trees "layed acrosse, one uppon an other" was erected near here by Pierre Radisson and Medart Groseilliers in 1659. The two French traders came to Chequamegon Bay from Montreal and Radisson's account of their journey reports "at the end of this bay we landed." This very profitable trip resulted in confiscation of their licenses and furs because they refused to share the proceeds with the French Governor of Canada. In anger Radisson and Groseilliers went to England and persuaded Prince Rupert to sponsor an expedition to Hudson Bay. The return of Groseilliers with a great cargo of beaver skins was soon followed by the issue of a royal charter to the Hudson's Bay Company. Thus the dream of two adventurers for exploitation of northern North America was to contribute much to the long conflict between England and France for control of the continent.

184

Ashland County

 NORTHLAND COLLEGE   Erected 1976
**Northland College Campus, Ellis Ave., on
Hwy. 13, Ashland**

North Wisconsin Academy, founded in 1892 by the Congregational Church, provided the first high school education available to young people of the small, isolated lumber camp, sawmill and farm communities in the area known as the Great Lakes Pinery, but commonly referred to as "A God-forsaken Waste." It stretched across the northern third of Wisconsin, Michigan, and Minnesota. The Academy was to be co-educational, to have a program of classical studies, to train both mind and character, and to be geared to the resources of the pioneer families it was intended to serve. The laying of the cornerstone of the Academy Building on July 14, 1892, was an historic moment marking the advance of educational and cultural opportunities into northern Wisconsin. In 1906 the Academy expanded its program to become Northland College, and on March 7, 1907, the Academy Building was renamed Wheeler Hall, a tribute to the Rev. E.P. Wheeler, first president of the Academy. This building, diagonally across from this site, is a landmark of progress to area citizens and a revered spot to every student who ever attended the Academy or College.

108 MADELINE ISLAND   Erected 1961
La Pointe, Madeline Island

Known to the Ojibway Indians as Moningwunakauning, "The Home of The Golden Breasted Woodpecker," the largest of the Apostle Islands was one of the earliest areas of Indian settlement, fur trade, missionary activity and commercial fishing in the interior of North America. It was discovered by French explorers in 1659. Trading posts were built here for the French by LeSueur in 1693 and for the British by Michel Cadotte in 1793. In 1834 this site and present La Pointe dock became headquarters for the Northern Outfit of the American Fur Company. Missionary operations began about 1830 with the erection of a Protestant Church followed by Father Baraga's Catholic Church.

View of the Village of La Pointe, Madeline Island, engraving ca. 1852.
SHSW Visual Materials Archive (X3) 25367.

Ashland County

054 **GREAT DIVIDE**   Erected 1956
Hwy. 13, 2.5 mi N of jct Hwy. 77, 10 mi. S of Mellen

You are now on the Great Divide which separates the two principal drainage areas of Wisconsin. Water falling to the north of the point finds its way into Lake Superior, then down through the Great Lakes and the St. Lawrence River 2,000 miles into the Atlantic Ocean. Water which falls to the south of here runs down the Chippewa River into the "Father of Waters," and after 1,600 miles reaches the Gulf of Mexico. The elevation here is approximately 950 feet above Lake Superior and 1,550 feet above sea level.

Ashland County

070 **THE BAD RIVER**   Erected 1957
Hwy. 2, Odanah

The Mauvaise (Bad) River was so named by the French due to the difficulties of its navigation. The Indians called it Mushkeezeebi or Marsh River. In 1845 the Rev. H. L. Wheeler, Protestant missionary at La Pointe, planned an agricultural settlement near the mouth of the Bad River where Indians had for many years made their gardens. He named the settlement "Odanah," a Chippewa word meaning "village". About 1850 a determined effort was begun to compel the Indians to move west of the Mississippi. Mr. Wheeler visited the lands to which it was proposed the Lake Superior Chippewa should go. He returned with the conviction it would be a deed of mercy on the part of the government to shoot the Indians rather than send them to the new region. In July, 1853, Mrs. Wheeler wrote her parents; "They (the Chippewa) are fully determined not to go. They have lived two years without their payments, and find they do not starve or freeze." Mr. Wheeler's pleadings were not in vain. The government resumed the payments, and his ideas of justice toward the Chippewa were substantially embodied in a treaty made with them in 1854 providing for them three reservations, at Odanah, at Lac Court Oreilles and at Lac du Flambeau.

Barron County

219 **PINE WAS KING** Erected 1976
Rest Area No. 34, westbound lane Hwy. 53, 2 mi. S of Chetek

Vast forests of virgin white pine were the treasure which brought the first wave of white settlers to Northern Wisconsin. The farms came later, but for half a century the forests were local history. In 1847, the Knapp, Stout and Co. purchased thousands of acres of pinelands from the Government for $1.25 per acre. In 1848 they began logging operations in Barron county and by 1870 the company was said to be the greatest lumber corporation in the world and the undisputed lord of the thousands of square miles comprising the Red Cedar Valley. In 1901 the Knapp, Stout & Co. mills became silent as the white pine of the area was gone and the denudation of the area was regrettably complete. Today Barron County ranks high in the state in forestry, but agriculture comprises the main industry of the area.

When Pine was King.
SHSW Visual Materials Archive (W6) 11608.

Bayfield County

 TRAGEDY OF THE SISKIWIT Erected 1955
Hwy. 13, 0.5 mi. E of Cornucopia

Once upon a time, according to an old Indian legend, the sand beach on the east side of this bay was a favorite camping ground. One spring a few lodges of Chippewa from La Pointe encamped here. When their chief, Bi-aus-wah, returned from the hunt, he found that a large party of Foxes had murdered all but two of his people. He trailed the enemy to their village and found them preparing to torture his young son. Chief Bi-aus-wah stepped proudly forward and offered his own life if the Foxes would release his young son, whose "tender feet have never trodden the war path." Fearing the consequences if they refused so noble an offer, the Foxes released the son and burned the father instead. The son returned to his relatives at La Pointe, and his story brought quick and decisive revenge.

Bayfield County

049 **MADELINE ISLAND**   Erected 1956
Hwy. 13, 2.3 mi. N of Washburn

To the east is Madeline Island, known to the Ojibways as Moningwunakauning, "The Home of the Golden Breasted Woodpecker." The French soldier Pierre Le Sueur built his post there in 1693. In 1718 a fort was erected which remained France's principal fur trading post on Lake Superior until New France fell to the English. In 1793 Michel Cadotte established a trading post and began permanent settlement. When Equaysayway, daughter of Chief White Crane and a member of the Ojibway aristocracy, married Michel Cadotte, she was given the Christian name "Madeleine." Her pleased father declared the island should be named in her honor.

Bayfield County

145 **SCHOOL CONSOLIDATION**   Erected 1964
Hwy. 13, Port Wing

As the 20th century began, logging operations were in full swing in this area and the small log schoolhouses could not handle the increasing number of students. Some classes were held in churches but additional facilities were needed. T.N. Okerstrom and James C. Daly conceived the idea of consolidating the rural districts and establishing a larger school with free transportation. It was a new idea and there was resistance, but after numerous meetings and much planning, a new school building for the consolidated district was completed in January 1903. S. A. Baxter was principal, with a salary of $70 per month, and teachers May Kinney and Nettle Trolander each received $40 per month. So far as is known, this was the first school district in Wisconsin to provide free, tax-supported transportation. Canvas-covered, horse-drawn wagons or sleighs, known as "school rigs," were used for this purpose.

Buffalo County

 BEEF SLOUGH Erected 1976
Hwy. 35, 0.5 mi. N of Alma

The Beef Slough was a sluggish branch of the Chippewa River that provided an excellent storage pond for the logs floated downstream by numerous logging companies. Here loggers were employed to arrange the mixed-up logs into orderly rafts to be towed by steamboats to sawmills down the Mississippi. The Chippewa Falls and Eau Claire sawmills felt threatened when the Beef Slough Manufacturing, Booming, Log Driving and Transportation Company was organized near here in 1867. Camp No. 1 built offices, a railroad depot, post office, church and dormitories to house 600 men during the rafting season. The competition between the Eau Claire and Beef Slough interests developed into a brief dispute in 1868, sometimes called the "Beef Slough War." The most important result of the "war" was the arrival on the scene of Frederick Weyerhaeuser, whose Mississippi Logging Company brought skilled management and seemingly unlimited capital into the picture and changed the logging operations on the Chippewa from locally operated activities into a major interstate industry.

Burnett County

CREX MEADOWS Erected 1976
**243 In Crex Meadows Wildlife Area, off Hwy. F,
N of Grantsburg**

During the last Wisconsin glaciation the advance of the Grantsburg sublobe blocked drainage, resulting in the formation of Glacial Lake Grantsburg. Natural succession eventually formed the extensive peat marshes known today as Crex Meadows. Prior to white settlement in the mid-1800's the Fox, Dakota and Chippewa Indians used Crex extensively. Large scale commercial drainage, begun about 1890, upset the entire ecological pattern. The vast operations of the Crex Carpet Company, started in 1911, involved harvesting and shipping the native wire grass, *stricta*, from which Crex probably derived its name. For two decades this industry was economically important to this area. Exploited to the fullest, Crex has withstood the ravages of time. Today, under the ownership of the State of Wisconsin, prescribed burning and water management are restoring the prairie flora and fauna of Crex the Meadows.

Chippewa County

 NATION'S FIRST COOPERATIVE GENERATING STATION
Erected 1976
Hwy. 124, 3 mi. N of Chippewa Falls

On Sunday, May 2, 1937, the Wisconsin Power Cooperative was organized by an assembly of farmers for the purpose of developing a generating and transmission facility to provide low-cost electric service for the rural areas of Buffalo, Chippewa, Clark, Dunn, Pierce, St. Croix, Taylor, and Trempealeau counties. Loans from the Rural Electrification Administration financed construction of the original station and transmission lines. Ground was broken on November 8, 1937, and on March 12, 1938, the nation's first cooperative generating station was ready for service. Transmission of electric energy into Buffalo and Trempealeau counties began on March 14, 1938, and into the remaining six counties by the end of that year. Additional generating units were added by late 1941, providing capacity to serve rural membership in Barron, Burnett, Eau Claire, Jackson, Polk, Rusk, and Sawyer counties. On December 16, 1941, Wisconsin Power Cooperative was merged with the Tri-State Power Cooperative of Genoa to form the Dairyland Power Cooperative of La Crosse. This historic plant was retired from service and dismantled during 1975.

Chippewa County

014 **OLD ABE, THE WAR EAGLE**   Erected 1954
Hwy. 178, 0.5 mi. N of Jim Falls

This wayside is part of the old McCann farm childhood home of Old Abe, the War Eagle. In the spring of 1861, a band of hungry Chippewa came to the McCann farm and traded a young eagle for corn. The eagle became a family pet. When Company C, Eighth Wisconsin was organized at Eau Claire for Civil War duty, the crippled Dan McCann offered his eagle's services as a mascot, feeling that "someone from the family ought to serve." On October 12, 1861, the Eagle Regiment started for the front. In action Old Abe spread his wings and screamed encouragement to his men. The louder the noise of battle, the louder and fiercer were his screams. The eagle served with the regiment in 42 skirmishes and battles and lost only a few feathers. After three years service, Old Abe was formally presented to the State of Wisconsin September 26, 1864. A room was equipped for him in the Capitol and a man employed to care for him. His last public appearance occurred at the National Encampment of the G.A.R. in Milwaukee in 1880, where he and General U.S. Grant were honored guests. After a brief illness, Old Abe died March 28,1881.

Old Abe, The War Eagle, artist unknown.
SHSW Museum Collection, negative in SHSW Visual Materials Archive (X3) 9698

331 **NORTHERN WISCONSIN CENTER FOR THE DEVELOPMENTALLY DIS-ABLED**   Erected 1996 **Jct. of Hwy. J and S Second St., Chippewa Falls**

Before the 19th-century social reform movement, developmentally disabled people were relegated to almshouses and county poor farms where the "indigent, insane, epileptic and idiotic" were housed together without regard to individual condition. Reformists advocated more humane treatment of the socially-dependent, and by the mid-19th century had demonstrated the educability of the "mentally deficient" and opened homes for their care and training. In 1895, Wisconsin allocated $100,000 for the establishment of its first institution for the developmentally disabled. Located in Chippewa Falls on 600 acres of land offered by the city, the "Wisconsin Home for the Feebleminded" opened June 17, 1897. The home, renamed the "Northern Wisconsin Colony and Training School" in 1923, provided care for children and adults and taught skills in self-care, farming, housekeeping, arts and crafts, and academics. In the 1970s, a new emphasis was placed on community care of the developmentally disabled, and the Northern Wisconsin Center for the Developmentally Disabled, renamed in 1976, began providing outreach services to individuals and communities.

Chippewa County

279 **THE COBBAN BRIDGE**   Erected 1986
W side of Hwy. 178, near Hwy. T

The Cobban Bridge, constructed in 1908 by the Modern Steel Structural Company of Waukesha, is a two-span Pennsylvania overhead truss type bridge and is the oldest of its kind in Wisconsin. Originally it crossed the Chippewa River just upstream from its junction with the Yellow River. The bridge was dismantled during the construction of the Wissota Dam in 1916, and through the efforts of Oscar Anderson, a Cobban store owner, the bridge was acquired to be placed on land donated by S.C.F. Cobban. During the winters of 1916 and 1917, the disassembled bridge was hauled here by horse and sled, with the movers receiving one dollar per ton for the fifteen mile trip. Footings were placed by the L.G. Arnold Company and reconstruction was done by Cromby and Thailacker of Milwaukee in 1918-19. The ferry that had provided a crossing to Cobban was discontinued, replaced by the Cobban Bridge, which soon was nicknamed the "Little Wagon Bridge."

The Cobban Bridge.
SHSW Visual Materials Archive (X3) 17678.

Clark County

161 **THE HOME OF COLBY CHEESE** Erected 1968
2 blocks W of Hwy. 13, Colby

At his father's cheese factory about one mile south and one mile west of here, Joseph F. Steinwand in 1885 developed a new and unique type of cheese. He named it for the township in which his father, Ambrose Steinwand, Sr., had built northern Clark County's first cheese factory three years before. The town had taken its name from Gardner Colby, whose company built the Wisconsin Central railroad through here. Colby is a mild, soft, moist cheese. Its taste became known in the neighboring areas and an 1898 issue of the *Colby Phonograph* noted that "A merchant in Phillips gives as one of the 13 reasons why people should trade with him, that he sells the genuine Steinwand Colby Cheese." After the turn of the century this area became one of the great cheese producing centers in the nation and Colby cheese a favorite in countries the world around.

Wisconsin Cheese Maker.
SHSW Visual Materials Archive (X3) 17678.

Wisconsin Cheese Factory.
SHSW Visual Materials Archive (X3) 8347.

N
O
R
T
H
W
E
S
T

Douglas County

298 **WARTIME SHIPBUILDING**   Erected 1990
Tourist Info Center, City Park, Hwy. 2, Superior

Wisconsin's shipyards made a significant contribution to Allied victory in World War II, setting national records for rapid and cost-effective production. Wisconsin shipyards built tugs, cargo vessels of various types, corvettes, frigates, and submarines worth 334 million dollars. Between 1942 and 1945, the builders in Superior produced eighty-one ships whose tonnage and total value exceeded that of all other Wisconsin shipyards. The Walter Butler Company built fifty-two ships, including eighteen coastal freighters, twenty-two ocean-going cargo ships, and twelve frigates employed as convoy escorts. In May 1943, Butler's 5,000 workers launched five large cargo ships in a single day. Globe Shipbuilding constructed ten armed ocean-going tugs, eleven 5,000 ton cargo ships, and eight Tacoma-class frigates. Globe workers developed innovative welding techniques that permitted construction to continue all winter. In 1944, some 230 of the company's 2,500 workers were women, including many who served as riveters. Ships built in Superior hauled portions of an artificial harbor to the Normandy beaches, towed damaged warships to port, and took part in anti-submarine warfare in the Atlantic.

Douglas County

OLD STOCKADE SITE Erected 1954
**Memorial Park, Hwys. 53, 13 and 2 at 17th
and 18th Aves., Superior**

The Sioux uprisings in Minnesota during the summer of 1862, culminating in the
New Ulm Massacre, caused great alarm in Superior. A Committee of Safety was
chosen, a Home Guard organized, and a stockade built on the bay shore here. An
inventory of all firearms in Superior revealed a total of 60 shotguns, rifles and pistols. The state sent 192 muskets and two cannon. To assist the Home Guard, the
Governor sent a company of Wisconsin soldiers that had been captured by the
Confederates at Shiloh and paroled. This Company was called back for Civil War
duty in the summer of 1863 and was replaced by other Wisconsin paroled soldiers.
The Chippewas residing in this vicinity remained friendly to the whites. By August,
1863, the Sioux in Minnesota had been overcome and most of the soldiers left
Superior. Eventually the stockade was abandoned.

Old Stockade, painting by William Olsen.
SHSW Visual Materials Archive (W6) 19139.

Douglas County

 ### *S.S. METEOR:* LAST OF THE WHALEBACKS   Erected 1974
Whaleback Museum, Barker's Island, Superior

The Great Lakes whaleback fleet was the revolutionary result of Capt. Alexander McDougall's attempts to improve conventional ship design. Between 1888 and 1898, 43 whalebacks were launched and became forerunners of the bulk fleet on the Great Lakes today. Thirty-nine whalebacks were built in Superior-Duluth, and most of them were launched from a site about one mile west of here, now the Fraser Shipyards. The *S.S. Meteor* was launched at Superior in 1896 as the *Frank Rockfeller* to carry iron ore. Later, as the *South Park*, she carried such diversified cargoes as grain and automobiles. In 1943 she was converted to an oil tanker and renamed *Meteor.* She has been preserved as a memorial to her builder and a tribute to Superior. As a boy, Franklin D. Roosevelt came to Superior with his father to watch the launching of a whaleback. In his enthusiasm to get a good view, he was swept into the slip by waves. A member of the Superior Fire Department rescued him before he reached deep water.

Douglas County

233 THE SUPERIOR ENTRY Douglas County   Erected 1976
Harbor Entry, off Hwy. 2 (53), Wisconsin Point Rd., Superior

The Superior Entry is the only natural opening through the longest fresh water sandbar in the world. Sand deposits from the lake and the rivers created the bar forming the harbor about 3000 years ago. The Entry, as first charted in 1861 was 1500 feet wide. The Army Corps of engineers completed the present 1500 to 2000 foot long concrete piers in 1909 and now maintains a channel 500 feet wide and 32 feet deep. Currents in the channel sometimes reach speeds of more than 3 mpg. The first ore shipped from the mighty Mesabi Iron Range passed through the Entry in 1893. Today the Entry serves one of the busiest ports in the United States, the western terminus of the St. Lawrence Seaway, and handles cargoes of iron ore, coal, petroleum and grain destined for ports throughout the world.

Douglas County

192 **BURLINGTON NORTHERN ORE DOCKS**
Erected 1974
Off Hwy. 2 (53), E. 37th Ave. and 1st St. at the docks, Allouez–South Superior

These docks, the largest in the world, consist of three structures of concrete and steel. The longest dock is 2244 feet long, 80 feet high, and contains 374 individual pockets which can hold 100,000 long tons of ore, or 7 average trains of 205 cars each. Ore is hauled 100 miles from Minnesota mines. The first dock was built of timber in 1892. The first cargo consisting of 2073 long tons of ore was shipped in Whaleback Barge No. 102 on November 11, 1892. Over one billion tons of ore have been shipped through these docks, the largest year's shipment being 32.3 million tons in 1953. In 1967 a conveyor belt system was installed for moving taconite pellets from trains to dock pockets. In the early years as many as 400-500 men worked on the docks; with modern equipment and reduced volume of ore, fewer than 140 men are now required.

Superior's Ore Docks.
SHSW Visual Materials Archive (X3) 48785.

NORTHWEST

Douglas County

210 **NORTHWEST PORTAL OF WISCONSIN**
Erected 1975
Rest Area No. 23, Hwys. 2 and 53, S limits of Superior

Over millions of years, the forces of nature have given Northwest Wisconsin some of the finest scenery in the world. The most striking feature is Lake Superior, largest freshwater lake in the world and the "Gitche Gumee" of Henry Wadsworth Longfellow's "Hiawatha." There are hundreds of species of animal and plant life: bear, beaver, deer, wolf, eagle, bluejay, grosbeak, shorebirds, waterfowl, grouse, chickadee. Plants include spruce, white birch, tag alder, popple, trillium, violet, daisy. For thousands of years before the white man came, the Indians ranged over the land in search of food and furs. In the 1600's the first coureur de bois was followed by hundreds of others. Men like Father Allouez, Duluth, Radisson, Groseilliers, Carver, Cadotte, Schoolcraft, came for exploration, missionary work and fur-trade. They were followed by the lumberjacks and the lumber companies, copper prospectors and miners. Welcome to beautiful and historic Northwest Wisconsin. As you travel, historical markers will offer brief chapters in Wisconsin history.

Douglas County

213 **SUMMER WHITE HOUSE—1928** Erected 1975
Superior Central High School, 1015 Belknap St., Superior

On May 31, 1928, President Calvin Coolidge accepted former Senator Irvine Lenroot's invitation to spend the summer in the Superior Area. Henry Clay Pierce had offered Cedar Island Lodge, part of a 4,000 acre Brule River estate, to serve as living quarters for the President and his family. Superior Central High School was designated the official White House offices for the presidential party and served in that capacity from June 15, 1928 until September 10, 1928. On July 16, 1928, President Coolidge welcomed presidential nominee Herbert Hoover to the area. The Superior visit was Mr. Hoover's first public appearance after his nomination. From the steps of Central High, President Coolidge announced his support of Hoover's candidacy to crowds of newsmen, visitors, and area residents. Hoover had taken a firm stand in favor of the Great Lakes Waterway and was hailed as the obvious choice for the presidency. During his stay here, President Coolidge also found time to fish on the Brule River, one of America's most famous trout streams.

Douglas County

 THE UNIVERSITY OF WISCONSIN-SUPERIOR
Erected 1993
**Between McCaskill Bldg. and Holden Fine Arts
Bldg., UW-Superior, Catlin Ave.**

Authorized by the legislature in 1893, the University of Wisconsin-Superior opened its doors in 1896 as the state's seventh Normal School to train teachers, drawing most of its students from ten northern Wisconsin counties. The original building, Old Main, burned in 1914 and was rebuilt in 1916. Educational offerings progressed from a one-year teacher training program, to a two-year program, to a four-year program for a bachelor's degree in education in 1926–27, to a four-year liberal arts degree program in 1946-47. A graduate program in school administration was added in 1950, and Master of Arts and Master of Science degree programs were established in 1968. By 1993, after four changes in name, the University of Wisconsin-Superior had grown to 18 buildings and outdoor athletic facilities on 230 acres. The University is known especially for its programs in the arts, business, education, humanities and sciences, and is a major cultural and intellectual resource for northern Wisconsin.

Douglas County

 EVERGREEN PARK COTTAGE SANATORIUM   Erected 1956
Hwys. F and B, Lake Nebagamon

Here, in 1903, Dr. W. B. Hopkins, Cumberland, opened the first tuberculosis sanitarium in Wisconsin. He built an office and three one-story frame buildings with screen sides–the men's ward, the women's ward and a dining hall. Hopkins treated tuberculosis cases here in summer. He wrote of the "pure air, day and night" and a program of close medical attention, good food and restrained exercise to keep the patient "cheerful and hopeful, temperate in all things." Weekly rates were $15, or a patient could build a little cabin on the grounds and get medical treatment for $10 monthly. Physicians volunteered their services, among them, Dr. F. G. Johnson, Lake Nebagamon. Operating losses caused the sanitarium to be abandoned in 1905. It was brave effort that stimulated inquiry into the treatment of tuberculosis in Wisconsin.

Douglas County

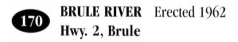

MAJOR "DICK" BONG   Erected 1957
Hwy. 2, Poplar

It was here that Major Richard I. Bong was born, received his education, and grew to manhood. After attending Superior State College where he received his first pilot training, he joined the U.S. Army Air Corps on May 29, 1941. Assigned to the New Guinea combat theater of operations on September 5, 1942, he quickly proved his mastery in the air by shooting down two enemy aircraft in his first air battle. By destroying a total of forty enemy aircraft in air combat he became American's leading air ace of all time. Awarded the Congressional Medal of Honor by a grateful government and winner of many other military decorations, he lost his life testing a jet plane in August, 1945, and lies buried nearby.

Douglas County

BRULE RIVER   Erected 1962
Hwy. 2, Brule

The Brule River flows in the former channel of a larger river which once flowed in the opposite direction and drained melting ice from glacial Lake Duluth. The receding glacier created Lake Superior and also carved the valley now occupied by the Brule. Instead of flowing southward out of Lake Superior, the Brule now flows northward into it. A short portage at Upper St. Croix Lake connects the Brule and St. Croix River systems. This route became know to French explorers in 1680 and became so important in the early fur-trade that France built forts at each end for its protection. The French lost their North American colony to England in 1763. Not far from here on October 1, 1842, a Sioux war party led by Old Crow penetrated this territory intent on seeking out small bands of Chippewa. Chief Buffalo of the Chequamegon Bay Chippewa quickly gathered 200 braves to meet the much larger Sioux force. The enemies met at sunset on opposite banks of the Brule. When the Sioux attacked the next morning, two groups sent by Buffalo above and below the Sioux attacked them from the rear. The Sioux suffered a bloody defeat and never again entered this territory. Long famous as a trout stream, the Brule also is noted for canoeing and for the "wild" beauty of its scenery.

Douglas County

120 **BRULE-ST. CROIX PORTAGE** Erected 1962
Hwy. 53, 1.5 mi. S of Solon Springs

The Brule and St. Croix rivers provide the natural water highway between Lake Superior and the Upper Mississippi. Daniel Greysolon, Sieur du Lhut, in 1680 was the first white man to use this passage. Traveling from Prairie du Chien in 1766, Jonathan Carver was advised by his Chippewa guide not to ascend the Mississippi and St. Croix rivers because he lacked enough gifts for the numerous and unfriendly Sioux along that route. Carver's party then detoured up the Chippewa River to Lac Courte Oreilles, portaged to the Namekagon, traveled down stream to the St. Croix and up that river to the passage north of St. Croix Lake. The two-mile portage between the St. Croix and Brule was used by another exploration party led by Henry Schoolcraft August 6, 1832. One of Schoolcraft's companions recorded that the Brule was a brook of clear, cold water "filled with brook trout." The Brule still is one of the best trout streams in the United States.

Dunn County

291 **MABEL TAINTER MEMORIAL**   Erected 1989
205 Main St., Menomonie

Erected to the memory of Mabel Tainter, daughter of lumberman Andrew L. Tainter and his wife Bertha, and given to area citizens on July 3, 1890, the memorial reflects advanced American architectural, social, educational and religious thought of the era. Designer Harvey Ellis, in the employ of St. Paul architect L.S. Buffington, created this important and sophisticated structure of local sandstone in the Richardsonian Romanesque style. Carvings, stenciling, leaded glass, brass and marble grace the interior, with a strong Moorish influence evident in the design of the ornate auditorium. The Memorial provided the community a reading room and library, club rooms, and an auditorium. It also served as the home of the original Menomonie Unitarian Society, whose minister, Henry Doty Maxson, inspired the Tainters to have it built as a center dedicated to the city's moral and social welfare. The Mabel Tainter Memorial continues to provide a cultural and educational focus for the entire community.

Mabel Tainter Memorial, interior.
SHSW Div. of Historic Preservation,
Paul Jakubovich, photographer.

Dunn County

307 **WORLD WAR I**   Erected 1991
Rest Area No. 62, I-94

The outbreak of war in Europe in August 1914 did not involve the United States directly. Americans expected to remain neutral in the struggle between Great Britain, France, Russia and Italy against Germany and its allies. The desire for neutrality was particularly strong in Wisconsin, with 25percent of the population of Germanic extraction. But by 1917, a majority of Americans favored the cause of Great Britain and France, and President Woodrow Wilson accepted the need to defeat Germany. The wartime period was stressful for Wisconsin. Some Americans vilified Wisconsinites as being pro-German. Superpatriots committed outrages against those suspected of "disloyalty." German culture was denigrated. Despite such tensions, Wisconsin citizens oversubscribed to their Liberty Loan quotas and responded enthusiastically to the call to arms. Over 122,000 entered military service, of whom 15,266 served in the Wisconsin National Guard, which became the Thirty-Second Division. By war's end on November 11, 1918, almost all of the 1,800 Wisconsinites killed in action and fully one-third of the 6,300 wounded were members of the Thirty-Second or "Red Arrow" Division, whose veterans earned over 800 medals for valor.

Dunn County

CHIPPEWA VALLEY WHITE PINE
Erected 1973
Rest Area No. 61, eastbound lane I-94, Menomonie

Here and northeast of here lies the vast Chippewa Valley. At the start of lumbering in Wisconsin, it held one-sixth of the nation's white pine. Surveyors estimated the total pine stand in the State at 136 billion board feet of prime lumber. Lumbermen considered the supply inexhaustible. Chippewa Valley white pine helped build the homes and cities of the corn belt, the great plains, Chicago after its fire. This valley made strong men, record log jams, tall tales, and prosperous cities, all while wasting 60 percent of its pine in stumps, slashing, culls, sawdust, slabs, and fires. The harvest here that began in 1838 with 5-foot diameter trucks 160 feet high ended 80 years later taking 5-inch logs. Today the Chippewa Valley is green again with farms and pine. Reforestation began before 1920. Early plantings are now merchantable timber. In time the Chippewa Valley will again stand with mature pine.

Rolling pine logs into the river.
SHSW Visual Materials Archive (W6) 6881.

Dunn County

 CADDIE WOODLAWN   Erected 1970
**Caddie Woodlawn Park, Hwy 25, 3.5 mi. S of
Downsville**

On this site during the Civil War Caroline Augusta Woodhouse, known throughout the world as "Caddie Woodlawn," experienced the excitement of growing up in pioneer Wisconsin. Her Tomboy adventures with her two red-headed brothers, and her fearless trust in the Indians who lived nearby, were faithfully recorded by her grand-daughter, Carol Ryrie Brink in her book, *Caddie Woodlawn*, and in its sequel, *Magical Melons*. In 1935 Caddie Woodlawn received the coveted Newbery Award Medal as "The most distinguished children's book of the year." It has since become a classic, read by thousands of children throughout the nation, and translated into more than ten foreign languages. Somewhere within the present park area, Mary, one of the eight children of the John V. Woodhouse family, is buried in an unmarked grave. Nearby stands the Woodhouse home which was moved in 1970 from the original site about 300 yards to the east. In January, 1940, "Caddie" died in Idaho at the age of 86.

Iron County

 GOGEBIC IRON RANGE   Erected 1962
Hwy. 2, 10 mi. W of Hurley

The Gogebic Iron Range, which may be seen to the south of here, extends for 80 miles from Lake Namekagon, Wisconsin, to Lake Gogebic (Chippewa for "place of diving") in Michigan. Prior to the discovery of iron ore, the area was relatively uninhabited as the land was ill-suited to agriculture. Nathaniel D. Moore uncovered ore deposits in the Penokee Gap near Bessemer in 1872, but it was not until 1884 that the first mine shipment was made. The news spread rapidly, attracting speculators, investors, and settlers. By 1886 there were 54 mines on the range and the area boomed having "inexhaustible deposits of uniformly high-grade Bessemer ores." For a brief period stocks rose 1200 percent. The crash in 1887 ended the extravagant prosperity.

NORTHWEST

Iron County

315 **IRON MINING IN WISCONSIN** Erected 1992
Wayside, Tourist Info Center, Hwy. 51, 1 mi. N of Hurley

Although iron mining in Wisconsin had its beginnings in Sauk, Dodge and Jackson counties in the southern part of the state in the 1850s, discoveries of vast new deposits shifted the focus to northern Wisconsin in 1880. The major iron mining area from the mid-1880s to the mid-1960s was the Gogebic Iron Range, which extends for 80 miles from Lake Gogebic in Michigan to Lake Namekagon in Wisconsin. Forty-five of the 70.7 million tons of ore produced from the Gogebic Iron Range in Wisconsin came from the Cary Mine near Hurley and the Montreal Mine at Montreal. The remaining ore came from smaller mines such as the Ottawa, Atlantic, Iron Belt, Germania and Plummer mines, most of which ceased operation before World War I. The Montreal and Cary mines closed in the 1960s when the steel industry changed from using high-grade iron ore from deep shaft mines to using abundant taconite ore that could be economically mined by the open-pit method. At the time of closing, the Montreal and Cary mines were producing ore from workings nearly one mile deep. The last iron ore from the Gogebic Iron Range in Wisconsin was shipped from the Cary Mine in 1965.

Jackson County

242 **SILVER MOUND** Erected 1977
Hwys. 121 and 95, 1.5 mi. W of Alma Center

This large, isolated hill is a famous site where prehistoric Indians gathered to quarry a particularly attractive quartzite for the manufacture of chipped stone tools. Several aboriginal quarries are scattered along the rimrock of this mound. Thousands of tons of waste rock from these pits indicated that quarrying was carried on selectively over many centuries. Fields surrounding this mound are littered with quartzite fragments and flakes which accumulated during the process of making and shaping trade blanks for transportation to out lying areas. Stone spearpoints, knives, and scapers made from this colorful material have a wide distribution throughout Wisconsin and portions of nearby states. It is known that the earliest Indians who migrated into the midwest, perhaps 10-12,000 years ago, made many spearpoints and knives from rock quarried here; thus this site is one of Wisconsin's oldest archeological monuments. History relates that the first white explorers mistakenly thought that the Indians were mining silver. Hence the name "Silver Mound."

Jackson County

204 **WISCONSIN'S INVISIBLE INDUSTRY**
Erected 1973
Rest Area No. 7 (eastbound lane),
15 mi. SE of Black River Falls

Marshy sections of Jackson, Monroe, Wood and Clark counties produce large quantities of Sphagnum moss, providing a major but little known state resource. The ability of Sphagnum to hold 20 times its weight in water makes it invaluable for keeping plants and nursery stock alive in shipment. It is also used in hydroponic gardening, for air shipment of flowers, and because it is sterile it is used in surgical dressings and in seed germination to prevent fungus attack in seeds. Sphagnum replaces itself in the central wetland marshes after harvest and is ready to be pulled again every three years. Harvest seasons run from spring until marshes freeze in the fall. Over 300,000 bales are pulled annually for shipment all over the world. No other state produces Sphagnum commercially.

Jackson County

249 **MARTIN W. TORKELSON (1878-1963)**   Erected 1978
Hwy. 27, 6 mi. S of Black River Falls

Martin Torkelson, born in Jackson County, served the State of Wisconsin for more than fifty years. He was a pioneer in the development for both land and air transportation. After graduating from the University of Wisconsin in 1904, Torkelson worked for the Wisconsin Geological and Natural History Survey, which was the forerunner of the State Highway Commission. His recommendations to the legislature in 1917 led to Wisconsin being the first state to set up a numbering system for its highways. Torkelson's work was not restricted to highway improvement. As Secretary and Executive Officer of the Wisconsin State Park and Planning Board, he published a recreational plan in 1939 to set aside land for public enjoyment. His report on airport development, published in 1945, provided the foundation on which the Wisconsin Department of Transportation has continued to build. Torkelson believed that adequate transportation was vital to commerce and that neither agriculture nor industry could flourish without it.

Jackson County

230 **BLACK RIVER VALLEY** Erected 1976
Bell Mound Scenic Overlook, westbound lane I-94, 5 mi. S of Black River Falls

White pine trees were growing here when Columbus made his voyage to America. In 1819 the first attempts to saw lumber were unsuccessful, but in 1839 Jacob Spaulding founded Black River Falls by erecting the first permanent sawmill and settlement on the Black River. This valley contained the largest pine trees, some of them up to six feet across at ground level, and the most pine trees per township in the state. Before logging ended in 1905, more than fifty sawmills had been in operation in Jackson County. Accurate records kept over a period for forty years reveal that enough lumber was sawed to have built a plank road nine feet wide and four inches thick around the world. Iron ore was smelted at Black River Falls in 1856 and again in 1886, but the old process proved too expensive and was abandoned. The Jackson County Iron Company, a subsidiary of Inland Steel, built a modern processing plant in 1969 that ships 2800 tons of taconite pellets every day of the year to its blast furnaces in Indiana. The mine buildings and open pit mine are visible from the overlook on top of this scenic Bell Mound.

Jackson County

301 **HIGHGROUND VETERANS MEMORIAL** Erected 1990
Rest Area No. 6, westbound lane I-94

Wisconsin Vietnam veterans provided leadership for the establishment of a memorial dedicated to the men and women of the state who served in America's 20th century conflicts. In 1985, the Wisconsin Vietnam Veterans Memorial Project acquired property near Neillsville, northeast of here. The site contains a strikingly beautiful elevated panoramic vista overlooking 500,000 acres of countryside. The site was soon dubbed "The Highground" by the veterans. During 1987, the veterans successfully attracted donations to support improvements that transformed The Highground into a memorial park. A national competition led to the choosing of Robert Kanyusik of Rhinelander as artistic designer. A Vietnam Veterans Memorial was dedicated in 1988 along with The Highground park. The memorial plaza and the associated art works evoke a sense of healing and of hope. The Highground is designed to recognize the experiences of Wisconsin veterans and serves as a reminder of their sacrifices.

066 MITCHELL RED CLOUD, JR. (1925-1950)
Erected 1957
Hwy. 54, 5 mi. E of Black River Falls

Corporal Mitchell Red Cloud was posthumously awarded the Congressional Medal of Honor for his courageous action in battle between U.S. troops and Chinese Communists near Chonghyon, Korea, Nov. 5, 1950. Red Cloud's Company was entrenched beside Hill 123. Early in the morning a large enemy force bore down upon them. Red Cloud shouted a warning and started shooting. In the exchange fire, he was critically wounded, but dragged himself up and, supporting himself by a tree, continued firing and gave his company time to reorganize before he was killed. Red Cloud was one of Carlson's Raiders in World War II. He was descended from a family of warriors. Chief Winneshiek, his grandfather, with others of his tribe, refused to be resettled in Nebraska and returned to this region. This marker is near Red Cloud's birthplace and adjoins the site of Winnebago powwow grounds. To the northwest 1 ¹/₂ miles is the Indian Mission and Old Decorah Cemetery, where he is buried.

Corporal Mitchell Red Cloud, Jr.
SHSW Visual Materials Archive (X3)
18417.

NORTHWEST

Jackson County

 THE PASSENGER PIGEON   Erected 1973
Rest Area No. 8, westbound lane I-94, 15 mi. SE of Black River Falls

Huge flocks of passenger pigeons once roamed North America. Larger than the mourning dove which it resembled, the passenger pigeon derived its name from an Indian word meaning "wanderer" or one who moves from place to place. Flying at a normal speed of sixty miles per hour, the pigeon moved hundreds of miles in migration and 50-100 miles a day during the nesting season, searching for food. The largest nesting on record anywhere occurred in this area in 1871. The nesting ground covered 850 square miles with an estimated 136,000,000 pigeons. John Muir described the passenger pigeons in flight. "I have seen flocks streaming south in the fall so large that they were flowing from horizon to horizon in an almost continuous stream all day long." Many reasons have been given for the extinction of the passenger pigeon. Each year millions were trapped, clubbed, or shot for food and pleasure. The last known passenger pigeon died in a Cinncinnati zoo in 1914.

Marathon County

 FIRST WORKERS' COMPENSATION LAW   Erected 1985
wayside, northbound lane Hwy. 51, 1 mi. S of Hwy. 153

The Wisconsin Workmen's Compensation Act of 1911 assured victims of work-related accidents or illnesses just compensation regardless of fault. With this law, enacted on May 3, 1911, Wisconsin became the first state to have a constitutional system for providing medical expenses, wage loss payments, or death benefits to employees or their families. The law is regarded as a pioneering act of social legislation and a major accomplishment of Wisconsin's progressive movement. On September 1, 1911, the date the law became fully effective, a mutual insurance company began operations in a one-room office in downtown Wausau. The company, which was formed by a group of central Wisconsin businessmen as a means of meeting their responsibilities under the new law, is today known throughout the world as Wausau Insurance Companies. The purchaser of the first policy issued by the fledgling insurer was the Mosinee Paper Corporation, then known as Wausau Sulphate Fibre Company. That contract is recognized as the nation's first valid.

Marathon County

180 **FIRST TEACHERS' TRAINING SCHOOL IN WISCONSIN** Erected 1972
UW-Marathon County campus, Wausau

Rural Teacher Training needs became apparent in Marathon County before the turn of the century. John F. Lamont, Marathon County School Superintendent, investigated the problem, urging Senator A. L. Kruetzer to introduce legislation in the 1887 session of the Wisconsin Legislature. The Marathon County Board appropriated $12,000 for construction of a building, completed in October 1902, to house classes for the Training School for Teachers and the Agriculture and Domestic Economy. Classes began September 11, 1899 in the Humboldt School in Wausau with Professor Oliver E. Wells as Principal at a salary of $1800 per year and Miss Rosalia Bohrer as Teacher at $1300 per year. In the ensuing 43 years, 48 faculty members graduated approximately 1444 teachers, most of whom taught in 365 rural schools to broaden the outlook, knowledge and social contacts for all people.

Marathon County

386 **WISCONSIN'S FIRST HOME-BUILT FLYING MACHINE**   Erected 1998
Rothschild Park, at the jct. of Grand Ave., Park St. and Kort St.,
Rothschild

On June 23, 1911, near this location, Wausau native John Schwister became a pioneer of Wisconsin aviation. Research indicates that on this date Schwister flew the state's first home built airplane capable of sustained, powered flight. Constructed of wooden ribs covered with light cotton cloth and powered by an early-model aircraft engine, Schwister's biplane flew for several hundred feet at a maximum altitude of twenty feet. Calling his plane the *Minnesota–Badger,* Schwister began the design and construction of his "flying machine" in St. Paul, Minnesota, but finished it in Rothschild, Wisconsin. Initially, Schwister flight-tested his biplane as a glider, towing it behind an automobile like a kite. He also built his own airplane hangar here. Schwister made many flights in 1911, including a 27-mile flight in which he soared to 2,000 feet, higher than nearby Rib Mountain. In 1912, Schwister was seriously injured in a plane crash, yet he continued to construct and fly his own airplanes making him Wisconsin's first successful "home-builder."

John Schwister and his Minnesota-Badger biplane.
Photograph from private collection.

Pepin County

 SITE OF FORT ST. ANTOINE 1686
Erected 1955
Hwy. 35, 3 mi. NW of Pepin

Nicholas Perrot was a daring adventurer, fur trader, and able diplomat. The handsome Frenchman built Fort St. Antoine on the shore of Lake Pepin near here in 1686. Alarmed by the aggressions of the English, the French government felt it was necessary to repeat their claims with sufficient pomp and ceremony to impress the Indians and to assure their allegiance. Accordingly, here at Fort St. Antoine on May 8, 1689, Perrot formally took possession of the entire region west of the Great Lakes "no matter how remote" in the name of Louis XIV. When A.W. Miller surveyed this area in 1855, he reported the fort site occupied "a space of about 60 by 45 feet, and stood about 70 feet back from the point of highest water mark on the lake shore."

Pepin County

157 **MAIDEN ROCK**   Erected 1966
Hwy. 35, 1 mi. N of Stockholm

The story of Maiden Rock has several versions. One by Mary Eastman was published in 1849. She heard the story from an old Indian friend, Checkered Cloud, who firmly believed the event happened around 1700. A more romantic version in verse was written by Margaret A. Persons. James Duane Doty accompanied the Henry Schoolcraft expedition into this area and on June 3,
1820, Doty wrote in his journal: "It is told that many years since, a young and beautiful Sioux girl was much attached to a young Indian of the same band, and who would have married her but for the interference of her relatives. They insisted upon her marrying another one whom she despised, and she contrived to avoid the connection for near a year. At length her relations, haveing sent away the young man she loved, on this point compelled her to marry the one they wished. It was evening, and she had not been united more than an hour, before they missed her from the lodge. Nothing could be found of her until morning, when they discovered her at the foot of this precipice, down which she probably precipitated herself."

Maiden Rock, Lake Pepin.
SHSW Visual Materials Archive (X3) 35305.

LAURA INGALLS WILDER   Erected 1962
Hwy. 35, Pepin Park, Pepin County

This park is named in honor of Laura Ingalls Wilder, author of the "Little House" books, which were awarded a medal in 1954 as "lasting contributions to children's literature." Laura Ingalls was born in a log cabin seven miles northwest of here February 7, 1867. In the 1870's her parents moved the family to Kansas Territory, then to Minnesota and finally to South Dakota. At 15, Laura was teaching school and three years later married Almonzo Wilder. They lived for awhile in South Dakota before settling on a farm near Mansfield, Missouri. Mrs. Wilder began her writing career when she was sixty-five. First in the series of eight books was *Little House in the Big Woods,* describing her experiences here in the Pepin area. The book was an immediate success. The author was surprised at her success and told an interviewer after writing her first book, "I thought that would end it. But what do you think? Children who read it wrote to me begging for more. I was amazed because I didn't know how to write. I went to little red schoolhouses all over the West and I never was graduated from anything." She died in 1957.

Laura Ingalls Wilder (standing to the right) and her sisters Mary and Carrie.
Courtesy of the Laura Ingalls Wilder Home Association, Mansfield, MO.

NORTHWEST

217

Pierce County

035 **LAKE PEPIN**   Erected 1955
Hwy. 35, 3 mi. W of Maiden Rock

This beautiful lake is 22 miles long, varies in width from 1 to $2^1/_2$ miles, and covers about 38 square miles. It was caused by the delta of the Chippewa spreading across the gorge of the Mississippi at the southeastern end of the lake. Because of its steeper grade, the smaller Chippewa was able to bring in more glacial debris than the Mississippi could carry away. This delta provided a natural dam and as the water backed up in the gorge of the Mississippi, Lake Pepin was formed. State Highway 35 hugs Lake Pepin along most of its Wisconsin shore and has been called one of the most scenic drives in America. One of Lake Pepin's admirers was William Cullen Bryant. He praised its natural scenery and declared the area "ought to be visited in the summer by every painter and poet in the land."

Pierce County

"BOW AND ARROW"   Erected 1979
259 **Hwy. 35, 1 mi. S of Wis. 63, SE of Hager City**

The rock outline you see on the distant bluff is an archeological curiosity. Jacob V. Brower, a Minnesota archeologist, observed this formation in 1902 and interpreted it as a bow and arrow. In 1903 he wrote, "Some of the stones representing the bowstring are displaced. The intention seems to have been to represent a bow and arrow drawn to shoot toward Lake Pepin." Modern archeologists think the boulders may form a bird effigy, but no one has reached a definite conclusion. Although it is an old, well-known landmark, perhaps even ancient, its origin and age are unknown and it is no part of the Indian lore in this region. Boulder alignments made by Indians exist in other states, but this is the only one known in Wisconsin. Was it made by Indians? Is it a bow and arrow or a bird? It remains a mystery.

Pierce County

165 **EDGAR WILSON NYE (1850-1896)**
Erected 1968
Hwy. 65, 3 mi. S of I-94

"Bill" Nye, journalist, lecturer, author, and humorist, grew to manhood in this quiet valley of the Kinnickinnic, which flows southwesterly through River Falls. The tall-tales of frontier humor were popular regionally before 1860. Sam Clemens (Mark Twain) and Bill Nye widely popularized similar exaggerations until they were considered typically American. In the country church, three-fourths mile eastward, Bill Nye practiced public speaking to empty pews. He was then a student at River Falls Academy, now State University. The family homestead is three-fourths mile south of the church. He delighted his audiences by referring to it as "a hundred and sixty acres of beautiful ferns and bright young rattlesnakes." Ferns are few and the snakes are gone, if they were ever there.

Pierce County

357 **PLUM CITY: EARLY HISTORY** Erected 1997
Spring Pond Park, Main St., Plum City

French traders and Native Americans traveled these rich hunting grounds over 300 years ago. When European settlement began in this area about 150 years later, many settlers followed the old St. Antoine Trail east from the Mississippi River to this location. Here, at the juncture of the trail and Plum Creek, speculator Frank Moser acquired and had surveyed forty acres of land in 1857. With great hopes for future development and inspired by the profusion of plum trees in the area, he named the new settlement Plum City. The entrepreneurial Moser and his brother constructed a dam and sawmill, but the isolated town developed slowly and after eleven years only ten log and two frame buildings had been built. The economy boomed in the 1870s when many pioneering farmers bought Plum City's fencing lumber for farms in eastern Minnesota. After 1900, Plum City became a prosperous farming community with a large business district. But throughout its history, the enduring heart of Plum City has remained this serene natural Spring Pond.

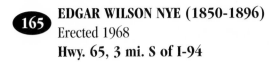

NORTHWEST

Polk County

132 **THE BATTLE OF ST. CROIX FALLS**   Erected 1963
Lions Park, Hwy. 87, N of St. Croix Falls

Here at the head of St. Croix Falls in about 1770, a war party of Chippewas led by Chief Waub-o-jeeg prepared for battle against their traditional enemies, the Fox and Sioux. The two parties met on the portage below this point in a fierce and valorous fight. As each side advanced all fell back, the dead and wounded warriors littered the crags and crevices of the dalles where the St. Croix River forces a passage through the narrow rocks. Many others plunged to a watery grave in the boiling floods below. "The voices of the war chiefs resounded above the rattle of musketry and yells of their warriors, as they urged them to stand their ground," according to Indian tales of the battle. First confident, finally desperate, the Fox and Sioux were routed. This was the last tribal battle of the Fox Indians. The few survivors retreated far to the south, their tribal fire extinguished, and begged to be taken into the Sac tribe. In the Battle of St. Croix Falls, the victorious Chippewas secured this territory, making it safe for the white settlers to come.

Polk County

171 **DANISH DAIRY COOPERATIVE**   Erected 1969
Hwy. 35, Luck

On March 28, 1885 one of Wisconsin's first incorporated creameries was organized as the Luck Creamery Company. The "Organization Artikler" were published in Danish in the Polk County Press on November 18, 1885, and printed in English about a month later on December 12. The seven Danish emigrants declared that only members of the corporation could own stock in it, and the sale of one hundred sixty shares at $15 per share was authorized. The first creamery was built eight-tenths of a mile west of here on the north shore of Little Butternut Lake. The first buttermaker was a Danish woman who made the butter in large wooden churns. In the early days the farmers brought their milk to the creamery in cans which had glass tubes or gauges on the side, marked down to one-eighth inches. The cream as shown by the gauge was measured and paid for by the inch. The cream was then skimmed off and the farmer kept the skimmed milk. Many groups of farmers adopted the cooperative principle to make dairying a leading industry in Wisconsin.

Polk County

143

STATE PARK MOVEMENT IN WISCONSIN—
INTERSTATE PARK
Erected 1965
Interstate Park, Hwy. 8, St. Croix Falls

In 1878 the Legislature set aside 50,000 acres of "Public Trust Funds Lands" as a "State Park." These were scattered timbered lands located in Lincoln, Iron, Vilas and Oneida counties. Because no effort was made to develop these lands, the Legislature in 1897 rescinded its previous actions and during subsequent years the lands were sold. Many Wisconsin citizens at that time believed that areas of statewide significance should be acquired for the use and inspiration of the people. Here at the Dalles of the St. Croix this public interest first took form. Harry D. Baker of St. Croix Falls and George H. Hazard of Taylors Falls headed groups from their respective states for acquiring land on both sides of the river for an Interstate Park. In 1895 their efforts persuaded the Wisconsin Legislature to authorize a Commission for the Interstate Park at the Dalles of the St. Croix." Under its direction in 1900, the first land was acquired. Still dedicated to the original concepts for public use, State Parks have now been developed in all parts of the state. They include sites of historic, archeologic, and geologic value as well as thousands of acres of the finest natural scenery in Wisconsin.

Portage County

121

DU BAY TRADING POST   Erected 1962
in Portage County Park, Hwy. E, 3 mi. S of Knowlton

In 1834 John Baptiste Du Bay established a trading post on the Wisconsin River one mile west of here, for the American Fur Company. His wife was Princess Madeline, daughter of Oshkosh, Chief of the Menominee Indians. According to tradition, Du Bay's father, John Lewis Du Bay, a French-Canadian voyageur, spent the winter of 1790 on the same site, which was known to the Chippewas as Nay-osh-ing meaning "the Point." Because of the underwater ledge, this was the first place north of Petenwell Rock where the river could be forded on foot and therefore became a strategic Indian crossing to the Black River hunting grounds to the west. In the 1860's stagecoaches operating between Stevens Point and Wausau took on passengers here. Lake Du Bay, created in 1942, covers the original site of the trading post. A monument marks Du Bay's grave in Knowlton Cemetery 2 $^1/_2$ miles north of here.

Portage County

324 **WISCONSIN'S GREATER PRAIRIE CHICKEN**
(Tympanuchus cupido pinnatus)   Erected 1993
Hwy. W, 8 mi. W of Hwy. 51, Buena Vista Marsh Wildlife Area

These open grasslands in the Buena Vista Marsh, Portage County, were one of the last remaining strongholds of the Greater Prairie Chicken in Wisconsin. Once abundant in the state, this impressive bird nearly disappeared when its grassland habitat was converted to croplands, pastures and forests. Many committed individuals and organizations worked to preserve the "chicken," purchasing nearly 15,000 acres of grasslands since 1954. Thanks to these conservation efforts, chickens can be observed gathering here on their territorial "booming grounds" each April. Hoping to attract a mate, the male birds frantically stomp their feet and spread their tails while inflating bright orange neck sacs and calling out with a low, mournful, booming sound that can be heard for great distances. After breeding, the birds disperse during the summer and early fall, gathering again in large flocks for the winter. An intensive grassland management and research program works to ensure the future of this important symbol of the prairie.

Price County

065 **PHILLIPS FIRE**   Erected 1957
Hwy. 13, Phillips City Park, Phillips

On July 27, 1894, forest fires racing through dry timber slashings descended on Phillips from three direction. Within a matter of hours the city of 2500 persons lay in smoldering ruins. More than 400 homes, the business district, a new tannery and the large sawmill were totally destroyed. Thirteen lives were lost, all in attempts to escape the flames by crossing the lake. Many families abandoning their possessions crossed the Elk River at the north end of the city to spend a frightening fire-reddened night at the water's edge protecting themselves from the heat and flying embers. Undaunted, these same valiant people built a new Phillips on the ashes of the ruins. Squaw Island, seen across Lake Duroy, is of historical interest. For many years before Phillips was settled and for some years after, it was an Indian burial ground.

Rusk County

 CHIPPEWA RIVER and MENOMONIE RAILWAY
Erected 1959
Hwy. 8, Weyerhauser

During the middle 1870's, when the great logging era of northern Wisconsin was in its infancy, the Mississippi River Logging Company attempted to float pine logs down the Soft Maple and Potato creeks to the Chippewa River but the streams were too shallow and crooked. To solve the problem the first logging railroad in Wisconsin was constructed in 1875-76 from Potato Lake to the Big Bend of the Chippewa River with a later extension northward. The town road which can be seen to the immediate west of this site follows that railroad grade. Sleds pulled by horses carried the locomotive, cars, and tracks overland from Chippewa Falls. In July 1884, this railroad and a subsequent line constructed through the Blue Hills were formally organized as the Chippewa River and Menomonie Railway Company.

Sawyer County

 NAMEKAGON-COURT OREILLES PORTAGE   Erected 1956
Hwy. 27, 5.5 mi. S of Hayward

Still visible here is the southeast terminus of the 2 $^{1}/_{2}$ mile portage that linked the St. Croix and Chippewa River system. Indians, explorers, missionaries and fur traders all used this "carrying place" to move their birch-bark canoes back and forth between the two great water routes connecting Lake Superior and the Mississippi. In 1784 Michel Cadotte established a fur trading post at the northwest end of the portage to control the trade at this pivotal point. From such interior locations as Lac Court Oreilles the Chippewa Indians carried over here on their trips to the south and west to gather rice and berries and on their war excursions against the Sioux.

NORTHWEST

223

Sawyer County

 PIERRE ESPRIT RADISSON AND MEDART GROSELLIERES
Erected 1960
Hwys. 27 and 70, 7 mi. W of Couderay

These brothers-in-law during the winter of 1659-60 camped with the Ottawa Indians two miles upstream from this point on Lac Court Oreilles (meaning "Lake of the Short Ears" in French). Early French explorers called the Ottawa Indians "Court Oreilles." Radisson's journal reports that among the gifts they brought to the Indians were "2 ivory combs, and 2 wooden ones" also some "red painte and 6 looking glasses of tin." The combs and paint were "to make themselves beautifull, the looking glasses to admire themselves." Radisson and Groseilliers were the first white men to discover and explore northwestern Wisconsin. When the French Governor General of Canada confiscated their rich cargo of furs because he claimed they did not have the proper credentials to trade with the Indians, Radisson and Groseilliers left the service of the French government. They went to England and were instrumental in the formation of the Hudson's Bay Company in Canada.

Sawyer County

 JOHN F. DEITZ: "Battle of Cameron Dam" Erected 1992
Hwy. W, 6.7 mi. SE of Winter

In 1904, John F. Deitz and his family purchased a farmstead on the Thornapple River about 2 miles south of here. Deitz soon discovered that Cameron Dam—one of many logging dams on this important tributary of the Chippewa River—lay on his property. He thereupon claimed that the Chippewa Lumber and Boom Co., a Weyerhaeuser affiliate, owed him a toll for logs driven downriver. For four years he refused to permit logs to be sluiced down the Thornapple, defending "his" dam at gunpoint and successfully resisting attempts to arrest him. At least one deputy and two of Deitz's children were wounded in confrontations. In becoming an outlaw, Deitz also became a folk hero with a nationwide following. In October 1910, a large sheriff's posse surrounded his house. In the ensuing gun battle, Oscar Harp, a deputy, was killed. John Deitz surrendered, stood trial for murder, and was sentenced to life imprisonment. He served 10 years, but public pressure eventually convinced Gov. John J. Blaine to pardon him in May 1921. Deitz died in 1924. Cameron Dam has long since disappeared.

Sawyer County

COURT OREILLES Erected 1955
Hwys. 70 and 27, Couderay

The area around Lac Court Oreilles has long been a favorite habitat of Indians because of the abundant game, fish, berries and wild rice. Radisson and Groseilliers were the first white men to visit this area (1659) and they found Ottawa Indians. Before that time the Sioux controlled this territory, and since 1745 the Ojibwa (Chippewa) Indians have lived here continuously. The Ottawa were called "Short Ears" by the French. Court Oreilles (Couderay) means "short ears." However, the Indians and early English and American explorers always referred to the area as Ottawa Sagaigoning or Lake. The Court Oreilles Indian Reservation contains nearly 70,000 acres and was set aside by the Treaty of La Pointe in 1854. There are approximately 1500 Chippewa Indians living on the reservation at this time.

Chippewa harvesting wild rice.
SHSW Visual Materials Archive (X3)
35386.

St. Croix County

051 **ST. CROIX RIVER**   Erected 1956
Hwy. 35, 4.7 mi. N of Hudson

Beginning in one Lake St. Croix approximately 125 miles north and emptying into another Lake St. Croix just south of here, this river is appropriately named. In 1680 Daniel Greysolon de Lhut, for whom the city of Duluth is named, with its small band of hardy voyageurs and Indians, started up the Brule River, seeking a water route from Lake Superior to the Mississippi. Following up the turbulent Brule he found the St. Croix, also a river of many rapids. The passage he discovered became so important in the early fur trade that the authorities of New France dispatched Pierre le Sueur to build a fort at each end of the route for its protection.

St. Croix County

200 **BRULE-ST. CROIX WATERWAY**   Erected 1973
Rest Area, Tourist Info Center No. 25, I-94 just E of Hudson

From early Indian days the St. Croix River and the Brule River, reached by a two mile portage, formed a waterway connecting Lake Superior with the Mississippi River. The first white man to travel the Brule-St. Croix route was the French explorer and trader, Daniel Greysolon, Sieur de Lhut, in 1680. Many traders followed in the next century and a half to harvest the beaver. They had hardly gone before the St. Croix carried the logs and the rafts of the lumbering days, now gone too. The primitive beauty and rugged landscape of the St. Croix earned its distinction by the United States Congress as a wild and scenic river. It is one of the best for recreation and for adventurous canoeing.

St. Croix County

NEW RICHMOND CYCLONE   Erected 1997
Campus Drive, Outlot #3, New Richmond

The New Richmond Cyclone of 1899 remains the most disastrous tornado recorded in Wisconsin history. On the hot summer evening of June 12, with little warning and amazing force, a tornado swept through the thriving agricultural community of New Richmond, a city of about 2,000 people. In the tornado's path lay the entire business district, several Victorian neighborhoods and a visiting circus. The destruction was swift and brutal. Within minutes structures collapsed and fires ignited, leaving 117 people dead, another 150 injured, 230 buildings destroyed and over 400 animals lifeless. The next day volunteers began arriving on relief trains followed by medical teams and the state militia. Many tourists thronged to see the destruction; a few came to loot. Despite the grief and loss, most of the surviving New Richmond residents remained in the city and rebuilt their homes, churches and businesses. Five months later the community had over one hundred new buildings.

New Richmond Cyclone.
SHSW Visual Materials Archive, classified files.

NORTHWEST

000 **RIB LAKE LUMBER COMPANY** Erected 1997
Hwy. 102, Rib Lake

In 1882, speculator J. J. Kennedy constructed a small mill here along the shores of Rib Lake, founding the Rib Lake Lumber Company. In spite of several mill fires, the company grew to produce over a billion board feet of lumber. At first dependent upon horse-drawn sleighs for hauling logs, the company developed into a large industrial complex when a railroad spur was constructed to connect Rib Lake to the Wisconsin Central Rail Road line. By the 1920s, the Rib Lake Lumbering Company included many specialized buildings and machinery, several lumber yards and an intricate tramway system and railroad servicing area. This area of Rib Lake was once known as the "hot pond," where mill steam thawed frozen logs before the bull chain pulled them into the mill. Two buildings remain from the original complex: a machine shed and lumber drying kiln. After the area's available timber was depleted, the mill closed in 1948, ending the era of huge logging operations in Wisconsin.

234 **RUSTIC ROAD** Erected 1976
Hwy. 102, 5 mi. NE of Rib Lake

This historical marker commemorates the first official Rustic Road in Wisconsin following state legislation authorizing the maintenance and identification of scenic roadways under the State Rustic Roads Board of the Department of Transportation. With its dedication September 27, 1975, this road became one of the first roads in the nation to be preserved for its rustic and scenic characteristics. Rustic Road Number One winds for approximately five miles from this site, through outstanding forested glacial topography. When originally laid out as a town road in 1895, the surveyors attempted to follow surveyed section lines, but the road had to be curved around the numerous lakes it encountered. The road has been witness to the cutting of the original pine and hardwood forest, the collection of hemlock bark for a now defunct tanning industry, and the creation and later abandonment of dairy farms. Rustic Road Number One is intended by the Rustic Roads Board to be the first of a statewide network of Rustic Roads maintained for "unhurried, quiet and leisurely enjoyment."

Trempealeau County

 133 **PERROT'S POST** Erected 1963
Perrot State Park, off Hwy. 93

One of the leading early French traders and diplomats among the Indians of the upper Mississippi region was dark and handsome Nicholas Perrot. After building Fort St. Nicholas at Prairie du Chien in the summer of 1685, Perrot moved north and spent the winter here "at the foot of the mountain behind which was a great prairie abounding in wild beasts." These "wild beasts" were buffalo, elk, deer, bear, cougar and lynx. Today, only deer are still common to this area. From here Perrot continued up the Mississippi to establish another fortified post on Lake Pepin and named it Fort St. Antoine. There on May 6, 1689, he formally took possession of the entire region west of the Great Lakes "no matter how remote" in the name of his king, Louis XIV. In 1731 Godefroy de Linctot built a small fort among the Sioux at "the mountain whose foot is bathed by water," sometimes written "La Montigne Qui Trempe a Leau" and now referred to as Mount Trempealeau. De Linctot's fort existed until 1736 and when its ruins were uncovered on this site in 1887, below them was found a hearth stone probably used by Perrot during the winter of 1685-1686.

Trempealeau County

008 **MISSISSIPPI RIVER PARKWAY: FIRST PROJECT** Re-erected 1994
Great River State Trail, Hwy. 35, 0.5 mi. E of Trempealeau

The first 5-mile-long section of the Great River Road project, or the Mississippi River Parkway as it was originally named, was built near here in 1953 and extended east across the Black River. Eventually, the Great River Road would follow the Mississippi through the scenic and historic heartland of the United States, from the river's source near Lake Itasca, Minnesota, to its mouth in the Gulf of Mexico, offering panoramic views and spectacular vistas to the traveler. Built by Wisconsin with federal aid and with the confidence that the other nine river states would continue the work, this section of the project symbolized the faith of Wisconsin in the integrity and permanence of the nation's institutions. The completion of the first part of the 2,000 mile project provided tangible evidence that the concept of a pleasurable riverside highway along the banks of the Mississippi River, from its source to the sea, would be realized.

N
O
R
T
H
W
E
S
T

229

081 DECORAH PEAK   Erected 1958
Hwy. 53, 1.5 mi. SE of Galesville

The rock-crested hill to the east was named after One-Eyed Decorah, a Winnebago chief who, according to tradition, took refuge in a cove near the peak after being wounded in a Chippewa attack on his village. He remained in hiding throughout the bloody engagement and then at nightfall made his way down the Black River to another Winnebago settlement. The next day he returned, surprised the celebrating Chippewa and routed them. With other Wisconsin chiefs Decorah signed a treaty with the United States at Prairie du Chien on August 19, 1825, establishing a tribal boundaries in the hope of securing "a firm and perpetual peace." He achieved his greatest renown after the Black Hawk War when he accompanied the defeated Black Hawk and the Prophet to Prairie du Chien, where on August 27, 1832, the two Sauk leaders surrendered.

 WINNEBAGO INDIANS Erected 1973
**Rest Area No. 5, eastbound lane I-94,
2 mi. SE of Osseo**

Winnebago Indians call themselves "Hochunkgra." A Siouan people, they once occupied the southern half of Wisconsin and the northern counties of Illinois. The Black Hawk War of 1832 and a series of treaties forced the Winnebago out of their homeland, and they were removed to reservations in Iowa, Minnesota, South Dakota, and finally to a portion of the Omaha Reservation in Nebraska. With each removal, small bands of Winnebago returned to Wisconsin, with the largest settlement in Jackson County. About seven miles east of Black River Falls is the historic Winnebago Indian Mission, founded by the German Reformed Church in 1878. The Mission includes about half of the Winnebago population of Jackson County, the pow-wow grounds, Indian Cemetery and Mitchell Red Cloud Memorial. Tribal traditions are preserved through the clan system, the Medicine Lodge, and War Bundle Feast.

Ho-Chunk (Winnebago) wigwams, engraving by Seth Eastman.
SHSW Visual Materials Archive (X3) 31266.

231

Washburn County

164 **YELLOW RIVER**   Erected 1968
Hwy. 70, 0.5 mi. E of Spooner

The Yellow River was called the "River Jaune" by early French explorers because of the bright yellow sand on the bottom of Yellow Lake through which it flows. Located in the heart of the "Folle Avoine" or wild rice country, it was one of the first tributaries of the St. Croix to be occupied by the Chippewa who (ca. 1700) in bloody battles drove out the Sioux and established permanent villages on Clam and Yellow Lakes. At the beginning of the nineteenth century, rival fur-traders for the Northwestern and the XY Companies competed fiercely with rum, trade goods and credit for the fur-trade of the Yellow River, Namekagon, Clam, and St. Croix bands of Chippewa Indians. Indian mounds indicate the residences of aboriginal Indians (ca. 300 A.D.) along the Yellow River and on Spooner Lake, two miles northeast of here. Succeeding the Sioux, the Chippewa maintained permanent villages on this lake from the early eighteenth to the early twentieth century.

Washburn County

162 **NAMEKAGON RIVER**   Erected 1967
Jct. of Hwys. 53 and 63, Trego

Here on the Great South Bend of the Namekagon was a natural camp-site, home of a band of Chippewa Indians and long used by explorers, missionaries, and fur-traders traveling the Namekagon route between the St. Croix and Chippewa rivers. In 1767 Jonathan Carver passed this way, downstream on his way from Prairie du Chien to Lake Superior via the Namekagon, St. Croix and Brule rivers. Henry Schoolcraft passed here in 1831 enroute from Lake Superior to the St. Croix. During the 1870's, ox teams hauled logging supplies on the tote road from Stillwater to Veazie Settlement, located two miles up river where the great Veazie Dam impounded water for log drives down the Namekagon to Stillwater.

Wood County

130 **POINT BASSE** Erected 1963
Riverside Park, Hwys. 54 and 73, Nekoosa

Five rapids covering a distance of about three miles in this area were referred to as Nekoosa (swift water) by the Chippewa Indians, who make their campground on high Swallow Rock overlooking these rapids. At the lower end of the rapids, Wakeley's tavern served as a rendezvous and resting place for the river traveler and lumber raftsmen. Wakeley's was the nucleus for the development of a settlement named Point basse (Low Point). The name was later changed to Nekoosa. The settlement became a key town during the colorful era when lumber was rafted down the river from the pineries of the North to Mississippi River markets. Daniel Whitney built the first sawmill on the Wisconsin River here at Whitney's rapids in 1831, making Nekoosa the birthplace of Wood County. From this first harnessing of the river's power developed scores of power facilities, making the Wisconsin River the hardest-worked river in the world.

NORTHWEST

086 ***CRANBERRY CULTURE*** Erected 1958
Hwy. 54, 5 mi. W of Port Edwards

For countless ages the wild cranberry flourished in many marshy areas of Central Wisconsin. In 1829 Daniel Whitney mentioned the purchase of three canoe loads of cranberries brought down the Yellow River by Indians from the area know known as Cranmoor. During the 1870's a few hardy souls literally carved out by hand the bogs in this area and, in spite of many hazards such as fires and lack of water, succeeded in establishing a new crop. With time the native vines were supplanted by higher producing selections which have given some of the highest yields per acre in the nation. At the turn of the century hand-picking predominated. Later, improved rakes replaced the colorful family groups together with their nightly entertainment. Today the machine has replaced hand labor in the operation of the bogs, and many of the simple pleasures and intimate association accompanying the laborious tasks of the cranberry bogs are now only memories of the past.

Fall cranberry harvest.
SHSW Visual Materials Archive (X3) 7703.

Wood County

296 **PRISONERS OF WAR**   Erected 1990
Wayside No. 4, jct Hwy. 10 and Hwy. 13

Prior to World War II, few Americans had ever been held as prisoners of war on foreign soil. But the surrender of U.S. forces in the Philippines in the spring of 1942 suddenly swelled the number of POWs into the thousands, and soon a network of support groups was formed in the U.S. to exchange information about loved ones held captive. At the war's end, the Bataan Relief Organization absorbed similar "barbed-wire clubs" and in 1949 became the American Ex-Prisoners of War. A Wisconsin department was established in 1977, and Stanley G. Sommers of Marshfield, a sailor captured at Corregidor, became national commander in 1980. Sommers was instrumental in compiling data regarding the effects of incarceration on ex-POWs, some of which informed the congressional debate over passage of the Former Prisoners of War Benefit Act of 1981. A total of 142,227 Americans were captured and held as prisoners of war during both World Wars, Korea, and Vietnam, including 1,929 Wisconsinites. Some 15,190 U.S. service personnel died in captivity, almost three-quarters of them in Japanese hands during World War II.

114 CENTRALIA PULP AND PAPER MILL Erected 1962
Hwys 54 and 73, S city limits of Wisconsin Rapids

Here the vast Wisconsin River paper industry began in 1887 when the Centralia Pulp and Water Power Company converted a saw mill into a pulp and paper mill. The pulp mill spanned the river to the island at the site of the present hydroelectric plant. The paper mill and boiler house were located on the island. Paper finishing and shipping facilities were located just south of this marker. Two paper machines were installed and five water-driven pulpwood grinders reduced logs to pulp. The paper mill operated until 1912 when it was destroyed by fire. The pulp mill was removed in 1920 to make room for an addition to the hydroelectric plant. From this beginning, the Wisconsin River area now has become the largest producer of printing papers in the United States.

Centralia Mills.
SHSW Visual Materials Archive (X3) 14690.

Markers
Northeast Region

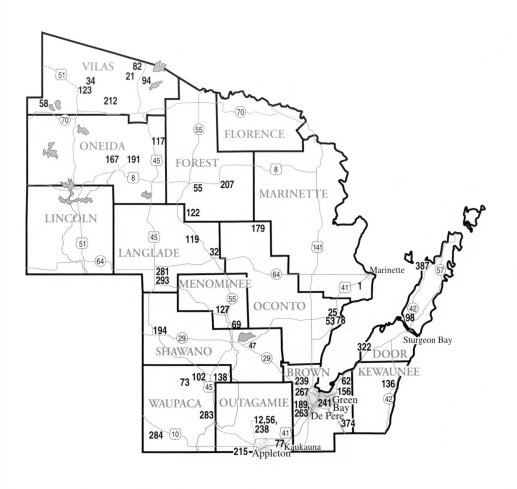

VILAS   82
34   21
123   94
58
212

70

51   70

117
ONEIDA   FLORENCE
167 191   55
45   FOREST
8   55   207
8
LINCOLN   122   MARINETTE
119   179
51   45
64   LANGLADE   32   64
281   141
293   MENOMINEE   Marinette   387   57
55
127   OCONTO
194   69   25   42
29   53 78   98
47   Sturgeon Bay
SHAWANO   29   322   DOOR
73 102 138   BROWN   KEWAUNEE
45   239 62
267 156   136
WAUPACA   OUTAGAMIE 189 241 Green 42
283   263 Bay
12,56, De Pere
284   10   238   374
77 Kaukauna
215-Appleton

41

0   10   20   30   40

Miles

June 1999   *University of Wisconsin Cartographic Laboratory*

NORTHEAST

237

Brown County

156 HAZELWOOD Erected 1966
1008 S. Monroe Ave., Green Bay

On this site Morgan L. Martin (1805–87) built this home in 1837, after his marriage to Elizabeth Smith of Plattsburgh, N.Y. It was a center of social, literary, and political accomplishment for nearly a century. Coming here in 1827 as a young attorney, he began to lay the foundation for Statehood. A member of the Michigan Territorial Council 1831–35, he returned in 1838–44 to serve on the Wisconsin Territorial Council. From 1845–47 he represented the Territory in Congress, at which time he introduced the bill "to enable the people of Wisconsin Territory to form a constitution and state government and for the admission of such state into the Union." The constitution submitted by the Convention of 1846 was rejected and Martin, elected president of a second Convention in 1847, did much of the preliminary revision here at Hazelwood. It was accepted by vote of the people, and President Polk approved the Act of Admission on May 29, 1848.
Wisconsin State Society Daughters of American Colonists

Hazelwood.
SHSW Div. of Historic Preservation.

Brown County

241 HERITAGE HILL STATE PARK Erected 1977
2640 S. Webster Ave., Green Bay

This park, built to portray and preserve Wisconsin's beginnings, is located on a site that is itself a part of history. On this 40 acre site stood Camp Smith—a temporary location of Fort Howard— part of the pioneer settlement known as Shantytown, and Wisconsin's first courthouse. Through this site passed the military road linking Fort Howard with Fort Winnebago at Portage and Fort Crawford at Prairie du Chien. Many of the buildings at Heritage Hill are original structures that were saved over the years by people of foresight and perseverance. Among these buildings are Henry Baird's law office, several original Fort Howard buildings, the Cotton House, a French fur trader's cabin, and the Tank cottage-Wisconsin's oldest standing house dating from 1776. The spread of civilization in Wisconsin was begun by the people who first made their homes here on the banks of the Fox River.

Brown County

 RED BANKS Erected 1957
Hwy. 57, 5 mi. NE of Green Bay

Many of the explorers who followed Columbus were more interested in finding an easy route to Asia than they were in exploring and settling this continent. In 1634 Jean Nicolet, emissary of Gov. Samuel de Champlain of New France, landed at Red Banks on the shore of Green Bay about a mile west of here. His mission was to arrange peace with the "people of the Sea" and to ally them with France. Nicolet half expected to meet Asiatics on his voyage and had with him an elaborate Oriental robe which he put on before landing. The Winnebago Indians who met him were more impressed with the "thunder" he carried in both hands as he stepped ashore firing his pistols. Nicolet reported to his superiors that he was well entertained with "sixscore beavers" being served at one banquet, but it was the pelts and not the flesh of the beaver that were to be highly prized by those who followed him.

Landfall of Jean Nicolet, painting by E.W. Deming.
SHSW Museum Collection, negative in SHSW Visual Materials Archive (X3) 30530.

Brown County

239 **GREEN BAY PACKERS** Erected 1977
Outside Packer Hall of Fame, SE corner Lombardi Ave. and South Oneida St., Green Bay

The Green Bay Packers, an institution and a legend, are unique. The only publicly-owned club in professional sport, they were founded as a town team in 1919 by E. L. "Curly" Lambeau, who coached them to six world championships. They acquired their first jerseys by persuading a packing company to put up money for equipment and, originally, played their games in an open field, where fans "passed the hat." Nurtured into a professional football power that has left a lasting imprint on the sport, they became the first team to win three consecutive National Football League titles (1929–30–31), a feat repeated under Vince Lombardi (1965–66–67) and unequaled. Overall, they have won 11 world championships, more than any other club in league history. Long a "state" team, annually playing games in Milwaukee as well as Green Bay, the Packers have become a national institution, with fans in all 50 states.

Brown County

263 **WHITE PILLARS** Erected 1980
403 N. Broadway, De Pere

This building was erected in 1836 to serve as the office of the Fox River Hydraulic Company, which was chartered by Wisconsin's first Territorial Legislature to construct a dam at Rapides des Peres. Following the 1837 financial crisis, notes issued by the company circulated as currency, making it one of the first de facto banks in Wisconsin. In subsequent years the building served as a barber shop, newspaper office, cabinet shop, private school, church and residence.

MARQUETTE-JOLLIET EXPEDITION
Erected 1973
**In park at NE corner of Broadway and
George Sts., De Pere**

Here in June 1673, an expedition headed by Jesuit priest Jacques Marquette and his companion Louis Jolliet departed from St. Francis Xavier Mission to find and explore the upper Mississippi River. In September they returned here to record their discoveries in their journals. The next spring Jolliet left for Quebec but the ailing Marquette remained at the mission until October. The mission stood on the bank of Fox River directly west of this spot.

Brown County

RAPIDES DES PERES-VOYAGEUR PARK Erected 1981
Voyageur Park, De Pere

The rapids at De Pere were well known to all early travelers along the Fox and Wisconsin Rivers, which provided the best access to the Mississippi. Despite Indian domination, the waterway served explorers, fur traders and voyageurs, missionaries, and soldiers, principally from France and from Canada (New France). Beginning in the late 1600's, the French sent various emissaries to maintain good relations with the Indians and to Christianize them; to seek a water route to the Pacific; and to barter with the Indians for furs. In 1668 Nicolas Perrot and Toussaint Baudry came here to establish fur trading; in 1671 Father Claude Allouez built the St. Francis Xavier Mission (hence the name Rapides des Peres); and in 1673 Marquette and Jolliet left from here to search for the Mississippi. Trouble with the Indians along the Fox River resulted in military expeditions in 1716 and in 1728. Until the completion in 1837 of the military road connecting forts Howard, Winnebago, and Crawford, the waterway was the only channel of communication linking Green Bay with other developing areas in Wisconsin.

374 DENMARK Erected 1998
Denmark War Memorial Park, Wisconsin Ave., Denmark

In 1848, immigrants from Langeland, Denrnark, seeking economic opportunity and plentiful farmland, settled in this vicinity. The Danes purchased land here and called their early settlement "Copenhagen," later changed to Denmark. In subsequent years, German, Irish and Czech immigrants joined the Danes, and Denmark grew to be a prosperous farming and trading community. After a railroad line reached Denmark in 1906, the area became an important center for Wisconsin cheese and dairy production.

R. Rasmussen Family, Danish settlers.
SHSW Visual Materials Archive 21254.

Brown-Manitowoc County Line

264 **WISCONSIN'S DAIRY INDUSTRY**
Erected 1980
**Rest Area No. 51, southbound lane I–43,
just S of Brown-Manitowoc line**

The growth of the dairy industry in Wisconsin is a story of remarkable transfer of scientific knowledge to practical use. As dairy farming developed, Wisconsin's agriculture underwent transformation in less than 50 years. Proposed as an alternative to wheat farming as early as the 1850's, dairying was common in southeastern and south central Wisconsin by the early 1860's. Farmers in other regions soon adopted diversified dairy farming, an enterprise favored by the state's geography. At first the "general purpose cow" provided milk, meat, and motive power, but milk production increased dramatically when farmers accepted the concept of the single purpose dairy cow and applied scientific methods of feeding, management, and selective breeding. Most milk was made into cheese and butter, which at first were made on the farm. In the 1870's, however, factories began dominating the cheese industry, and in the 1890's the butter industry. Wisconsin had 245,000 dairy cows by 1867 and more than 2,000,000 by 1925. By 1907, Wisconsin, 13th largest state, produced nearly half the cheese and a tenth of the butter in the nation.

Barnyard of a family farm, Oconto ca. 1900.
SHSW Visual Materials Archive (X3) 23303.

Modern dairying, ca. 1933, at the Horlick Co.
SHSW Visual Materials Archive (X3) 8326.

Brown-Manitowoc County Line

269 **WISCONSIN'S MARITIME INDUSTRIES** Erected 1980
Rest Area No. 52, northbound lane I–43, just S of Brown-Manitowoc County line

Since about 1840 the lakeshore area from Manitowoc to Sturgeon Bay has been a center for shipping, fishing, and shipbuilding on the upper Great Lakes. Early shipping was characterized by sail and steam vessels docking at small private piers extending into the lake. In the 1860's, lakeshore communities improved their harbors so that ships could dock farther inland. Completion of the Sturgeon Bay Canal in 1880 greatly shortened the Lake Michigan Green Bay passage. Manitowoc and Kewaunee became car ferry terminals in the 1890's and remain so today. As shipping increased, certain port cities developed shipbuilding industries. Manitowoc was the leading builder of wooden ships on the western shore of Lake Michigan in the late 1880's and still produces small craft. Sturgeon Bay began in the 1890's and is now the largest shipbuilding center on the Great Lakes. Commercial fishing began at Two Rivers in the 1850's and later in Kewaunee and Algoma. These ports still have fleets actively engaged in commercial fishing-one of the maritime industries that help to sustain Wisconsin's economy.

Door County

 THE ORCHARDS OF DOOR COUNTY Erected 1960
Hwy. 42, 0.5 mi. N of jct. Hwy. 57

In 1858 Joseph Zettel, a native of Switzerland, acquired the farm directly south of this station and established the first commercial orchard on the Door Peninsula. The high yields and quality of his fruit aroused the interest of Emmett S. Goff of the University of Wisconsin and Arthur L. Hatch, orchardist, and led to the discovery that the Peninsula is remarkably suited for fruit growing. In 1892 Goff and Hatch planted a small acreage to cherries, apples and plums. Commercial production of red cherries began in 1896. The University of Wisconsin established this research station in 1922 to help advance the fruit industry. Progressive growers, community leaders, and thousands of pickers form distant places have shared in bringing Door County national recognition as a fruit producing area.

Door County

 BELGIAN SETTLEMENT IN WISCONSIN Erected 1993
Namur, Hwy. 57

Wisconsin's and the nation's largest Belgian American settlement is located in portions of Brown, Kewaunee and Door counties adjacent to the waters of Green Bay. Walloon-speaking Belgians settled the region in the 1850s and still constitute a high proportion of the population. A variety of elements attests to the Belgian American presence: place names (Brussels, Namur, Rosiere, Luxemburg), a local French patois, common surnames, unique foods (boohyah, trippe, jutt), the Kerrniss harvest festival, and especially architecture. Many of the original wooden structures of the Belgian Americans were destroyed in a firestorm that swept across southern Door County in October 1871. A few stone houses made of local dolomite survived. More common are 1880s red brick houses, distinguished by modest size and gable-end, bull's-eye windows. Some houses have detached summer kitchens with bake ovens appended to the rear. And the Belgians, many of them devout Catholics, also erected small roadside votive chapels like those in their homeland.

Door County

387 **THE ALEXANDER NOBLE HOUSE** Erected 1998
Noble Square, 4167 Main St., Fish Creek

The Alexander Noble House was built in 1875 on land purchased from Asa Thorp, the founder of the Village of Fish Creek. This Greek Revival Style-influenced residence is the Village's oldest existing dwelling still in its original location. Born in Scotland in 1829, Alexander Noble immigrated to Canada in 1840 and settled in Fish Creek in 1855 where he lived until his death in 1905. He was a blacksmith by trade and served for many years as town chairman, postmaster and member of the county board.

Forest County

055 **NORTHERN HIGHLAND** Erected 1956
Hwy. 8, 1.8 mi. E of Crandon

Sugarbush Hill, which you see across the valley, is one of the highest points in the northern highland geological province. This province, which includes some 15,000 square miles in northern Wisconsin, is underlain by the crystalline rock on an ancient mountain range comparable to the Rockies, the peaks of which were ground down by glacial and other geological processes extending over almost infinite time. Because it is particularly suitable for the growing of timber, extensive forests of hardwoods and conifers cover most of its area. Within this forest region lies one of the greatest concentration of lakes in the world, similar to that of Finland. Its cool climate and myriad of lakes make it an ideal summer vacationland.

Forest County

 LAONA SCHOOL FOREST Erected 1975
Hwy. 32, 1 mi. S of Laona

In 1927 this tract of land was purchased for the Laona School Forest, the first in Wisconsin and the United States. It was dedicated April 22, 1928. Motivated by the suggestion of Dean H.L. Russell, of the College of Agriculture, University of Wisconsin, and by the encouragement of the Forest County land use planning committee, the people of this county adopted the idea of school forests to activate a reforestation program. The Laona School Forest, consisting of 80 acres, was logged off in 1921–1922. In 1928, this area, like much of northern Wisconsin, was covered with blackened stumps left by previous fires and cuttings. Today, this growing forest and others like it are living memorials to the interest and work of students and adults in many communities.

Forest County

 BATTLE OF MOLE LAKE Erected 1962
Hwy. 55, 0.5 mi. N of Mole Lake

This is the home of the Sokoagon Band of the Chippewa tribe. According to tradition handed down from one generation to the next, the first chief of the Band was Getshee Ki-ji-wa-be-she-shi, or the Great Marten. Each summer the Sokoagon Band came to Mole Lake to fish and hunt, and in the fall they harvested the wild rice before they followed the deer herds into the swamps of the Peshtigo River for the winter season. About 1806 bands of Sioux from the north and west tried to gain control of the rice boats. A fierce hand-to-hand battle resulted. The Indians, armed with bows and arrows and clubs, fought a long, hard battle. Over 500 Chippewa and Sioux were killed and were buried here in a common mound. The battle was expensive for the Sioux, who retreated westward and never again attempted to return.

Kewaunee County

CAR-FERRY SERVICE Erected 1964
Ferry yard, Kewaunee

Kewaunee, Green Bay & Western Railroad Ferry slip No. 1, to your right, is the point where car-ferry service across Lake Michigan began. On Sunday, November 27, 1892, Ann Arbor Railroad car-ferry No. 1 loaded 22 cars of flour which originated at Minneapolis and were destined for England, Scotland and Ireland—the first boatload of box cars to be transported across Lake Michigan—a service later extended to other ports.

Langlade County

LANGLADE COUNTY FOREST: WISCONSIN'S FIRST COUNTY FOREST
Erected 1990
Wayside, Hwy. 45, 3 mi. S of Antigo

By the 1920s, the once vast forests of Wisconsin had been reduced from more than 30 million acres to about 2 million through farm clearing and lumbering practices that left large cut-over areas. In 1927 the Wisconsin legislature passed the County Forest Reserve Law, which permitted counties to acquire lands because of tax delinquency or other reasons for the purpose of establishing county forest reserves. On November 6, 1928, the voters of Langlade County passed a referendum to establish the first county forest in Wisconsin, leading the way for a permanent program of county forest management. The Langlade County Forest now totals over 125,000 acres. An additional 27 county forests statewide totaling nearly 2.3 million acres have helped once threatened forests develop into highly productive lands. These county forestry programs provide a stable basis for the state's forest products and recreation industries and serve to enhance water quality, improve wildlife environment, and ensure public enjoyment of a vital Wisconsin resource.

DE LANGLADE Erected 1955
032 Jct. of Hwys. 55 and 64, Langlade

The Village of Langlade and Langlade County were named for Charles Michel de Langlade, who has been called the "Father of Wisconsin." Born at the trading post of Mackinac in 1729, de Langlade's character, military ability, and influence left a commanding impression on Wisconsin's early history. He was among the first permanent settlers to locate on the present site of Green Bay about 1745. During the French and Indian War, de Langlade led Wisconsin Indians against Fort Duquesne, and from there to Fort Cumberland, where Braddock was in command, and where George Washington served as a young lieutenant. In 1759, De Langlade fought under General Montcalm in the Battle of Quebec, which ended the French Empire in North America. After active service with the British in the Revolutionary War, de Langlade returned to Green Bay. He died there in 1800.

Langlade County

ANTIGO SILT LOAM, STATE SOIL OF WISCONSIN Erected 1987
281 Hwy. 52, near jct. Hwy. 64

This plain was made thousands of years ago by rivers of water flowing from hills of melting glacial ice that lay a short distance north and east of here. The summer flood waters first laid down gravel, which was then covered by four feet of fertile windblown silt. The silt was slowly changed into productive soil by the action of forest roots and leaf fall. Under careful management by farmers, the soil has been further enriched since settlement and supports a versatile agricultural and forestry economy. Antigo silt loam, first identified through a resource inventory conducted in Langlade County in 1933, was named after the nearby city and occurs in areas across a dozen counties from Green Bay to Minnesota. In 1983 the Wisconsin legislature designated the Antigo silt loam as the official state soil to represent the soil resources of Wisconsin that serve as the foundation of life upon which plants, animals and human beings depend.

NORTHEAST

Langlade County

119 **OLD MILITARY ROAD** Erected 1961
Hwy. 55, 3.5 mi. N of Lily at Wolf River

In March, 1863, Abraham Lincoln signed an Act of Congress which enabled the states of Michigan and Wisconsin to begin construction of a road between Fort Howard at Green Bay and Fort Wilkins near Copper Harbor. It took one year to build the road from Fort Howard to Keshena. By 1869 it had reached the Michigan state line. First used for transporting federal troops and supplies, the road also was used by explorers, settlers, trappers and hunters. By the turn of the century it became an artery for the lumbering interests who kept the road repaired until it became a part of the state trunk highway system in 1923. Along this road are many points of historic legendary interest. Nine Mile Creek, Langlande and Lily were important logging centers. Way stations were established during the 1880's at the Otter Slide, three miles north of Sullivan Falls, the Gauthier Place near Shotgun Eddy, and Mag Lawe's station, two miles north of Keshena Falls, served both the lumber trade and weary travelers.

Marinette County

001 **PESHTIGO FIRE CEMETERY** Erected 1951
Peshtigo Cemetery, Oconto Ave., Peshtigo

On the night of October 8, 1871, a booming town of 1700 people was wiped out of existence in the greatest forest fire disaster in American history. Loss of life and even property in the great fire occurring the same night in Chicago did not match the death toll and destruction visited upon northeastern Wisconsin during the same dreadful hours. The town of Peshtigo was centered around a woodenware factory, the largest in the country. Every building in the community was lost. The tornado of fire claimed at least 800 lives in this area. Many of the victims lie here. The memory of 350 unidentified men, women, and children is preserved in a nearby mass grave.

Pestigo Fire, from *Harpers Weekly,* 1871.
SHSW Visual Materials Archive (X3) 96.

Menominee County

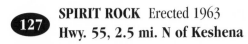

127 **SPIRIT ROCK** Erected 1963
Hwy. 55, 2.5 mi. N of Keshena

One night long ago a Menominee Indian dreamed that Manabush, grandson of Ko-Ko-Mas-Say-Sa-Now (the Earth) and part founder of the Mitawin or Medicine Society, invited him to visit the god. With seven of his friends the Indian called on Manabush who granted their request to make them successful hunters. One of the band, however, angered the god by asking for eternal life. Manabush, seizing the warrior by the shoulders, thrust him into the ground and said, "You shall be stone, thus you will be everlasting." The Menominee say that at night kindly spirits came to lay offerings of tobacco at the rock and that if one looks closely he can see their white veils among the trees. The legend is that when the rock finally crumbles away the race will be extinct.

069 MENOMINEE RESERVATION Erected 1957
Hwys. 47 and 55, S county line, 5 mi. N of Shawano

When Nicolet in 1634 stepped ashore not far from the present site of Green Bay, the Menominees were living in peace with their neighbors on both sides of the Menominee River, on the present sites of Menominee, Michigan, and Marinette, Wisconsin. Language and legend stamp them as Algonquians. Their name was bestowed upon them by the Chippewa and means "The People of the Wild Rice." As white settlers encroached on their lands and treaties were made with the U.S. Government, the Menominees moved reluctantly from one place to another. By 1831, they had transferred to eastern Indians half a million acres at 4 $^1/_2$ cents per acre and another half million acres to the Government at 5 $^1/_2$ cents per acre, the money to be paid in annuities. When Wisconsin became a Territory in 1836, they were compelled to sell 184,320 acres through the Fox River Valley for settlement and lumbering at 17 cents per acre, and they had to move again. In 1848 the Government sought to move them to the Crow Wing country of Minnesota, but this time the Menominees under the leadership of Chief Oshkosh refused to move. In 1852 they moved up the Wolf River where in 1854 they were granted ten townships, and the present Menominee Indian Reservation.

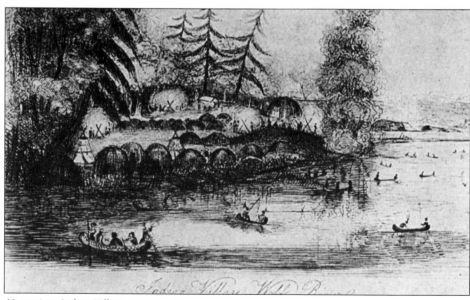

Menominee Indian Village.
SHSW Visual Materials Archive (X3) 20034.

Oconto County

 OLD COPPER CULTURE CEMETERY
Re-erected 1978
Copper Culture State Park, Oconto

At this site approximately 7500 years ago, Wisconsin Indians gathered to bury their dead. They were of the Old Copper Culture, the earliest known people to inhabit Wisconsin. Because of their use of copper tools, weapons, and ornaments, this group became known as the Old Copper people. They fashioned spearpoints, knives, and fishhooks from pure copper nuggets that may have been transported from mines as far away as Isle Royale in Lake Superior. Through a process of heating and hammering, the nuggets were made into tools and various other objects. Old Copper people lived by hunting game, fishing, and collecting plant foods. They interred some of their dead in graves and cremated others in pits. Implements of copper, stone, bone and shell were buried with them. This particular site was excavated in 1952 by the Wisconsin Archeological Society and the Oconto County Historical Society.

Oconto County

 FIRST CHURCH OF CHRIST SCIENTIST Erected 1954
Chicago and Main Sts., Oconto

This church was organized June 10, 1886. The first service was held here October 31 of the same year. Seven years earlier Mary Baker Eddy, the Discoverer and Founder of Christian Science, had founded the Church of Christ, Scientist, in Boston, Massachusetts. Services were held elsewhere in the United States before this church was built, but it is the first edifice erected solely for this purpose. It was dedicated in February, 1887.

Oconto County

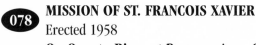

MISSION OF ST. FRANCOIS XAVIER
Erected 1958
On Oconto River at Brazeau Ave., Oconto

On December 2, 1669, the Eve of St. Francis, Father Claude Allouez arrived at Oconto, then a village of about 600 Indians. Here Allouez founded the Mission of St. Francois Xavier, the first mission in northeastern Wisconsin. Six French fur traders happened to be here at that time. The primitive chapel made of bark and cedar boughs remained until 1671 when the mission moved to Red Bank on the east shore of Green Bay.

Oconto County

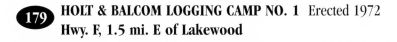

HOLT & BALCOM LOGGING CAMP NO. 1 Erected 1972
Hwy. F, 1.5 mi. E of Lakewood

Generally called "Depot Camp," it is the oldest standing lumber camp in Wisconsin. It remains where originally built in 1880, in what was one of the greatest white pine regions of the middle west. Expert woodsmen built the camp as is evidenced by the skilled workmanship on the hewn corners, floors, and bunks. The winding trail along McCaslin Brook was the supply road over which countless lumberjacks on foot and on bobsleds entered and left the woods for over half a century.

Oneida County

 NICOLET NATIONAL FOREST Erected 1962
**W edge of Nicolet National Forest, off Hwy. 32,
E of Three Lakes**

You are in the original Oneida Purchase Unit that marked the beginning of Nicolet National Forest. The first tract of land, acquired from the Thunder Lake Lumber Company in 1928, contained 12,940 acres. Today there are 640,000 acres rich in scenic, recreational, historical and economic resources. Under the multiple-use management program of the United States Forest Service, the forest offers resources for industry and a wide variety of recreation. Thousands of acres whose trees were removed through logging or were ravaged by fire were reforested by the Civilian Conservation Corps in the 1930's. The Nicolet National Forest is named in honor of Jean Nicolet, who in 1634 was the first white man known to have traveled into what is now Wisconsin.

Oneida County

 FIRST RURAL ZONING ORDINANCE Erected 1969
Oneida County Courthouse grounds, Rhinelander

The Oneida County Zoning Ordinance, adopted May 16, 1933, was the first comprehensive rural zoning ordinance in the United States. In the early 1930's most Northern Wisconsin counties were in financial difficulties. The Oneida County Board of Supervisors resolved the costs of transporting school children, and the construction and maintenance of new roads, by adopting a zoning ordinance prohibiting settlement in remote areas. The purpose was to promote public health, safety, and welfare, and to regulate, restrict, and determine the areas within the county where various activities could be conducted. The Ordinance became a model for other counties in Wisconsin and throughout the United States. It was a new concept in rural land management. It demonstrated that careful planning, by local people, involving joint discussions and joint decisions with many agencies of the County, State, and Federal Governments, is essential for wise use of our natural resources.

Oneida County

191 **THE HODAG** Erected 1973
Hodag Park, Rhinelander

This mythical creature is the official symbol of Rhinelander. It was created in 1896 by "Gene" Shepard, Rhinelander pioneer timber cruiser and famous prankster. Shepard claimed to have discovered the animal in the woods near Rice Creek. He "captured" it by blocking the mouth of its den with rocks and rendering it unconscious with a chloroformed sponge on a long pole. Actually fashioned by a skilled woodcarver named Luke Dearney, the original Hodag was seven feet long and thirty inches high, black and hairy, with two horns on its head, twelve horns along its spine, and short powerful legs armed with long claws. For years Shepard exhibited the Hodag at county fairs in a dimly lighted tent, controlling its movements with wires. Many spectators believed the animal was real. Shepard would assure them that he had captured it on "Section 37" and that it ate "nothing but white bulldogs and those only on Sundays."

Outagamie County

283 **BIRTHPLACE OF THE AMERICAN WATER SPANIEL** Erected 1988
Beacon Ave. and Division St., New London

Of all the breeds of dog recognized by the American Kennel Club, only five were developed in the United States and one, the American Water Spaniel, originated in Wisconsin. The development of the Water Spaniel as a purebred was due largely to the efforts of Dr. F.J. Pfiefer of New London, Wisconsin, who perfected and standardized the breed and obtained official recognition by the United Kennel Club in 1920 and the American Kennel Club in 1940. The Water Spaniel is characterized by its ability not only to retrieve waterfowl but also to act as a flushing dog in upland hunting. Smaller than other retrievers, the versatile Water Spaniel stands from 15 to 18 inches at the shoulder, weighs 25 to 40 pounds and has a chocolate brown or liver-colored coat with an abundance of tight curls. In 1986, the American Water Spaniel was designated as Wisconsin's official state dog.

Outagamie County

 TREATY OF THE CEDARS Erected 1958
Hwy. 96, 0.1 mi. W of Little Chute

The Treaty of the Cedars was concluded on the Fox River near here September 3, 1836. Under the treaty, the Menominee Indian nation ceded to the United States about 4,000,000 acres of land for $700,000 (about 17 cents per acre). The area now contains the cities of Marinette, Oconto, Appleton, Neenah, Menasha, Oshkosh, Wausau, Wisconsin Rapids, Stevens Point and many others. The six-day meeting ended in a spirit of mutual respect and fairness. Governor Dodge said "I view it as a matter of first importance to do the Indians ample justice in all our treaty stipulations." And Menominee Chief Oshkosh later affirmed, "We always thought much of Governor Dodge as an honest man." The treaty was proclaimed February 15, 1837, and the Indians began moving to their new homes west of the Wolf River.

Outagamie County

 REVOLUTIONARY WAR VETERANS Erected 1976
Thelen Park, Kaukauna

In this area, part of the Statesburg settlement, are the graves of Hendrick Aupaumut and Jacob Konkapot, Stockbridge Indians of Massachusetts. Captain Aupaumut won the notice of George Washington. Able tribal counselor, he served as envoy to western tribes and fought to redress Indian grievances. Konkapot served with the army stationed around Boston. A prosperous New York farmer in the 1780's he employed white labor. At Statesburg he operated a sawmill.

Outagamie County

012 **WORLD'S FIRST HYDROELECTRIC CENTRAL STATION** Erected 1953
600 Vulcan St., Appleton

Near this site on September 30, 1882, the world's first hydroelectric central station began operation. The station, here reproduced, was known as the Vulcan Street Plant and had a direct current generator capable of lighting 250 sixteen-candle power lamps, each equivalent to 50 watts. The generator operated at 110 volts and was driven through gears and belts by a water wheel operating under a ten foot fall of water.

Outagamie County

215 **SOUTH GREENVILLE GRANGE NO. 225** Erected 1975
Just N of jct. Hwys. BB and 45, 4 mi. W of Appleton

Oliver Hudson Kelley organized National Grange, Patrons of Husbandry in Washington D. C., December 4, 1867. The Wisconsin State Grange was organized October 24, 1872 by National Deputy J. C. Abbott. South Greenville Grange No. 225 was organized by State Deputy James Brainerd, October 27, 1873. Of 500 Granges organized in Wisconsin, South Greenville Grange No. 225 is the oldest continuously active grange and in 1973 was the first to celebrate its Centennial. The Grange is unique for it first organized on the national level and then on the local level. Patrons of Husbandry, the Grange, is America's and the world's oldest and only rural family fraternity. It aims to serve all the interests of rural and urban people. The "Grange Laws" regulating monopolies and Grange sponsorship of cooperatives has greatly influenced agricultural and industrial growth.

Outagamie County

 FIRST ELECTRIC STREET RAILWAY
Erected 1956
807 S. Oneida, Appleton

On August 16, 1886, the Appleton Electric Street Railway Company began operation of the world's first commercially successful electric street railway. The cars were driven by Van Depoele direct current motors, which received power from a hydro-electric generator through two trolley wires. In 1930, the expanded electric street railway system serving the cities of Appleton, Neenah, Menasha and Kaukauna was retired when bus service was begun to better serve the transportation needs of these communities.

Shawano County

 SHAWANO Erected 1956
Hwy. 22, 3.5 mi. E of Shawano

Shawano is both a Chippewa and a Menominee Indian term signifying "to the South." Shawano Lake first was given this name because it was the southern boundary of Chippewa tribal territory. The city and county later were named after the lake. Like many Wisconsin cities, Shawano was the site of an Indian village before the white men came. In the 19th century a band of Menominees moved westward from Green Bay in search of a lake that would provide good fishing. They found Shawano Lake and settled nearby. State Trunk Highway 55 which passes along the main street of Shawano was part of the Military Road which was built from Green Bay to Ontonagon on Lake Superior. This road was authorized by an Act of Congress in 1863. After the Civil War it was used extensively by loggers and lumbermen as a supply road.

194 THE HOMME HOMES Erected 1973
Hwy. 45 at city limits of Wittenberg

Deep concern for the needs of people in the wilderness brought The Rev. E. J. Homme from Winchester, Wisconsin, to this location in 1879 where he could accomplish his dream of social services to orphans, the aged and Indians in an atmosphere of peace and tranquility. Homme convinced the Milwaukee, Lake Shore and Western Railroad to change the name of its station from Carbonero to Wittenberg. He then recruited friends and former parishioners to come and settle. By 1885 there were forty families in Wittenberg. In a decade Homme built a church, a home for the aged and an orphanage. The orphanage, built just south of this point, served homeless children of all ages from the Upper Midwest. The financial demands of his service programs led Homme to run a farm, publish three newspapers, operate four schools, raise and sell garden seeds and sell a patent medicine of his own making called "Wittenberg Drops." The pond you see was formed when Homme dammed the Embarrass River to run his sawmill. Homme died June 22, 1903, at the age of 59 and was buried in Wittenberg.

Vilas County

 LAC DU FLAMBEAU Erected 1956
Hwy. 47, Flambeau Lake

Lac du Flambeau (Lake of Torches) has been a permanent settlement of the Chippewa Indian nation since about 1745, when Chief Sharpened Stone led his band to this lake. Nearby lakes furnished a fine setting for Indian life, with wild rice in season and plentiful fish which were taken at night by the light of flaming torches, hence the name "Flambeau." The tribe was loyal to the American colonies, never taking sides with the British or French and fought with the Union forces in the Civil War. Old Abe, American Eagle mascot of the Eighth Wisconsin in the Civil War, was captured a few miles below this point by a Flambeau Indian. In 1792 the Northwest Fur Trading Co. established the Lac du Flambeau department for the Wisconsin River area trade. Forts and posts remained on this shore for about fifty years.

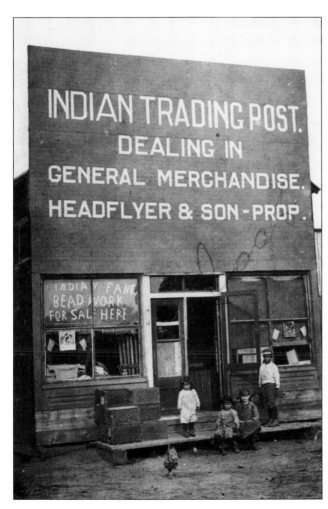

Lac du Flambeau Indian Trading Post, ca. 1910.
SHSW Visual Materials Archive (X3) 25456.

Vilas County

 WISCONSIN RIVER HEADWATERS Erected 1954
Hwy. 45, 1.5 mi. S of Land O' Lakes

About two miles east of here, the Wisconsin River has its source in Lac Vieux Desert. Several spellings and meanings were given to the name of the stream in early days. The Algonquian "wees-konsan" means "the gathering of the waters." The Winnebago "wees-koos-erah is quite different, meaning "river with flowery banks." With its partner, the Fox River, the Wisconsin provided a super-highway for Indian, explorer, adventurer, missionary, and settler and was a "main street" for the fur trade. The Wisconsin River travels nearly the entire length of the state and empties into the Mississippi just below Prairie du Chien, about 300 miles from here. Because there are nearly 50 power and storage dams along its route today, the Wisconsin has been called "the hardest working river in America."

Vilas County

082 **THIRTY-SECOND DIVISION MEMORIAL HIGHWAY** Erected 1957
Hwys. 32 and 45, 0.5 mi. S of Land O' Lakes

The 32nd Division was organized in 1917. Originally it was made up of National Guardsmen from Wisconsin and Michigan. World War I: Fought in Alsace, Aisne–Marne, Oise-Aisne and Meuse-Argonne Offensives. Vanquished 23 German Divisions. Served in the Army of Occupation in Germany. Deactivated in 1919. World War II: One of the first to be called. Fought offensively in the Buna-Sananda Operations. Saidor, Aitape, Morotai, Biak, Leyte and Luzon campaigns. 654 days in action in the Pacific Theater. Served in the Army of Occupation in Japan. Deactivated in 1946. THIS HIGHWAY IS DEDICATED TO THE GALLANT MEN OF THE THIRTY-SECOND RED ARROW DIVISION WHO MADE THE SUPREME SACRIFICE IN BOTH WARS.

Vilas County

 LAC VIEUX DESERT Erected 1960
Lac Vieux Desert Park, West Shore Dr.,
0.5 mi. N of Hwy E, near Land O' Lakes

Here rises the Wisconsin River. Many feet have trod this spot in many kinds of shoes from moccasins to French traders and Indians, boots of loggers, early settlers and the Army to sport shoes of today's tourists. This procession began before the first map of this lake was published in Paris in 1718. Jean Baptiste Perrault wintered here in 1791. Capt. Thomas Cram, surveyor, parleyed with Chief Ca-sha-o-sha in 1840. In the 1850's the Drapers built the first white settler cabin. Leonard Thomas married Draper's daughter and in 1884 built the first summer resort. In 1860 the Wausau Ontonagon road crossed here, joined later by the military road from Green Bay. Indian trails, canoe and mail routes, log drives and oxen hooves marked this spot as the hub of pioneer activity. Known as Kat-ik-it-i-gon and Old Planting Ground, the French name of Lac Vieux Desert is accepted for this beautiful body of water.

Vilas County

 FIRST FOREST PATROL FLIGHT Erected 1955
Hwy. M, 6 mi. S of Boulder Junction

The first forest patrol flight was made from Trout Lake by Jack Vilas June 29,1915. Vilas was commissioned "Official Aviator" by the Wisconsin State Board of Forestry (now Wisconsin Conservation Department) and on his own request received no salary other than "many thanks." During July and August, 1915, patrol flights were made almost daily in a Curtiss Flying Boat. Vilas had shipped his plane from Chicago to Trout Lake by train. In those days the 350 mile flight from Chicago would have taken several days and a crew of special mechanics following in a train, to keep the "flying machine" going. The flights from here by Jack Vilas marked the first time anywhere that an aircraft was used in detecting and locating forest fires and patrolling large forest areas.

Vilas County

123 **FOREST RESTORATION—THE BEGINNING** Erected 1963
At Trout Lake Nursery, Hwy. M

This place on Trout Lake was selected by E. M. Griffith, Wisconsin's first State Forester, as the headquarters for the program in forest restoration of the State Board of Forestry. Early in 1911, a civil service examination was given and the first forest rangers were appointed. Their primary duties were to initiate a tree-planting program and to protect forest lands from fire. Both of these activities have now spread over the entire state. It was on this site that the first seed beds (pine of local origin) were sown. Although some preparatory work had been done in 1910, the ground was actually broken in 1911. The first planting stock was lifted in 1913. Any measure of success which has been or will ever be attained in the restoration of the forest resources in this state had its tangible beginning here.

Vilas County

212 **SNOWMOBILE** Erected 1975
Sayner Park, Sayner

Wisconsinites experimented with over-snow vehicles before 1900, trying bicycles on runners with gripping fins, steam-propelled sleighs and later Model T Fords converted with rear tractor treads and skis in front. In the first races held near Three Lakes in 1926, 104 of these "snowbuggies" started. Carl Eliason of Sayner developed the prototype of the modern snowmobile in 1924 when he mounted a small gasoline-powered marine engine on a long toboggan, steered with skis under the front and driven by a rear, single, endless track. Patented in 1927, Eliason made 40 snowmobiles. Upon receiving an order for 200 from Finland, he sold his patent to the FWD Company of Clintonville. They made 300 for military use, then transferred the patent to a Canadian subsidiary. There are 2 $^1/_2$ million snowmobiles in North America now. Annual sales exceed $1 billion and result in 100,000 jobs. Used even above the Arctic Circle, they provide not only recreation but mobility for utility repairmen, forest rangers, game wardens, mail carriers, policemen, etc.

Waupaca County

102 **FOUR-WHEEL DRIVE** Erected 1960
Walter Olen Park, Clintonville

In this machine shop, in 1908, Otto Zachow and William Besserdich developed and built the first successful four-wheel drive automobile. Their first car, the "Battleship," soon proved that it "could go anywhere a team of horses could go" and led to the founding, in 1909, of the Badger Four-Wheel Drive Auto Company (word "Badger" dropped in 1910 and name changed to FWD Corporation in 1958). Government interest in motor vehicles and the success of the four-wheel drive in early military tests caused the company to switch from cars to the manufacture of motor trucks. In two World Wars, U.S. and Allied armies won the battle of transport with military vehicles of four-wheel drive design. As civilization moves on to new horizons, transportation and progress are served by trucks invented and built in this community using the Zachow-Besserdich principle of applying power to all wheels of a vehicle.

Waupaca County

138 **BIRTHPLACE OF AN AIRLINE** Erected 1964
Municipal Airport, Clintonville

It was here in Clintonville that Wisconsin Central Airlines, now known as North Central Airlines, was founded in 1944. Fostered and promoted by the Four-Wheel Drive Auto Company, the airline was an outgrowth of the company's need for air transportation. Four-Wheel Drive had been operating a non-scheduled airline service to Chicago for months before making application for scheduled airline service to the civil Aeronautics Board in June 1944. Since beginning service on February 1, 1948, with a fleet of three nine-passenger twin-engine aircraft, North Central has become one of the largest of the local service air carriers in the country. Its routes provide the basis of Wisconsin's airline system serving all of the state's air carrier airports.

Waupaca County

073 **CHIEF WAUPACA** Erected 1957
Hwy. 110, 3.5 mi. S of Marion

Chief Waupaca, better known as Sam Wapuka, was a friendly Potawatomi Indian who lived in this vicinity about the time the first white men arrived. Although he was friendly to the settlers, his tribesmen were bitterly opposed to the invasion of the white man. Once on a trip with several of his warriors, they stopped where the present city of Waupaca is located. His men were eager to massacre the entire small settlement and Waupaca talked long and eloquently to prevent it. He succeeded but when he remounted his pony to continue on his way, he suddenly fell dead from his horse. His companions hurriedly buried him almost where he fell. Later relatives purchased several acres of land, including this site, and brought the body here. His sons Shopodock and Hongkoot, stepson Jake and at least sixteen other relatives are buried here with him.

Waupaca County

284 **GRAND ARMY HOME** Erected 1988
Marden Memorial Center, Wisconsin Veterans Home, King

The Grand Army Home was established in 1887 by the Wisconsin Department of the Grand Army of the Republic, a nationwide organization of Union veterans of the Civil War (1861–1865). The Home provided care for indigent veterans and their wives in a pleasant community setting. The city of Waupaca donated seventy-eight acres along scenic Rainbow Lake to the veterans, and the local branch of the Women's Relief Corps (an auxiliary of the G.A.R.) constructed several cottages on the site. This was the first veterans' home in the nation to allow women to become members. Dr. Frederick A. Marden, a G.A.R. member from Milwaukee, originated the concept of a co-educational veterans' retirement community. He also devised the Home's cottage plan. Marden believed that elderly soldiers and their wives were owed a debt of gratitude for their service to the imperiled Union and that they would find contentment in the modest cottages and tree-shaded lanes at King.

266

NUMERICAL LIST OF OFFICIAL WISCONSIN HISTORICAL MARKERS

(Please note that missing numbers designate removed markers.)

1. Peshtigo Fire Cemetery
2. Jefferson Prairie Settlement
5. Shake Rag
6. Radisson-Grosseilliers Fort
7. Village of Dover
8. Mississippi River Parkway: First Project
9. Old Wade House State Park
10. Villa Louis
11. Aztalan State Park
12. World's First Hydroelectric Central Station
13. Home of Governor Harvey
14. Old Abe, the War Eagle
15. Old Stockade Site
16. Castle Rock
17. Lizard Mound State Park
18. Brigham Park
19. Lake Ripley
20. First State Fair, October 1-2, 1851
21. Wisconsin River Headwaters
22. Site of Fort St. Antoine
23. Gays Mills Apple Orchards
24. Wisconsin Lead Region
25. First Church of Christ Scientist
26. Dawn Manor - Site of Lost City of Newport
27. Knaggs Ferry
28. Tragedy of the Siskiwit
29. John Muir View
30. Wisconsin Central Railroad
31. Nation's First Watershed Project
32. De Langlade
33. Battle of Bad Axe
34. First Forest Patrol Flight
35. Lake Pepin
36. Watertown Plank Road
37. State Historical Society
38. Old Military Road
39. Court Oreilles
40. Butte des Morts
41. Meadowmere
42. Ringling Brothers Circus
43. Invention of the Typewriter
44. Dutch Settlement
45. Auto Race - Green Bay to Madison
46. Highway Marking
47. Shawano
48. Poygan Paygrounds
49. Madeline Island
50. Namekagon - Court Oreilles Portage
51. St. Croix River
52. Masonic Home
53. Old Copper Culture Cemetery
54. Great Divide
55. Northern Highland
56. First Electric Street Railway
57. Oneida Street Station, T.M.E.R. & L. Co.
58. Lac du Flambeau
59. Octagon House
61. Fort Winnebago
62. Red Banks
63. Marquette
64. Major "Dick" Bong
65. Phillips Fire
66. Mitchell Red Cloud, Jr. (1925-1950)
67. Upper Fox River
68. Red Cloud Park
69. Menominee Reservation
70. The Bad River
71. Thirty-second Division Memorial Highway
72. The Spark
73. Chief Waupaca
74. First Kindergarten
75. Belmont - Wisconsin Territory 1836
76. Dams on the Mississippi
77. Treaty of the Cedars
78. Mission of St. Francis Xavier
79. Admiral Marc A. Mitscher
80. The Gideons
81. Decorah Peak
82. Thirty-second Division Memorial Highway
83. Governor Rusk
84. 9XM-WHA
85. Oldest Lutheran Church in Wisconsin
86. Cranberry Culture
87. Hop Raising
88. Tomah
89. The Baraboo Range
90. Chippewa River & Menomonie Railway
91. Museum of Medical Progress
92. Horicon Marsh
93. Route of Abraham Lincoln 1832 and 1859
94. Lac Vieux Desert
95. Albion Academy
97. Radisson and Groseilliers
98. Orchards of Door County
99. Panther Intaglio
100. Hamlin Garland (1860-1940)
101. Hamlin Garland
102. Four Wheel Drive
103. Nelson Dewey
104. Wisconsin Dells
106. Potters' Emigration Society
107. Milton House

215. South Greenville Grange No. 225
216. Civilian Conservation Corps
217. Chief Win-no-shik, the Elder
218. Coles Bashford House
219. Pine Was King
220. The Name "Wisconsin"
221. Bernard "Bunny" Berigan (1908-1942)
222. General Mitchell Field
223. Nation's First Cooperative Generating Station
224. Wisconsin's First Nuclear-Fueled
     Generating Station
225. Northland College
226. Samuel N. Rogers, Sr., Soldier
     of the American Revolution
227. August W. Derleth
228. Wisconsin Progressive Party
230. Black River Valley
231. Storrs Lake, Milton
232. Beef Slough
233. The Superior Entry
234. Rustic Road
235. Allen Family
236. Milwaukee Interurban Terminal, 1905-1951
237. Luther College
238. Revolutionary War Veterans
239. Green Bay Packers
240. Shot Tower
241. Heritage Hill State Park
242. Silver Mound
243. Crex Meadows
244. Spence Park
245. Seils-Sterling Circus
246. St. John's Military Academy
247. Clare A. Briggs - Cartoonist
248. Manitowoc's Maritime Heritage
249. Martin W. Torkelson (1878-1963)
250. Great Divide
251. Kemper Hall
252. Iowa County Courthouse
253. Winnebago Trail
254. Elroy-Sparta State Trail
254. Elroy-Sparta State Trail
255. MacArthur Square
256. Lannon Stone
257. Golda Meir
258. Drumlins
259. "Bow and Arrow"
260. Rest Areas on the I-Roads
261. Roche-a-Cri State Park
262. Birthplace of GTE
     (General Telephone & Electronics Corp.)
263. White Pillars
264. Wisconsin's Dairy Industry

265. The Upper Mississippi
266. Carl Frederick Zeidler
267. Rapides des Peres - Voyageur Park
268. Valley View Site
269. Wisconsin's Maritime Industries
270. The Wisconsin River
271. The Sand Counties - Aldo Leopold Territory
272. Rock River Industry
273. The Driftless Area
274. Carrie Chapman Catt
275. First Workers Compensation Policy
276. Bay View's Rolling Mill
277. First State Normal School
278. Adrian "Addie" Joss
279. The Cobban Bridge
280. Wisconsin's Lime Industry
281. Antigo Silt Loam, State Soil of Wisconsin
282. First Swedish Settlers in Wisconsin
283. Birthplace of the American Water Spaniel
284. Grand Army Home
285. Wisconsin's Oldest Newspaper:
     The Milwaukee Sentinel
286. Manitowoc Submarines
287. The "Dinky"
288. National Soldiers Home
289. Civil War Camp
290. Historic Cedarburg
291. Mabel Tainter Memorial
292. Medal of Honor
293. Langlade County Forest-Wisconsin's
     First County Forest
294. First African-American Church
     Built in Wisconsin
295. Korean War
296. Prisoners of War
297. Major General C.C. Washburn
298. Wartime Shipbuilding
299. Janesville Tank Company
300. Wisconsin Military Reservation
301. Highground Veterans Memorial
302. World War II
303. Father Caspar Rehrl
304. Lorine Niedecker
305. Fleet Admiral William D. Leahy
306. Cordelia A.P. Harvey
307. World War I
308. Mormons in Early Wisconsin
309. The University of Wisconsin-Milwaukee
310. Pabst Theater
311. Third Ward Fire
312. Captain Frederick Pabst
313. The Iron Brigade
314. In Service to Their Country

INDEX

Number in **boldface**: indicates there is an entire marker devoted to that subject on that page.
Number in *italics:* refers to an illustration on that page.
Number in ***bold italics:*** means there is both an illustration and a marker for that subject on that page.

Adams, Alva, 81
Adams County, 128
African Americans, 33, 114; first Wisconsin church built for, **33**; Pleasant Ridge community, *141;* settlers in Cheyenne Valley, ***178***
agriculture and agricultural settlement, 4, 16, 40, 47, 48, 53, 57, 67, 70, 84, 91, 92, 93, 97, 99, 102, 112, *113*, 118, 128, 135, 141, 148, *149*, 170, *178*, 180, *234, 242, 243*, 245, 248, 249. *See also* state fair; 4-H Club; Grangers; *names of specific crops*
airplane, Wisconsin's first home-built, ***214***. *See also* aviators
Albee, George S., 71
Albion: Albion Academy, **81**
Alexander, Rev. William R., 33
Algoma, 244
Alim (Fox leader), 130
Allen, Philip, and family, **124**
Allouez, Claude, 200, 241, 254
Alma, 191
Alma Center, 208
Almond, 126
American water spaniel, birthplace of the, **256**
Anderson Mills, 140
Antigo, 248, 249
Antigo silt loam, **249**
antislavery efforts, 3, 72, 114, 178
Apostle Islands, *186*
Appleby, John, 148
apple-growing. *See* orchards
Appleton, 24, 257, 258-259
Appleton Electric Street Railway, 259
archeology, 102, 169, 171, 218, 253. *See also* Indian mounds
Arena, 148

Arms, Samuel, and family, *178*
artists, 174
Ashland, 184-185
Ashland County, 184-187
athletes and athletics, 98, 156, 240
Atkinson, Gen. Henry, *107*, 108, 115, 117, 121, 134, 147, 172
Aupaumut, Hendrick, **257**
authors. *See* literary figures
automobile-makers, 51, *60*, 265
automobile race, from Green Bay to Madison, **95**
aviators and aviation, 28, 39, *41*, 72, 179, 202, 209, *214*, 263; Wisconsin's first aviator, **119**
Aztalan State Park, ***102***

Babcock, Stephen Moulton, **82**
Bad Axe, Battle. *See* Battle of Bad Axe
Badger (car ferry), **14**
"badgers," origin of nickname, vi, 163
Bad River/Bad River Reservation, **187**
Baker, Harry D., 221
Bangor, 166
Baraboo, 46, 79, 80, 173, 176
Baraboo Range, **174**, 176
Barron County, 188, 192
Bashford, Coles, and house of, **72**
Battle of Bad Axe, 94, 107, 122, **181**
"Battle of Cameron Dam," **224**
Battle of Mole Lake, **247**
Battle of St. Croix Falls, **220**
Battle of Wisconsin Heights (Black Hawk War Trail), **94**; other mentions, 95, 122, 134, 167, 177, 181
Bayfield County, 189-190
Bay View (Milwaukee): rolling mill in, **23**; immigrants in (Ethnic Trail), **30**
Beaumont, Dr. William, 131
Beaver Dam, 96, 139
Beckman, August, and family, 116
Beef Slough, **191**
Belgian settlement, **245**
Belgium, 48
Belleville, 85
Belmont, ***161***, 162
Beloit, 119, 120-122, 115, 117
Beloit College, 81, ***119***, 124

271

inns, hotels, and lodges, 59, 82, *88,* 114, 138, *139. See also* resorts

"In Service to Their Country" (Veterans marker), **103**

insurance industry, 212

interstate highways. *See* roads

Interstate Park, **221**

Interurban Bridge (Cedarburg), **45**

inventions and inventors, 15, 24, 72, 75, 95, 101, *111,* 120, 148, 264, 265

Iowa County, 142-148, 163; courthouse, **147**

Ioway people, 154

Irish immigrants, 16, 17, 18, 19, 30, 37, 43, 47, 70, 164, 242

iron and steel production, 23, 198, 199, 207, 210; first iron smelter in Wisconsin, **97**; iron mining on the Gogebic, **208**

Iron Brigade (Veterans marker), *150*, 151

Iron County, 207-208, 221

Italian immigrants, 18, 30, 122, 164

Jackson County, 192, 208-212, 231

James, Ada, *168*

Janesville, 40, 117, 118, 120, 139

Janesville Tank Company (Veterans marker), **120**

Jefferson County, 101-110, 115

Jefferson Prairie settlement, **116**

Jenkynsville, 53

Jim Falls, 193

Johnsburg, 8

Jolliet, Louis, 11, 75, 100, *132*, 156, **241**. *See also* Marquette, Jacques

Joss, Adrian "Addie," **98**

journalists and journalism, 19, 219

Juneau, 98

Juneau, Solomon, *xiii,* 19, **96**

Juneau County, 148-153

Kaukauna, 257, 259

Kemper, Bishop Jackson, 8, *63*

Kemper Hall, **8**

Kendall, 153, 167

Kennedy, J. J., 228

Kenosha, 8-9, 29, 124

Kenosha County, 8-11

Keokuk (Sac leader), 122

Keshena, 250, 251

Keshena Reservation, 68

Kewaunee, 244, 248

Kewaunee County, 245, 248

Kewaunee, Green Bay and Western Railroad, 248

Kickapoo people, 90, 94

Kickapoo River, 135

Kilbourntown (precursor to Milwaukee) (Ethnic Trail), **31**

kindergarten, first in the U.S., *105*

King, 266

King, Rufus, *150*

Kingsley Bend Indian Mounds, **80**

Kingston, 111

Kinnickinnic River, 219

Kinzie, John and Juliette, 71, 74

Kissel Motor Car Co., *60*

Knaggs Ferry, **71**

Knapp, Stout and Co. (logging), 188

Knowlton, 221

Konkapot, Jacob, **257**

Korean War (Veterans marker), **112**; other mentions, 103, 115, 151, 155, 211, 235

Koshkonong, 128

Krause, L. F. E., 49

labor history, 6, 19, 23, 30, 50, 149, 180, 212, *234*

Lac Court Oreilles, 203, 223, 224, 225

Lac Court Oreilles Reservation, 187, 225

Lac du Flambeau, *261*

Lac du Flambeau Reservation, 187

La Crosse, 11, 53, 154-156, 182, 192

La Crosse County, 153-160

Lac Vieux Desert, 148, 262, **263**

Lady Elgin, sinking of the, *17*

Lafayette County, 161-165

La Follette, Robert M., Sr., *83*

Lake Church, 48

Lake Geneva, 125

Lake Koshkonong Effigy Mounds, **109**

Lake Mendota, 89

Lake Michigan, 11, 12, 14, 15, *17,* 27, 28, 34, 50, 244, 248. *See also* shipping; ferries

Lake Mills, 101-102

Lake Monona, 89, 90

Lake Namekagon, 207, 208

Lake Nebagamon, 201